The Accidental Captain

The
Accidental
Captain

GLENN PATRON

To Gale,
Wife. Grandmother, sailor, cook and much more.
Thank you for your support, your patience and your love.

Contents

1

How Did I Get Here?

Splashing through ankle deep water, I rushed to the twin engine room access doors to check the bilge. Snatching them open, I could see, even in the dim light, an ocean of water sloshing back and forth in the bilge, the level nudging but not yet quite reaching the terminals on the battery tops. Damn, if it goes up another inch, we'll lose the use of the pumps and engine.

Oh, shit. It's midnight. I'm on my sailboat in the Atlantic Ocean with three people who are with me because they trusted me. And we're sinking. Damn. How did I get into this mess?

Well, that's pretty much what this book is about. How I got into that mess, and a few others, while learning to sail, survive, and enjoy being a long-distance sailor.

If you bought this book expecting sage advice on keeping your sailboat in perfect running condition, the best way to sail through a storm, or how to find your position with a sextant, I suggest you rush back to the bookstore; they still might return your money.

Yes, you might stumble onto some information about how to get around in your sailboat and not get into the kind of trouble that I have. While I can't quite say "Everything I know I learned on my sailboat," I can tell you that learning to keep my craft sound and navigate safely over long distances to exciting places profoundly changed me. These experiences created the bridge that spans the chasm between the boy I was and the man I became.

The stories I share in this book are the same ones I tell when we're sitting in the cockpit, having drinks with guests. My second drink in hand, I feel as though I'm Jerry Seinfeld reciting a hilarious account of his last disastrous date. Probably, thanks to their second drink, the sailors in my audience seem to think my stories are funny, or maybe instructive, or perhaps just pathetic.

So I hope you sit back, relax, and enjoy reading this book. But if you don't find it interesting, try reading it after a drink … or two.

An Unlikely Sailor

I guess I should begin by telling you that I was born on the wrong side of the docks. Unlike celebrated nautical figures such as Captain Fatty Goodlander, who was raised on his parents' schooner, or Ted Turner, scion of a wealthy yachting family, my father was a New York City boy who, during the depths of the Depression, traveled the country in search of work and adventure. He panned for gold, was a cub reporter, and even made it as a Triple-A professional baseball player. All very exciting, but after the adventure ended he again found himself with empty pockets.

By the time he met my mother, he was ready to settle down, so he bit the bullet and went into partnership with his stern, German-born father to achieve some financial security—if not excitement—in industrial supplies. Early success allowed him to move his young family from New York City to the Long Island suburbs to become a "golf-weekend" and "good-school-for-the-children" family and to live the American dream.

He and my mother chose to live in the town of Great Neck ("West Egg" in *The Great Gatsby*). No longer known for millionaires' estates, developers had broken up the properties into one-acre lots, which were snatched up by second generation Jewish strivers for whom education and material success were paramount. My father savored the admiration he received as an excellent golfer and successful businessman: achievements he felt came from his toughness and hard work, and not what others ascribed to natural ability. He did his best to instill those values in me.

My mother, on the other hand, was his diametrical opposite. She, a soft, brown-eyed brunette who lived then—and even today at 96 still lives—to be connected to the world of art and culture. She was an intellectual, a talented painter, exceptional singer, and avid reader, but she always seemed to be dealing with asthma or some other illness that impaired her ability to live a normal life. But nothing inhibited her crusade to bring me up as a sensitive, artistic, non-aggressive young man.

Later on I realized that the only way I could please both my parents would be to grow up to be a hard-bodied, violin-playing Buddhist champion boxer who made tons of money selling his oil paintings.

To my father the fact that Great Neck was surrounded by water on three sides was purely incidental. His focus was more on his growing small business and excellent golf game. He understood— and had just about as much interest—about boating as he did about Chinese embroidery. I think that the only thing my parents had in common, with the exception of quick forays into the warm ocean during our annual one-week winter vacations in Miami Beach, was a total lack of interest in the sea.

Wait, it gets worse.

As a child I was a passive, asthmatic, pudgy, sickly kid who was a bit intimidated by the rough and tumble games the other neighborhood kids played. My days as a pre-teen were mostly spent reading at home. On school days I liked to pretend I was sick—with no opposition from Mom—so I could stay home in my cozy, safe room with my books and collections and practice my clarinet. Unlike the other Jewish kids in the town who had to take violin or piano lessons, my parents, fans of the great Benny Goodman, shoved his complicated woodwind at me and ordered me, "Learn."

Frankly, the most memorable experience I had as a clarinet student was a wild demonstration ride down a sinuous country road with my clarinet teacher in an MG-TC he brought back from England when mustered out of the Army. What a difference from my father's ponderous 1954 Cadillac or my mother's feeble Chevy Bel Air. This experience soured me on these lumps of American iron that could hardly get out of their own way and piqued my interest in sports cars and the different perspectives towards motor cars found in Europe.

Hiding out at home gave me an opportunity to become an avid reader. I devoured every book that came into the house, including my dad's recommended reading list, which had a strong effect on me. Books with titles like *Navy Diver, Struggle is Our Brother, Some Follow the Sea,* and *Street Rod,* which provided young male readers like myself with vivid portraits of youths living exciting, adventurous lives in war and peace, were my favorites. I could not escape the realization of the stark differences that were all too obvious between me and the heroes in the books.

Then a vigorous, athletic man in his thirties, my dad tried to interest me in the outdoors and the exploits of others by bringing home books about men like flyer Richard E. Bird and explorer Robert Peary. And to make sure I was well rounded fiction-wise, he threw in the Hardy Boys mysteries and Zane Grey's tales of the Old West. When he commanded me to read them, you can be sure I did. No one disagreed with my father.

You see, my father was always right.

If by some miracle there existed some overwhelming proof that he was wrong about something, his defensive smokescreen and counter-attack were so disagreeable that, as my mother and the three subsequent wives were to learn, it was better never to question him.

For example, one summer day my sister and I were playing in the front yard when my father arrived home from work. After glancing at our cocker spaniel sprawled out, sleeping on the concrete path in the warmth of the late afternoon sun, he pro-claimed, "The dog looks dead," and continued into the house to enjoy his drink and *The New York Times*. Resigned to the reality that if the dog showed any signs of life the results would be unpleasant, my sister and I looked at each other, wondering which one of us would have to accept the onerous job of killing the poor pet.

Summer held a special terror for me because, even when Dad came home late from work, there was still enough daylight for him to say, "Let's go out on the lawn and have a catch." An activity that I absolutely dreaded. He was 6 ft. tall, red hair just beginning to recede, practically a legend because of his past as a professional baseball player, and I was supposed to play ball with him. Every time I dropped the ball or threw it over his head, I felt like a dismal failure and just wanted to run away and hide.

I spent my most pleasant times each summer alone and un-chal-lenged in the shallow end of our community pool. I hid out there for many a summer day.

While father may have been an excellent athlete and astute busi-nessman, he had a big hang up about manual labor or any task in which one worked with one's hands. I assume this came from the humiliation he felt growing up as the son of a wretched mechanic. He tended to ignore any possibility that anything in the house might need fixing. The "tool drawer" at home was bare except for a hammer, screwdriver, a pair of pliers, and some string. With the old man mostly absent, working or spending his weekends at the golf course, it fell to me, as the default man of the house, to try to repair stuff that broke.

I tried fixing my bike, a folding chair, the lawn mower, toys. But rusted bolts defied my pliers, and because no one told me that wood construction requires wood screws not nails, the cart I built out of wood collapsed. Somehow, nothing I worked on seemed to turn out right. Finally, with no tutor and inade-quate tools, in frustration I gave up any repair projects. All I ever achieved was to convince myself I was unable to deal with

I had the boat, the hat and the sails. All I needed was water

mechanical or electrical tasks. This would come back and haunt me years later.

My Bar Mitzvah in the fall of 1955 marked a subtle bend in my life's path when, to reward me for this important ethnic achievement, my dad offered to buy me a small sailboat. The offer came with a very important caveat. He would buy the boat, but I couldn't *use* the boat until my grades improved. Excited to have arrived at the first step up the ladder to the level of my literary heroes, I concentrated on the search for the best boat, not so much on the best scholarship.

Examining the classifieds every day, I soon found a Blue Jay—14 ft. class boat—for sale at a sailing club just across Manhasset Bay from our town. We went to see it. The price was right, my dad said okay, and within a few days the seller delivered it on a trailer, barely making it through the gate into our fenced-in backyard, where it awaited my delivery of good grades for its return to its element. I named her *Vireo*.

Despite our agreement there was no miraculous change in my educational motivation, so it sat high and dry all winter and spring. When school ended the following June, it was still secluded in my backyard, a casualty of all the Ds and C-minuses on my report card.

Not willing to completely forego the adventure of sailing, I used time that perhaps should have been dedicated to studying to invent a wooden frame that supported the boat and rested each corner on a stack of old tires. Thus mounted, with main and jib up, even a light breeze would allow this vessel, although trapped in the backyard, to heel as though we were on the bay. Without having to suffer the indignities of getting wet or having to deal with navigation hazards.

While my backyard boating did connect me somewhat with the sea escapades in the books, it had really been my trip to the sailing club to inspect this little craft that had made the greatest impression on me.

The neat club grounds had been teeming with trim, healthy boys and girls dressed in white, purposefully engaged in rigging and launching their small sailboats and beating their way out into Manhasset Bay to experience … well, the kind of undertaking I had only dreamed about. These were real people, not characters from one of my books. They were living lives so different from mine, and I envied them immensely.

With another summer approaching—and my report cards still looking dismal—my old man, admitting—a rare—defeat, sold the Blue Jay, nearly but not completely nipping in the bud my growing enthusiasm for sailing.

That summer, one of the few I didn't have to go to summer school, my parents decided to send me to the same summer camp in upstate New York my sister, Lisa, had attended. Having no choice, I went. I played softball on hot, dusty ball fields—I was the permanent right fielder—went along on hikes through woods where I was sure child-eating bears lurked, and swam the two laps needed to win my "Novice Swimmer" certificate. But my passion was the old, wooden, 24-foot, gaff-rigged keelboat that was tied to the camp's rickety dock on the lakefront. I climbed aboard every free moment I had, but as a 14 year old—camp rules permitted only those 16+ could sail it—I could only sit in it and daydream. However, this vessel was to play an important role in my maturing into a young man.

There in its cockpit one starry summer night, I had my first sexual experience. Unfortunately, I was alone when this happened. But it did give me my first exposure to "single handing."

The balance of my teen years passed without much change for me at school. While I did make the football team, I wasn't a very good player. I wasn't angry and aggressive enough. I didn't acquire these traits until I was married. I never made the Honor Roll nor was I invited to join the Debating Society. I did achieve everlasting local fame one warm May day by climbing out the classroom's open third-floor window onto a long, narrow ledge when the teacher stepped out into the hall to talk to someone. Edging away from the window, I became invisible to those in the classroom.

Upon her return, Miss Estabrook, picking up the lesson where she left off, must have noticed the lack of my usual wisecracks, because through the open window I could hear her inquire, "Where is Glenn?" The class erupted into a gale of laughter, and it was great fun until the little shit who *was* on the Honor Roll and Debating Society squealed on me.

Higher Education

I felt a great sense of relief when, after attending summer school my senior year, I received my High School diploma in the mail. But now I faced another challenge. My school, full of Jewish over-achievers, boasted an almost 100% rate of college admission. Somehow, I had to find an institution of higher learning that would accept me. I did much better than that. I found a whole string of them.

First, there was Olivet College where I got expelled during freshman orientation. This early departure allowed me to make the first day of classes at my next hall of knowledge, Mexico City College. This institution of learning was, like a cheap Mexican hooker, willing to let anyone in and not charge very much for the experience.

I wouldn't be alone in Mexico City though. My grandfather's sister Paula, unable in 1920 to get permission to immigrate to the U.S., chose Mexico as an interim stop that had become permanent.

Before emigrating from Europe, she had been an actress in Yiddish theatre, and her stories of the Belle Epoch, culture, and style in the Old Country are what planted the seeds of my later, incurable case of Europhilia. I worshipped her. She was a Jewish Auntie Mame. To make a living in Mexico, she had worked as a writer, real estate agent, and contractor. She had guts and connections and a million great stories to tell.

Paula made sure I found a place to live in the Polanco section near her friends so they could keep their eyes on me. To get to school I would leave my rooming house each morning and walk four blocks through the thin, cold air to a designated spot on Avenida Reforma. Once there I would wait for the arrival of the college's broken-down bus. Climbing aboard, I would find it about half filled with other gringos on their way to being deposited at the grimy campus. Windows open, we inhaled the smoggy, diesel fume-laden air of Mexico's capital (which masked the student's symptoms of "Montezuma's Revenge").

Once at class I was expected to take in vital information, in English, that would help prepare me for a successful career in …?

However, the most useful knowledge I acquired was that, only a $12 bus ride away in the resort town of Acapulco, there existed an establishment on Condesa Beach called "El Catalejo. By day its little, thatched beach huts with hammocks were rented to tourists. When the sun went down, the tourists returned to their stainless steel, concrete, and glass hotels to be replaced by a small group of hippies and vagabonds who, for the grand sum of $2.00 US, got the hammock at night and two ample Mexican meals each day.

At first I spent only a weekend. Then a long weekend. Then, well, I just didn't go back to school. Obviously, English Literature, World History, and Contemporary Psychology back at the college didn't stand a chance of competing with my life on the beach. I spent my days chatting with people I found on the wide palm-fringed beaches. Tourists, backpackers, beatniks—that's what hippies were called in those days—musicians, gays, druggies, artists. I met fathers who wanted me to meet their daughters … and fathers who made sure I didn't. My perspective of what the world was like changed immensely from what it had been as a suburban teenager.

My body changed too. From a pale-skinned, pudgy 220 lbs. to a bronzed, slim 175. The young female tourists I met appreciated my local knowledge and loved the wild stories I made up and told them. The clincher for me was the purchase, from a skinny Mexican teenager, of a shoebox full of marijuana for only $5.00 US. Regrettably, my supply of grass outlasted my supply of money; by spring I still had marijuana but had run out of cash. And since now even Mexico City College wouldn't let me back in, I had no choice but to go home.

The Virgin Islands Dream

Home was, however, no longer on Long Island. In a crazy twist of fate, my parents had moved to a different island: St. Thomas, U.S. Virgin Islands.

Why this strange turn of events? An old Jewish rumrunner who had used St. Thomas as his base during prohibition decided after World War II to invest his ill-gotten profits in the island's potential for tourism. He built a large luxury hotel in the early '50s and gave his sons-in-law—golf buddies of my dad—the job of moving to St. Thomas and managing it.

Their first winter vacation in the Virgin Islands convinced my parents they wanted to spend more time there. The weather was perfect for a winter get-a-way, and my mother's persistent asthma seemed to disappear while breathing the warm humid air.

When my father found a way to start a small manufacturing business that took advantage of the island's free port status, the deal was sealed. Six months in New York, then six in the Virgins. While I was squandering my time in Mexico, they had commenced building their dream vacation home.

My arrival coincided with the midpoint of one of those third-world nightmares one encounters in the Caribbean. Building a home in the Virgin Islands 50 years ago was a very challenging exercise.

Their north shore waterfront lot sat high above the blue sea and had a stupendous view. St. John, Jost Van Dyke, and Tortola were jewels tied together like a necklace of emeralds by the smaller islands that connected them in a setting of blue Caribbean waters. The trade winds brought a constant breeze to the lot's perch about 100 feet above sea level. A short walk down a path from the house to the rocky shore gave me access to clear waters where I could snorkel and spearfish whenever I wanted. Though my time there was spent on land, the memory of the divine view of that tropic scene was, later on, to dovetail with my desire to sail and to change my life.

It was here that their local contractor, Mr. Torres, had begun constructing their perfect dream house. Sadly, it was only after putting down a hefty deposit and work commenced that my parents realized their contractor was not very good at reading blueprints. Or English for that matter. Their periodic visits from New York to check on Torres' progress were continuous bouts with disaster and frustration.

For example, upon discovering that the concrete walls of the first floor had been poured without provision for windows, my parents angrily confronted their contractor with this deficiency. "*No problema,*" was always Mr. Torres' reply. He handed my parents a piece of chalk, and once they outlined the locations of the designated apertures, he sent in his three workers, Larry, Curley, and Moe, who with sledge hammer and chisel created the desired openings.

The fluency in Spanish I gained from time in Mexico came in quite handy because, while he could make himself understood somewhat in English, Mr. Torres was only able to completely express himself in his native language. For example, after assuring my parents that the bathroom tile work would be finished the next week, he confided in me, *"Se me acabo' el dinero y no puedo comprar los azulejos."* So I had to tell my parents he was too embarrassed to tell them he'd run out of money and couldn't pay for tiles and materials. They advanced the necessary funds, and on we would go.

After a year of shuttle diplomacy, the house was finally finished—to island standards—and it was decided by my parents that since my job was over, instead of languishing in paradise, I should try another college—any college—that would take me. And lo and behold, they found one.

University number three was CW Post College. It was a fairly new institution on Long Island that had such low standards even I could get in. My father, taking no chances, took care of the paperwork, drove me to the campus in Brookville, Long Island, and personally deposited me in my dorm room. But once he was gone I went back to my old tricks. Classes were a drag and there were much more interesting things to do outside the classrooms.

Me, a Family Man

Quite soon I had an additional distraction: a very determined, very beautiful young lady who thought I would make a good husband. (Wrong.) 1963 found me, at 21 years of age, undiplomaed, unemployed, and about to blight my troth to this dark-eyed beauty. Since there were expectations from our families that I be able to pay for food and a roof over our heads, I would need to bring in some money on a regular basis. Despite having sworn never to become one of the family business serfs, it looked like the only job I could be sure to get would be working for my father in his industrial supply business.

Working for my father was not a stroll in the park. He was an early pioneer of "flextime." Employees could come in any time before 8 a.m. and leave any time after 7 p.m. Confident because of the success he had achieved, my father was a tough boss.

I guess he had to be. Returning to New York with empty pockets at 25, he found himself working as a mechanic's helper to my muscular, uneducated grandfather, whose trade as a millwright was installing machines for people who had factories in the loft buildings of lower New York City.

My grandfather, the black sheep of his cultured, Jewish-European family, having no other prospects, joined the German Merchant Marine in his teens. Even many years after jumping ship in New York, he had trouble reading and writing English, so he was relieved to be able to send my father out to find or order the motors, belts, chains, etc. needed to make the installations for his customers.

Seeing the inefficiency of scurrying around in search of these components every time they were needed for a job, Pop chose to buy some of the most common components in advance, creating an inventory available for his father's work. Soon other millwrights came looking for equipment, and within just a few years, he had invented a new type of industrial supply establishment: the power transmission distributor.

So here I was at 21, and unlike the characters in the books I had read, I was not an explorer, sea captain, or adventurer. I was a guy who did what most guys did: look for a way to support a family. My fiancé, a far more practical person than I, spent a lot of time one afternoon pressuring me to ask for a place for myself in the family business. Now. Though I dreaded it, she convinced me to raise the subject that night after dinner at my father's country club.

Excellent meal now finished, I followed my father to the "Lounge," where we settled into plush armchairs and he lit his cigar. For a few minutes there was only silence. Then gathering up sufficient courage, I timidly opened my gambit with, "Pop, I've been thinking …"

Leaning back in the luxurious chair and confidently blowing a thick cloud of aromatic cigar smoke, he looked at the ceiling and replied, "Yeah, well, that's something new."

Trembling inside, and acutely aware of the disparity between my penury and the sparkling luxury that surrounded me, I desperately looked for a way to be convincing on his level. "Pop, I think I can be a big help at your office."

Without even lowering his gaze, he absolutely demolished my foray. "What would you do? We already have Willie the janitor."

What little dignity I had maintained up till then crumbled from just these two glancing blows, and I found myself just where my father liked having everyone: helpless and begging. "Okay, okay. I'm getting married and I'll need a job. I have no diploma or experience. (I didn't think that my days on the beach in Acapulco would count.) Will you please give me a job?"

Leaning forward, and with a bearing so rigid even the ash on his cigar wouldn't fall, he looked at me and said, "I don't want any of my grandchildren starving. You can work for me, but you're going to start at the bottom."

Not realizing at that point how far down the bottom could be, I agreed.

The "Bottom," since I wasn't black, was to start as a stock boy. My job was to fill orders for the grease-covered machine parts from racks in the five-story building my father owned in Lower Manhattan. Today it's an upscale area known as SoHo, but back then it was "The Machinery District." I remember how proud I felt when I brought home my first paycheck and handed it to my wife.

"What happened to the rest of the money?" she asked. "Is this just tips?"

Now that I was a husband and soon to be a father with a small rental apartment in Queens, it was time for me to take this opportunity seriously. I left home each morning at 6 a.m., proud that I, the kid who was often late or cut class, arrived first and worked harder than any of the other stock boys. I still revered and read books like Sterling Hayden's *Wanderer* and Heyerdahl's *Kon Tiki*. There I was, day after day, in my gray uniform, picking those greasy parts from shelves that filled five floors of the creaking old building in Lower Manhattan. I filled the orders that made my father prosperous enough to pay me more than I was worth.

Car Top Sailing

I felt gratified that I was finally earning my own money, and if there were any surplus, I could do any goddamn stupid thing I wanted with it. And I did. I bought an 11 ft., car-top sailboat called a PB-II. Sort of like the popular Penguin class boat but with the quality of an early model Yugo. Now all I had to do was get it into the water and sail it.

With sailing facilities in New York City pretty much nonexistent, I decided to take advantage of the obligatory weekend trips to my in-laws' house on Long Island to try out the boat. So, hull and rigging bound to the top of our Chevy II station wagon, we left on our usual Friday pilgrimage through rush hour traffic to the south shore town of Patchogue, arriving just in time for dinner.

My father-in-law, a short, round, very traditional Jewish patriarch, was more familiar with the important religious figures of 19th century Budapest than boat ramps on the south shore of Long Island. However, he thought there might be water deep enough to launch my craft at the end of nearby Old Muck Road. I jumped at the chance to actually sail my own boat. On water.

Anxious to get the failure monkey off my back, I was up at dawn the next morning, and as soon as there was enough light, I spread out all of the boat's components on my in-laws' back lawn in an effort to understand where and how they fit together and how they worked. Pretty confident I had it figured out, I piled the components into the station wagon and set out for the launch site.

Initially frustrated by a few dead ends, I finally found the recommended street where the road parted the swamp grass and descended into the water of Great South Bay.

Cautiously reversing the station wagon, I got as close to the water's edge as I could and set the parking brake. Carefully sliding the small craft off the luggage rack to the water's edge, I pushed it through the rusty clothes hangers, old milk crates, and condoms at the shoreline until it floated.

Thrilled, I stepped the mast, positioned the boom, then returned to the car for the rudder, only to realize I must have left this key component in my in-laws' backyard and would have to return to retrieve it.

Leaving the little craft tied to a cinder block that protruded from the dirty water, I rushed back to the house to pick up the missing piece. Leaving the engine running, I threw the rudder into the car and hurried back to the launch site. As I drove, visions of wavelets lapping the bow as my vessel heeled under a brisk breeze filled my imagination. The sliver of water visible in the distance only served to raise my expectations as I picked my way back to the launch site.

Nearing the waterside, the potholed road doglegged around a junk yard, and as it straightened I anticipated my return to this portal to sea adventure. However, instead of my precious craft, there was nothing but a huge emptiness at the end of the road. I faced the jaw-dropping realization that either I was in the wrong swamp or someone had swiped my splendid sloop.

Sadly, the latter was the case. I was crushed. Once again I was a stymied sailor. Worse, I had to return empty handed to face the scorn of my in-laws.

Bad luck followed me all the way back to their house. I had hoped to park the car down the street so they would not notice my dearth of sailboat. But there was my father-in-law, sitting on a folding chair on the front lawn where he could see me as I slid into a parking space.

"So, did the boat sink?"

"No, Dad, it didn't sink," I said in my most annoyed, defensive manner.

"I don't see it. Did it shrink? Maybe we should all be so lucky you sold it."

"No, I didn't sell it."

"So tell me, Sir Francis Winchester—he never got anything right—what happened to your noble craft?"

"I'm sorry, I lost it."

"You lost a boat? Nobody loses a boat! People lose keys, dogs, maybe the World Series. Only Glenn Patron would lose a boat! Go inside, your mother-in-law made brisket and matzoh ball soup for dinner."

There was little I could do or say at this point except put my tail between my legs and go inside. I had confirmed their opinion that I was wasting my time on foolish, childish schemes. I should be concentrating on being a good Jewish husband, father, and provider instead of some sort of two-bit swashbuckler. At that moment I had to concede they were probably right, and my future looked depressingly domesticated. Once more I had screwed up, and the adventure I so desired had again slid out of my reach.

I guess should have paid more attention to the Bible stories we read as kids at religious school. Like the Passover story. When Moses and the Hebrews found their escape thwarted by the Red Sea, what did Moses do? Did he raise his arms and ask God for a thousand boats? No, sir. He knew his people and said, "Lord, dry land, please. We're walking!"

The Call of the Caribbean

After a year of running up and down stairs in a greasy uniform, my father promoted me from the warehouse to an office position. My initial joy at the ten dollar raise and being able to wear clean clothes every day was tempered by my realization that now, in the same office with him, my father could see what I was doing all the time.

I must say that by this time the birth of my daughter, Ivy, had transformed me into a more responsible adult. I worked even longer hours to prove myself and was constantly on the lookout for ideas that would help the company be more efficient or grow. My father and I clashed often as I tried to advance faster than I probably deserved. I felt unappreciated. He felt pushed.

At this point my ability to speak fluent Spanish, one of the skills—besides smoking grass—I acquired during my sojourn in Mexico, was about to liberate me from this stalemate and toss me into a new life and new challenges.

It was 1967 and one of our customers, a two-employee firm in Ponce, Puerto Rico, called South Puerto Rico Bearings, was going bankrupt. I heard opportunity knocking … in Spanish. Their misfortune could provide me with a chance to get out on my own. Maybe I could pick up this failure cheaply so I could have my own business and also live in a place with a different culture and language.

Steeling myself for the withering opposition I expected, I declared my intention to buy the company and leave Dad's employ. Stunned with his affirmative reply, I was pleased and also a bit confused by his genuine approval of my plan. Why was he suddenly agreeing with me? Did he really love and support his son, or was he just glad to get rid of me?

I'd offered the people in Ponce $3,000 to take the concern off their hands. They accepted and suddenly, I owned a business a couple of thousand miles away. I had a lot of arrangements to make.

Ponce in 1967 was in the midst of a profound transformation. What had been a sleepy Caribbean city, controlled by a dozen or so conservative wealthy families who owned most of the land on the agricultural southern plain, was becoming a humming industrial zone, thanks to the diversification program of the Puerto Rican government. Though surrounded by new petrochemical plants, cement factories, and busy electrical assembly operations, the social life still had an Old World, traditionalist Spanish flavor. Children's birthday parties were always attended by both parents and siblings, and random crime was rare. But there was one major drawback: the climate. It rarely rained and it was hot as hell.

How hot? I once saw a dog chasing a cat … and they were walking.

I fantasized about my future, supposing that I would spend a couple of years becoming wildly successful. Then seeing my real talent and value, my old man would repent and beg me to return to New York with dignity and a salary commensurate with my accomplishment.

Whatever. Since the Ponce business was about to go under, I could hardly make things worse. Right?

Our arrival in Puerto Rico on June 23, 1967, to start a new life was followed shortly after by a message from my mother saying she was flying down from New York to see us, arriving the next week on the Caribair 10 a.m. flight.

Just after noon—the usual arrival time for the Caribair 10 a.m. flight—the DC-3 dropped from the sky and bumped its way through the waves of July heat down the airstrip to the small concrete-block shelter that served as the terminal of the Ponce Airport. The engines coughed and flapped to a stop. The oven-like silence was marred only by the screech of the ungreased wheels of the small stairway being pushed over the shimmering tarmac to the plane.

The door opened, revealing my mom, who proceeded to elegantly make her way down the three steps and across the baking asphalt for perhaps ten steps before she tottered and then fainted. This incident immediately drew a crowd of people who rushed out to where she had fallen and began shouting out suggestions:

"Fan her," said one.

"Get her some water," said another.

"Call a doctor," was proffered.

"Take off her mink," said I.

Once revived she explained she had come to find out if I was all right. Was I? I wasn't so sure.

Imagine the size of the challenge I was facing. I had chosen to rebuild an already failing business in an unfamiliar place in a culture and language not my own. I knew no one and had no business administration schooling or university education whatsoever. I was now slowly beginning to comprehend what it would take to run my own business here. Experience would teach me that to survive I would have to modify my values and behavior to match a very different culture and environment.

For example: While in the midst of my drive to "make it big" and acquire the material symbols of success, I had an enlightening experience. While riding in a sugar mill's company pickup truck on my way out to the cane fields to measure parts needed to repair field machinery, we passed settlements of field workers shacks. I was intrigued to note that scattered amongst the old, warped wooden cabins were newly built, substantial, concrete homes.

I asked the driver, "What's with the nice homes amongst the shacks?"

Looking at the road as he drove, he explained, "They belong to people who have gotten good jobs outside the mill and have made enough money to tear down their old cabins and replace them with nice homes."

Accustomed as I was to the American style of upward mobility, where one leaves a poor area for a better environment to be surrounded by others who also have attained more material wealth, this seemed strange, and I said so to my companion.

Obviously baffled by my remark, he turned and looked me in the eye. "I don't understand you," he said. "Just because now they have more money, why would they want leave the place where they grew up? Where their family and friends still live?"

I had to admit he had a good point.

I learned a similar lesson soon afterwards. I was visiting a store downtown, and when the clerk kept me waiting for a couple of minutes while she carried on a personal conversation instead of tending to me, I called her attention to this serious breach of customer service.

Taken aback and seemingly mystified by my complaint, she replied, demonstrating a humanity that I lacked, "But I was talking to my friend!"

These were attitudes that reflected very human values of local culture and manners. So different from the hard-charging lifestyle I had learned in New York, they gave me pause.

How to Spend Free Time

I realize I am a guy who keeps choosing "the road less traveled." It might be a good idea, every once in a while, for me to question why the hell nobody else is on the road with me. In this case it would have been a damn good idea to have asked why the company I now owned was going under and why no one else had wanted to save it. I learned the answers to these questions slowly and painfully.

In the end I beat the odds and turned the company around, but it was a real struggle. After five intense years of scraping along, I was finally earning enough to buy a house and had sufficient free time to enjoy a hobby.

What hobby? Wood turning? Gardening? Cooking? No, *dirt bikes*.

Why dirt bikes?

As I traveled the island of Puerto Rico each day, visiting customers—I was, in those early days, our best and only salesman—my weekly routine was to drive from factory to factory, selling myself and my company. Week after week, as I traveled the same roads, retracing the same routes, trying to talk the same people into buying my stuff, I was intrigued by the many dirt roads and trails that led off the highways into the distant mountains and spreading cane fields. Where did they go? Who used them?

Though immersed in my obligatory routine, I yearned for an opportunity to take one of these paths: a route that would take me away from the paved roads of civilization. Away from my tedious struggle to make a living and follow them to…? A stream? A farm? A hidden valley?

Who knows what awaits the pathfinder who dares? While I didn't dare while using my company car, I thought that perhaps a motorcycle might be a better way to explore. Of course it would have to be a motorcycle that I could use on the road too. Practical... you know.

I bought all the motorcycle magazines I could and my research convinced me that a Kawasaki Big Horn would be my magic carpet to Puerto Rico's secret places. Next I purchased some National Geodetic Survey maps from the Department of the Interior and set out to explore the trails that ran through the mountainous countryside around Ponce. It was magical.

The Jibaros, mountain dwellers of Puerto Rico, walking and driving their cattle before them, had over the centuries, created shaded, narrow trails along the step mountainsides. For them these journeys on foot from their small subsistence farms, tucked into a valley or mountain hollow, to one of the small towns was just a way to sell their produce and buy goods they could not make themselves. They took for granted the bright colors of the orchids and other flowers that studded the dense tropical green that lined the paths or the literally breath-taking views of the foam-fringed Caribbean coastline thousands of feet below us. The cool streams that were to them just impediments to travel were to become, to us, havens where we washed mud and sweat from our bodies.

As I explored more and more territory and added to my catalogue of trails and routes, I also added disciples to my cult. With time, our group became more proficient at trail breaking and improved our riding skills. Soon we found ourselves racing each other along sections of trails that in the beginning we fearfully traversed only by getting off and pushing our motorcycles.

Within a year there were Enduro and Motocross competitions every couple of weeks somewhere on the island, and I suppose because of all the trail riding I was doing, I had the skills to win often. I was even featured in the bible of the sport, *Dirt Bike*

Magazine, when Editor Chet Heyberger came from California to Puerto Rico to ride with us. We became fast friends. (See *Dirt Bike Magazine* articles on my website, www.accidentalcaptain.com.)

My wife didn't think much of my trophies and renown. She complained about the amount of time I was spending away from my family and strongly suggested I take up a more family-oriented sport. One that would include her, my ten-year-old daughter, Ivy, and seven-year-old son, Andrew. She suggested bowling. I proposed boating.

I asked her, "Come on! Do you really want to spend your time in a dank, noisy bowling alley or be surrounded by tropical islands, beaches, and the blue sea? After all, here we are on an island in the gorgeous Caribbean. Don't you think we should take advantage of all that while we're living here?" Overwhelmed by my argument, she gave in.

It's just like they say: What's the difference between rape and seduction? Salesmanship.

Nautical Baby Steps

In spite of all my history of nautical calamities, I still had enough confidence in myself to believe that now, older and wiser—theoretically—and somewhat more cautious, I should try sailing again.

My vanity said "big boat." My budget said "small boat." My wife, suspicious of any craft smaller that a cruise ship, expressed the opinion that, if it had to be a sailboat, she wanted one with a large flat deck so she could spread out comfortably and get some sun. And it had to have a cockpit big enough for the children. And a nice "kitchen" for cooking.

Since every husband knows that a happy wife makes any undertaking more pleasant, I made these requirements my priorities, leaving other qualities like seaworthiness and safety a bit further down the list.

We had joined what in our town was considered *the* yacht club and social center, the Ponce Yacht and Fishing Club,

The Cal 28 "Family Boat"

basically a bar with docks on a sand spit. There, on my first day of searching, I found a 12-year-old Cal for sale. It had a wide, flat deck, a big cockpit, and a nice galley with a dining room table. Perfect. When the owner proudly told me about all the races he had won with this boat, I was sold, and so was the Cal.

My bank agreed that my new hobby was creditable, so with cash in hand I closed the deal. I was now the proud owner of what I was to find out later was one of the tenderest small sailboats made at the time.

With the self-assurance I had gained by my mastery of cars, motorcycles, and riding lawn mowers, and the 20 years of being "involved" in sailing, I was sure that, even though I had never actually sailed any of my previous boats, I was ready to step into my third craft for the first of what would be many wonderful voyages.

The following Sunday found my family, who I now referred to as "crew," at the dock in boating attire, laden with lunch and our Labrador retriever, Sloppy. Why the dog? Well, because it seemed like the nautical, family thing to do.

They say a dog can sense imminent danger long before humans do. Perhaps that's why our big black Lab whimpered, dug her claws into the wooden dock, and stubbornly refused to be shoved aboard my new acquisition. Finally hauled into the boat, we were to find out her intuition was spot-on.

With family and supplies aboard my perky little craft, I pulled the cord on the 10-hp Johnson outboard and pushed the shift lever to reverse to leave the slip on my maiden voyage. The commencement of our adventure was slightly delayed by a loud *thong* sound and a rebound because I had failed to let loose one of the dock lines.

Details. So annoying.

Unfettered now by this minor setback, the whole kit and caboodle now headed away from the marina's dock and into the small bay where I planned to raise the sails.

I managed to get the main up with only a little difficulty and a few "salty" imprecations. But somehow the jib had become twisted around the forestay. Handing the tiller to my daughter, I snapped the boom tight amidships—the main was flapping and all that noise didn't seem right—stepped upon the foredeck, and strode forward to get the little sail sorted out.

That's when the ship hit the fan.

Abruptly, the bow fell off just as the wind gusted, and the capricious Cal unexpectedly and violently heeled to port. With the deck at an angle of about 45 degrees, my feet went out from under me, and I slid across the "wide flat deck"—that my wife had so desperately wanted—towards the water, stopping only when my crotch came to rest against the port shroud.

Ignoring the waves of pain that washed over me—as well as the saltwater that washed over my dangling toes—I desperately tried to find some way to get my weight off the shroud and more onto the boat's center of gravity. I saw a line lying on the deck within reach. What luck. I'll use it to pull myself towards the boat's center. Bad news. The line I used to try to save myself was the not properly belayed main halyard. The good news was that, as the line slipped through my hand, the mainsail came hurtling down and the boat righted itself.

From the beginning I had planned for my family to be involved in my new hobby, and I must say that as disaster unfolded they did not just sit around doing nothing. No, my wife screamed. My daughter cried. My son ducked into the cabin, and the dog threw up all over the cockpit.

Overwhelmed by the chaos I had created, I crawled back into the cockpit and recognized at that point I had no alternative but to put the helm over and take my victims home. I knew the score and it was Boats 3 - Glenn 0.

I did get the family safely off the boat, and I came back the next day after work and cleaned up the mess. I can understand how others might view this incident as total failure. But since I had never actually moved any of my previous craft across the water before, I considered this experience a small victory. At long last I had my own sailboat. I had taken it out *and* returned it in one piece. Barely.

Miraculously, I did convince my family to sail again by promising them a wonderful trip to a popular nearby destination, the beautiful, nearby isle called Isla Caja de Muertos, referred to in English as "Coffin Island." But after the anchor dragged, the outboard wouldn't start, and we lost the dinghy, they all decided they had had enough. Even though we made it safely back to the marina, to my great embarrassment my family crew informed me they didn't have enough confidence in my ability to sail with me again.

The mutiny by my crew didn't mean I couldn't *use* the boat. In the weeks that followed, I spent quite a few afternoons alone, sitting in the cockpit, morosely drinking away my misery while still fast to the dock. Then one afternoon while I was drowning my sorrows in the cockpit, a guy stopped by to chat. He told me he had learned to sail on a Rhodes 19, he now felt he was ready to step up to something bigger, and had heard — word gets around — that the Cal might be for sale. Befuddled by drink as I was, I could still see there was a logical process here I had missed when I bought the Cal.

Now he could take this wobbly curse off my hands, and I could buy his Rhodes and learn the basics in a simple boat, sailing *alone*. And that's exactly what I did.

As humiliating as it was, I actually went out, bought, and read a book about learning to sail.

After studying the book, with theory now on my side, I started taking out the Rhodes and practicing. With just the mainsail she sailed beautifully. After a few weeks of positive sailing experiences, the jib was hanked on, and the true excellence of this daysailer, on which so many others have learned to sail, became apparent.

From our base in Ponce, I began exploring all the waters and bays along the south coast of Puerto Rico. Going as far east as Humacao and as far west to La Parguera, with each outing I gained knowledge, honed my skills, and built confidence.

My family, noting that I did in fact return from my solo trips unbloodied, were again willing to try a trip or two in the smaller craft but were still too traumatized from my initial attempts to feel comfortable enough to become real sailing aficionados. I was mostly still a solo sailor. Then fate, a four-letter word, grabbed the tiller and put me on another course.

It was 1979, and that year's Pan American Games were to be held in Puerto Rico, with the sailing competitions in Ponce. Again my competitive juices began flowing. A year of successful sailing had by now convinced me that I was the Jewish version of Dennis Conner. The games would be a perfect opportunity for me to add some fame and sailing trophies to my collection of motorcycle-racing awards.

Looking over the list of one design class boats scheduled to compete, I decided that the Snipe class boats were within my budget and ability, so I bought one and successfully coerced my teenaged daughter, Ivy, into being my racing crew.

Although she was only 15, she was, in addition to being a top student, an athletic blonde with a bold spirit. This time things would be different. To be certain we would be properly prepared to compete, I signed us up for classes at the famed Steve Colgate Racing School in City Island, NY.

Over two summer weekends we, along with a dozen other aspiring racers, spent our mornings immersed in theory in a classroom whose walls were replete with trophies, posters, and flags that cried "competition" and "win-win-win." The afternoons were devoted to racing a class boat—Solings— against our fellow students on the surprisingly warm, attractive waters of a little New York coastal town called the Bronx. The results were very heart-ening. Puffed up with the knowledge that on the two consecutive weekends of school we triumphed in every race but one, I was sure we had what it took to take home the gold back in Ponce.

However, the skills and tactics so sharply honed in the Bronx didn't seem to translate to the same success back in Ponce where there were four crews competing for the honor of Puerto Rico. The Olympic Committee had hired a sailing coach—we called him Genghis Khan—who kept us busy with drills and practice races. The sad truth is that we never finished better than third, and when a surprise jibe slammed the boom into Ivy's lovely mouth, thus breaking a front tooth, I knew the jig was up, and I sold the Snipe.

I must admit I never understood the passion these guys have for racing. (In my opinion sailboat racers are the Taliban of sailing). A few years later I was asked to crew on a sailboat in the important Virgin Islands Rolex series of races. There the idiocy of this kind of competition was really brought home to me when I saw *Evergeen*, a 40-ft., Class A racing sloop, costing millions of dollars and boasting a uniformed professional crew, easily being passed by a teenage girl in a bikini on a windsurfer.

Getting Into Cruising

Okay. Racing was out, but I was still fascinated by the idea of cruis-ing by sailboat. I voyaged vicariously by devouring every sailing magazine I could get my hands on: *Sail, Cruising, Sailing, Yachting,* and even some of the more obscure publications like *Gay Navigator* and *Pakistani Wooden Boat Quarterly*. Stories of sailing off to exotic places filled my imagination. But unlike the cruising sailboats I saw anchored in the Club's harbor, with my 19-ft. daysailer, I really couldn't go very far.

Every year from November until the next year's start of hurricane season in July, boats cruising to and from the Caribbean would stop and anchor in the little bay off the Club docks. Hoping to learn some inside stuff about voyaging to faraway places, I approached anyone at the club bar who looked out of place—the scruffy ones—as they were probably cruising sailors and had stories that would be instructive.

Often I would come upon a disheveled couple hiking in the heat on the two-mile walk along the highway to Customs—sometimes it was hard to tell the homeless from the cruisers—and I'd give them a ride or help them find the part or supplies they needed. And along the way I would listen to their tales.

I learned a lot that way.

First: I found the majority of these sailors were not wealthy. They had found ways to finance their dream of making it to the Caribbean—and perhaps beyond—on a modest budget. (Something I was never able to accomplish.)

Second: They knew how to deal with stuff that needed fixing on their boats because being away from the normal world also means being away from professional help.

Third: No one—at least none of the husbands—no matter what travail, danger, or misery they suffered, regretted having made the choice to cruise.

I also noticed that flabby cruisers seemed to be a rarity, so I assumed sailing long distances kept the participants in good shape. Only much later did I find out that the lack of softies had less to do with exercise and more to do with the fact that cruising kills off the weak.

While at that point I could only dream about having the time, money, and vessel necessary to travel like them, I could live like they did, even if only for a week or so, with a bareboat charter. So why not try my hand at the Holy Grail of sailing aficionados, a one-week charter in the Virgin Islands?

I began perusing the dozen or so sailing magazines that arrived each month for ads for bareboat charters. I was looking for a boat that was small enough for me to handle, big enough for four people, but wouldn't break my bank account. I would open each newly arrived issue, working my way through the splashy display ads from the major charter companies showing classy couples on 40- or 50-footers, towards the "classifieds" section. There I would search for someone who offered what I wanted. Scanning the ads one day, the words "Bargain Bare Boat" jumped out at me. It was a small charter company located in Frenchtown on St. Thomas, USVI, that offered a Pearson 26 at a reasonable price that was affordable.

Now who to invite to join me for this historic experience? My wife refused—thank God—to join us. So I looked elsewhere for companionship. Still seeing myself more as a motorcycle guy than a yachtie, my choices for crew were Charlie—the owner and chief mechanic of the local Honda shop—who came with his loud, blonde, pudgy, blue-collar wife, Tina. And to make it an even four, my new pen pal and friend Chet Heyberger, editor of *Dirt Bike Magazine*.

Agreeing on a date to sail, I sent off my $140.00 deposit check and anxiously awaited the arrival date of our departure to St. Thomas.

That First Charter

The clear blue water raced under the wings of the small plane as it descended towards touchdown at the St. Thomas Airport. When the clatter of the propellers—yes, old radial engines—ended, I stepped out of the cool dark cabin into the almost painful brightness of St. Thomas. I was ecstatic; it was really going to happen.

Loading our soft luggage and canned goods into a taxi, I answered the driver's, "Where to?" in a commanding tone, declaring, "Take us to Bargain Boat Rentals."

"Mistah, I take lots of people to chartah places, but I nevah heard o' dat one."

Great, my first yachting trip, and I get a loser for a cabbie. Trying to sound knowledgably annoyed, I told him, "Just take us to Frenchtown. Frenchtown. Got it!"

The charter company's location was one of the things that had influenced me to choose them. Ah, Frenchtown. I had visions of boutiques, sidewalk cafés, and tall, thin, topless women wandering the streets.

After a trip of only about five minutes, the taxi turned off the paved road and stopped. "This be Frenchtown," the driver said and got out to remove our luggage from the back of the van. I paid him and turned to survey the environment. While one could say that today's Frenchtown is gentrifying, the 1970's version would better be described as putrefying.

Undaunted, I surveyed the area, looking for the charter company's marina. Since a charter company would logically be on the waterfront, we picked our way through the jumble of old shacks to the water's edge where we found a hastily whitewashed house, and on one wall were the hand-drawn initials B.B.R. over an anchor. This was the establishment we were seeking.

Looking back now, I marvel at how simple everything was in those days. No credit cards; instead, you paid cash for everything. No pesky insurance regulations or deductibles. The "Captain's Orientation" consisted of an explanation of where the two-stroke oil for the outboard was stored, and the chart briefing was confined to the simple statement, "Here's the chart." Then off we went. Wow. All this for only $700. Such a deal.

Now checked out, with crew and supplies aboard, we started the 6-hp Johnson outboard and began an easy, outboard-motor sail across Charlotte Amalie Harbor towards the open sea. It wasn't until we turned west, shut down the engine, and found ourselves outside the protection of the Frenchman's Reef promontory that we learned what the Caribbean currents and winds really were like.

Awaiting us out there was 15 knots of wind and about two knots of current, which strongly opposed our plans of spending that night in Caneel Bay. However, the south shore of St. Thomas was beautiful, and we got to know it very well as we tacked our tiny cruiser back and forth, arriving at pretty much the same point on land each time our tack took us back to the green, hotel-dotted coast.

Surrendering to practicality, we lit up the outboard again, and with its help we were able to make more progress. But even with this mechanical assistance, at 5 p.m. we had only gone as far as Christmas Cove. The calculation that we had only traveled seven miles in six hours convinced us to stop for the day and that taking shelter off the beach of this low, dry island was the better part of valor. Sails down, we putt-putted in, dropped the toy anchor, and broke out the booze.

So ended Day One.

Day Two would be the second day of our one-day trip to Caneel Bay on St. John. The learning process for me had begun.

Today, as a veteran boat owner and Caribbean sailor, I sneer at people who come to the Virgins to charter and seem to think that an integral part of the experience is to tie a handkerchief around their heads and become drunken, loud yahoos at the anchorages. (Although I graciously give a pass to the topless ladies, gentleman that I am.)

But it would do me well to remember my first charter ... and Tina. There she was, an abundance of flesh and blonde hair, knocking down Scotch whenever it was calm enough to do so. Next to her, sitting quietly on a blue cushion, was her husband Charlie, a dead ringer for Bob Denver's perpetually shipwrecked Gilligan, in his old "Hondas are Hot" T-shirt. Tina was enjoying the trip to the fullest and had no qualms about letting everyone know it.

After an all-day sail in the relatively sheltered waters of St. John, we reached our chosen destination: the bay and beach in front of the elegant Caneel Bay Hotel. In the gloaming's dying breeze, we soundlessly floated to a stop, quite close to where white-coated waiters were serving cool drinks to guests in cocktail clothes at the beach bar.

Suddenly, before I could even drop the anchor, Tina came alive. Knocking down her fourth Scotch of the day, poured into a bikini but forgetting to say "when," all engines on forward and jiggling all her "rigging," Tina jumped to the deck and leapt into the water, bellowing as loudly as she could, "THIS IS FUCKING FANTASTIC!" Normally, I would have been mortified, but I was so stoned myself I could only nod my head and say, "Yeah."

The rest of the week continued pretty much along those same lines: a series of hangovers and heavenly bays. Surrounded now by the Bali Hai panorama that I had only seen from a distance from my parent's terrace, I truly felt as though I had arrived in paradise.

Luckily, the Pearson was small enough and shallow enough that we managed to spend the week missing the reefs and rocks that we should have been looking for but weren't, thus avoiding any "incidents." The engine did die on the third day out, but as a paean to my planning, having Charlie, a professional two-stroke mechanic, on board turned what could have been a calamity into just a bump in the road to a perfect first sailing vacation.

Comfortably exhausted, the boat safely returned to its slip, we boarded our return flight to Puerto Rico. I watched through the small window as St. Thomas disappeared under the wing and thought about what the previous seven days had meant to me.

I realized that while my general competence as a captain or my sailing skills had not really been challenged or proven on this trip, my fantasy about the trip had been completely realized. The incredible beauty of the land and sea, and the sensory pleasures of nearly perfect sailing conditions here, were all anyone could ask for.

I knew that I had to do this again.

Getting My Wife On Board

Who wouldn't enjoy a trip like the one I had just completed, I thought. I just need to get my wife turned on to this wonderful pastime then we'll be able to enjoy sailing as a family. But in the euphoria of the moment, I had failed to take into account her aversion to frightening situations, her distaste for heavy drinking, and abhorrence for physical discomfort.

This fallacy in my logic may be obvious to the reader, but obsessed as I was by the dream, it wasn't evident to me at the time. I decided to begin my sales pitch at a low level, steadily increasing the intensity until I finally broke through her stubbornness by promising her a luxurious week in the Grenadines on a comfortable Gulfstar 50 from a charter company I found in St. Vincent.

Why do we men do this over and over again? We promise a woman the world to get her to agree to do what we want, then damn. They expect us to deliver.

Now I had to deal with three problems.

First: How was I going to convince the charter company to rent me a boat almost twice as long as the only sailboat I had ever successfully commanded?

Second: How was I going to *pay* for this?

Third: How would I make sure my spouse would enjoy every moment of the voyage?

The obvious solution to all three challenges: Use deception and manipulation.

First: To qualify for this impressive yacht, I convinced my friend Dr. Bill Fleming, Puerto Rico's famous dirt bike-riding psychiatrist, to join us. Bill looks more like Man-Mountain Dean the wrestler than Sigmund Freud, but he is as gentle as an old Labrador retriever. (And based on our previous family sailing experiences, his psychiatric skills might come in handy at some point.)

Owner of a 42-ft. sport fisherman, and a Caribbean native, Bill had the chops to be the captain, so I put his name on the contract as "captain" instead of mine.

Two: To share the financial load, I also invited my old journalist buddy Chet, who would bring along his girlfriend Gina—rhymes with Tina?—and a female friend from work. We solved the financials by doing a three-way split of the charter fee.

Two down and one to go.

Departure Day. My reunion that Sunday morning with Chet at the San Juan Airport was warm and heartfelt. With him were skinny, straggle-hair Gina and her statuesque work buddy, the Swedish blonde bombshell Elsa.

My wife and Bill completed our crew, and we all felt a tremendous sense of anticipation as we boarded the modern jet to Barbados. There we would spend the night and catch a puddle jumper the next morning to arrive at our destination, St. Vincent. Once there I felt it would be safe enough to tell Bill I had put him down as captain. When the time came, Dr. Bill not only handled the deception well, he made it a reality—a good thing in the end—so we had no problem convincing the charter company to let us have this sleek, commodious yacht.

The big sloop was a quantum leap from the little 26 footer that had been our first charter boat. Unlike the Pearson, whose interior smelled like gasoline and unflushed toilet, the Gulfstar's cool, shady cabin surrounded us with the fragrance of its fine woods and rich, white-upholstered settees. Dishes and glasses had their place, and the brass and stainless steel fittings shone. A refrigerator assured ice and cold drinks. Seen from the cockpit, the mast seemed to reach to the heavens, and the bow disappeared into the distance.

Once the charter company's orientation was over, we split into two groups. Chet, Bill, and my wife went to the supermarket for supplies while Gina and I stayed on board to get everything put away, prepared, and shipshape. However, before we began our labors, I decided to introduce Gina to my double booze, double sweet Puerto Rican Rum Punch. I watched as she drained the glass, licked her lips, and then suddenly pressed them hard to mine. Grappling and stumbling, we found our way forward. Oh, boy, what a trip this was going to be, I thought as I felt my way to the V-berth.

All too soon our efficient team of shoppers returned, and with luggage now stowed we raised anchor, setting our sights and sails for the anchorage at Admiralty Bay, Bequia, only seven miles south of our Blue Lagoon base.

Essential Supplies

With our destination due south and the 15 kts. of wind 60 degrees off the port bow, the short hop was over in no time, and the afternoon found us anchored off Port Elizabeth before we could fully enjoy the great sail we were having.

This miniature, low-rise town arrayed along the curving beach was the perfect place to start what would be a very different cruise. Unlike the busy Virgins, the Grenadines are a scenic, sparsely populated string of about a dozen islands. This archipelago trails south from St. Vincent 60 miles to the major island of Grenada, a place that would later become the scene of a lopsided American military victory over the nefarious forces of Communist evil.

Grenada was too far for us to reach and return in the week we had available, so we decided to go only as far as Palm Island—about halfway—a pilgrimage to meet the author of the famous sailing saga *Desperate Voyage* by John Caldwell.

Quaint and low key aptly describes the small cluster of pastel-painted restaurants and bars along the Admiralty Bay beach, so when Elsa said, "Hey, let's go ashore and party!" I wondered if we would find as much excitement ashore as I already had experienced on board. We went but found the village was so sedate and quiet we were soon back on board for more fun. The conversation turned to motorcycles and how much everyone was enjoying my special, alcoholic rum confection. My wife, a teetotaler and non-rider, was, though I barely noticed at the time, a bit aloof.

Mysterious hangovers again the next morning. How can all that pineapple and orange juice give us headaches? Must be the ice. Even at our reduced level of alertness, we were able to raise anchor and sails and turn again south towards our next stop: the primitive—in those days—nearly uninhabited island of Canouan, a hop of less than 20 miles.

Again Aeolus was on our side, and the big, sleek yacht, unperturbed by 20 kts. of wind and 5-foot, sunlight-flecked seas, had us in Charlestown Bay in three hours. Some small wooden houses were scattered along the water's edge. A poet would describe their exteriors as pastel—I call them faded—against the backdrop of a small hill covered with parched grass, beyond which any sign of habitation was negligible. Jeez, Bequia was like Times Square compared to this place.

Fortifying ourselves with a lunch of sandwiches and beer, we discussed strategies for dealing with a serious problem we had encountered. After only two days, the orgiastic consumption of my rum punches had exhausted our supply of the main alcoholic component: rum.

Elsa, blonde-haired and perfectly bikinied, declared, "You bums have been knocking down so many punches that we're out of rum." This announcement was met with three gasps. (My wife couldn't have cared less.) Looking at me with gray eyes that had gone from delicate to steely, Elsa said, "Who's going ashore to get some more?"

Silence.

"Glenn, you weren't part of the St. Vincent shopping party." (How could I forget?) "It's your turn." My protestations that putting the dinghy in the water and mounting the outboard were too much trouble were answered with, "So swim."

After splashing the dinghy, I pulled it up onto the beach and looked around. The sand road that ran behind the beach was empty of people and vehicles, but to my left, maybe 100 yards away and nestled in a copse of mangroves, I could see a wooden shack with a hand-painted white sign with the word "GROSERY" in red. I could think of nothing more gross than being out of rum, so I trudged over and went in.

The light that leaked in through the door illuminated wooden shelves painted blue and sparsely populated with products like Marmite and Twinings and Smarties. No rum in sight.

Behind the counter, overflowing an aluminum beach chair, was a huge black woman, not just sleeping but snoring loudly. With some trepidation I called out, "Hello, hello, ma'am." I was relieved to see that she stirred a little. My "Ma'am, do you sell rum?" caused her to open one eye and say something I couldn't make out.

My question, "Excuse me, what did you say?" provoked a heaving of flesh from the sagging chair to her feet. Reaching under the counter, she took out a funnel, placed it on the dusty counter, looked me in the eye, and said, "Where's you bottle?"

Now I get it. Rum in bulk. Just what we needed.

Not wanting to have to return to the boat for a container, I bought six bottles of something called Ribena, emptied them onto the sandy road, and had them filled with a vicious-smelling white stuff she called *Ba-bush*. The bill was minuscule, and with the bottles tied together with a piece of string, I clanked my way back to the yacht. With the main ingredient again in plentiful supply, we set about testing a new recipe.

Word must have gotten out via the Tobago Telegraph that there were customers in town because a few minutes later a pirogue with two guys in threadbare bathing suits appeared next to us.

"Lobstah. Hey, mon, you want lobstah? Fresh, jus' dis mawnin."

The crew exchanged glances that said, "Wow, this is really Caribbean. Fresh lobster from the fishermen who just caught them."

"Let's see them," Chet demanded. The guy in the bow held up a whole Caribbean lobster of about 5 lbs. in each hand, and the guy in the back said, "Bot' for ten dollah."

What a deal. I had turned to go below and get my wallet when Gina grabbed my arm and said, "Wait. In places like this you never pay the first full price. I'll handle this."

Turning back towards the water, and looking down at the two men in the dugout from the heights of our stately vessel, she said,

"Ten dollars? That's too much money."

There was a long silence during which the man who quoted the price just stared at her from his seat in the engineless, hand-hewn little craft. Then he turned his head towards the high, proud bow of our noble yacht and slowly moved his gaze along the teak toe rail, cabin top, and shiny, stainless steel dorades, all the way to the fiberglass dinghy and outboard in the stern davits.

His gaze returned to our bunch of pale-faced visitors, and shaking his head, his voice dripping with sarcasm, he told us, "You be shame you isn't got ten dollah to pay for our day's work."

We "shame" and coughed up the $10.

The lobster was delicious, and our enjoyment of Tuesday evening in Canuoan was greatly enhanced by the joints Chet had hidden in his suitcase and slipped past Customs. While we puffed and giggled and planned future outrageous escapades, the mother of my children sat on the poop deck, as far away from the fun as possible, watching out for any sign of the authorities she was sure would appear at any moment to drag us away to some terrible West Indian dungeon.

Abandon Ship

The next day, Wednesday, dawned bright and fresh, a description that could not be applied to most of the crew. Nevertheless, with Palm Island, our turn-around point, practically in sight, we had some time to relax and recover that morning. But when 11 a.m. rolled around, I—aka Captain Blighstein—was forced to rouse the group to weigh anchor so we would have time to make a stop at The Anchorage, a hotel and marina on the east side of Union Island recommended by our cruising guide. The crew may have been slow, but thanks to another nice, close reach, we covered the short distance quickly and were sitting at the marina bar by 2 p.m.

We were on our second round and having a great time when I realized that my wife, who quite some time ago had said she was going to the bathroom, had not returned. Puzzled, I left the group, who were trying to learn bawdy songs in Swedish from Elsa, and began a search that ended when I found her in earnest conversation with the marina manager in his office.

It seems our plan for skinny dipping at Mayreau had broken the camel's back for her, and when the hotel said it could arrange her immediate departure via a pricey charter flight to Barbados and then home, she jumped at the chance and ordered the plane.

Although I tut-tutted the expense a bit, I have to admit that elimination of this drag on our fun was, as my four-times-married father used to say about divorce, "expensive but worth it." Thirty minutes and $300 dollars later, she was in the co-pilot's seat of a small plane as it taxied down the runway.

It was while standing there in the long grass that bordered the Union Island airport, watching the plane carrying my straight-laced wife grow smaller and smaller, that I realized cruising is not so much an activity as a state of mind. A state of mind involving an intoxicating mixture of adventure, skill, and the acceptance of Mother Nature's will and human nature's imperfections. My wife would never understand why this pastime held such a strong attraction for me, let alone participate or appreciate why I wanted to spend my time with others who felt the same way.

Ergo, my life was about to undergo yet another, even more traumatic change.

2
Second Chance

My natural ability as a sales/marketing person had created dramatic sales volume increases for my company. But this growth in sales had quickly outstripped my meagre administrative abilities. So as Ronald Reagan began to put his stamp on the American economy, my three-location distribution enterprise was out of control and deeply in debt. At the same time, my marriage was also ailing.

Despite our best intentions, my wife of 18 years and I were now headed down paths that were increasingly diverging. Intensely wrenching for my children and a huge misfortune for my wife, my decision to end the marriage was for me a matter of emotional survival. Unable to convince my wife to reconsider the rules and goals we had set for ourselves as teenagers 20 years before, I felt my only choice now was to go it alone.

My feelings of guilt obligated me to leave our home with everything in place. I considered myself fortunate to find a very modest, two-story waterfront vacation home rental along the tranquil mangrove-lined shore just west of Ponce.

The area, called El Boquete, was a tiny settlement of fishermen. The house also came with a small dock, and there, nestled amongst the mangroves, I and the Rhodes 19 planned to dwell for the near future.

Healing

During the tumultuous year of my near bankruptcy and the strains of my domestic break-up, I was battered by a constant stream of problems, aggravations, and trials. I would have given up if not for the one really big thing I had in my favor: Dr. Bill Fleming.

My friend Bill was not just a trail-riding, hard-drinking sailing companion, he was also a very astute observer of people and a talented therapist. During this seemingly endless period of depressing misery, he worked hard to help me put all my broken pieces back together, never asking for a penny for all the hours he spent—in and outside his office—taking the shattered person I was and helping me to create a new, better human being.

Because there were lawyer's fees and child support to pay, not to mention reviving the business that was my only source of income, I couldn't "go away" and rehabilitate myself. I had to buckle down and find a way to mend my business while Bill was mending me.

I had married at 21 and become a father at 22. Now for the first time in my life, I had a place of my own and was not obligated to negotiate or compromise with anyone about what I did in my home. Initially, the only small, bright light I could see was this wonderful opportunity to experience life as an unmarried adult. Would I be a hermit? A swinging bachelor? Was this new life going to be "My Oyster?" Or just a bad clam? I planned to find out.

After other priorities were dealt with positively, I could look at pleasures available to me. One of these was to get reacquainted with women.

As a married man it seemed as though the world was just full of fabulously interesting, good-looking women. Tall ones, short ones, smart or sexy. They were everywhere. Now that I was single, I wanted to get to know them all. But like so many of my other fantasies, I found the reality was very different.

My dentist's assistant, who looked so sexy I literally drooled over her, turned out to be a dolt. The sexy, tall, skinny girl I met at the Holiday Inn bar just wanted to go dancing every night. The divorced wives my age whom my friends promoted were boring, and neither they nor any other female I met wanted to go sailing. So when I acquired a steady girlfriend across the island in San Juan, and started sleeping there, my sad little sailboat languished, jilted at her little dock.

The big city had restaurants, hotels, and culture, and after provincial Ponce, I found them very exciting. As time went by I began spending more and more time there. I turned what had been my branch office in San Juan into the company headquarters, and since my Ponce friends had rallied around my discarded wife, and my kids hated my guts, I spent most of my time enjoying the new, urban, sophisticated life available to me in the capitol city.

My new romance didn't last, but who cared. I was single in the big city. I found an apartment in Old San Juan—the Historic District—that overlooked the center of the old city's social life, Plaza San Jose. Covering the entire third floor of a 19th century building, it had a huge terrace from which I could observe, every night, hundreds of people—tourists and locals—hanging out. Booze, music, and romance were there, waiting right at my doorstep.

The big city also gave me a chance to indulge an ambition I had harbored for years. I became involved in some amateur theater groups. Although I had no formal acting training—except for what I learned about drama during the 18 years I lived with my mother—after a few walk-ons, I was given some choice roles. This exposure led to paid gigs doing ads and voice-overs for TV and radio.

My big break came when I began getting parts in the local TV soap operas—*telenovelas*—which had a large following in the Spanish-speaking world. While I played supporting roles, I worked with Gisele Blondet, Alba Nydia Diaz, and Daniel Lugo, some of the biggest Latin American stars of the day.

Working surrounded by cameras, monitors, crew, and the make-up girl touching me up was so exhilarating that each time I left the studio I felt as though I were walking on air.

But acting with a live audience out there in the dark theater was the best. It gave me a hugely satisfying, visceral emotional response every time I got a laugh from the audience. I was just a small fish in a smaller pond, but that pond had become my world, and performing made me feel alive in a way nothing else did. While, thankfully, my company's financial condition was slowly improving; nevertheless, the money I earned from performing came in very handy and validated me as a professional.

The struggle to rebuild the source of my income filled my days, and discovering so many new opportunities filled my nights. All this time the Rhodes sat, tied to the little dock in Boquete, gathering barnacles and patiently waiting for me. She knew I'd never abandon her completely. She was right, but something would have to happen before then.

I was returning from work one day, and as I opened the door to the building on Plaza San Jose, one of my fellow bachelor Lotharios walked by and said, "Hey, Gringo, you gotta check out the Manager's Cocktail party at El Convento Hotel tonight."

Puzzled, I turned and asked, "Why? What's so special there?"

"Gringa tourists. They go every Thursday. Lots of them! It's *La Vida Loca*."

Well, since I wasn't working that night, didn't have any acting to do, culture to take in, or clothes to wash, I decided what the hell, go for it.

El Convento is a small, chic boutique hotel housed in what used to be an old Spanish nunnery in the most picturesque part of the Historic District. Surrounded by the quarter's Spanish colonial buildings and blue cobblestone streets, it looks more like a piece of Seville than a building in the Caribbean. I checked and found that the weekly Manager's Cocktail Party for the hotel's guests was held at 6 p.m. on the third floor's "Sunset Terrace" overlooking the bay. Though not a guest, I knew I could talk my way in.

So that night, showered, perfumed and dressed in my best flowered shirt, I walked the three blocks from my house to the hotel and

Charming El Convento Hotel

nonchalantly pressed the 3 button in the small antique elevator.

Leaving the hotel's shaded interior hallway, I was temporarily blinded by the golden glow of the setting sun as I stepped out onto a wide terrace. As my eyes adjusted, the light receded, revealing a long, purple shape that slowly identified itself as a long, flowing, wine-colored dress adorning a slim blonde with a graceful profile, sitting on the low wall at the edge of the terrace. She was amazingly beautiful in an angular but soaring way. I thought, Wow, if Eero Saarinen—who created the TWA terminal at JFK and the Arch in St. Louis—had been commissioned to design a woman, *this* is what he would've produced.

Fascinated and intimidated at the same time, I decided to try a flanking operation. Finding a temporary haven chatting with a tourist couple from England, I studied the lithesome blonde. The object of my attention never moved nor did she engage in conversation with anyone. Perhaps her aloofness was an indication she was so stuck-up she wouldn't have anything to do with the likes of me.

Gathering my courage and steeling myself for rejection, I excused myself and approached her. Sucking in my gut, I smiled and said, "Hi, would you care to join us?"

"Oh, thank God," she exclaimed, "You're the first person I've met here who speaks English!"

Well that explained the aloofness.

Okay, so she wasn't attracted by my looks or suave manner but rather by our common language. It was a start. And when I took out my pack of Merit cigarettes, her eyes lit up. "I smoke Merits too," she proclaimed. Connection #2.

Unbelievably, as though I had written the script, she, Gale Wilson, told me she was from New York, worked in the theater, and enjoyed sailing. She had lived for many years in the Cayman Islands before her divorce and loved getting back to the Caribbean whenever she could to visit her friends who lived in ... the British Virgin Islands.

Bingo. This was too good to be true.

Setting my charm and bullshit to peak output, and checking to see if I still had one credit card that was not over the limit, I rustled up all my *savoir faire* and asked, "Hey, how about joining me for dinner once they stop serving the free food and booze here? I know a wonderful *tapas* place nearby."

I nearly fainted when she smiled and said, "Yes." But then she added—cue the screeching sound of brakes—"But my two daughters are in our room, and I can't go to dinner and leave them alone."

Now this was a major bummer. All I had in mind at the time was, "How do I get her alone and naked?" But from some previously undiscovered well of decency deep inside me, I produced, surprising myself, the statement, "Great! Can I meet them? I love children. We can all go out to dinner together," and down we went to her room.

When the object of my interest opened the door to her room, the two girls, caught in the middle of a shrieking pillow fight, froze in mid-swing and stared at the bearded stranger standing next to Mom in the doorway.

Gale's daughters, Jill and Adrienne, then 13 and 12 years old, were at the peak of their prepubescent cuteness. I found myself totally overwhelmed by this feminine threesome. My life was already full of exciting things, but unexpectedly, I was overcome by the sudden desire to share my world with these three delicious human beings.

My reverie was broken when Gale asked the girls, "Is it alright if Glenn and I go out to dinner?"

Jumping up and down again on the bed, they sang out, "Yes, Mommy, have fun," and, "Oh, Mommy, yes. It's Love Boat!"

Our dinner that night was a big success, and I went on to spend the next three days showing them around the island. This first visit was followed by a 12-month whirlwind, long distance courtship with alternating monthly trips of me flying to New York or Gale coming to San Juan.

Both recently divorced, we didn't have much money. (Unable to find an affordable apartment in Manhattan, Gale had spent the previous winter living with her girls in an unheated houseboat at Manhattan's 79th Street Boat Basin.) But we felt sure we could blend our families successfully, and the money issues would work themselves out somehow.

Jill, dark haired, tall and slim and intense, was the striver who would later go as far as being Director of Marketing Services for *The New York Times* before dropping out of the business world to raise her children.

Adrienne was her opposite. An indifferent student, she struggled her way to a BA and then, out in the real world, broke all sales records at Johnson & Johnson's Surgical Products Division. An out-of-the box thinker, I will never forget how once when we were living together in San Juan, she solved the "Senior Prom Dress" dilemma.

It was Jill's Senior Prom, and as is customary in Puerto Rico, siblings also attend. The parents of the boys had it easy. Just rent tuxedos for the kids. But we couldn't compete with the other parents of daughters at Jill's upscale, private school in San Juan who were spending thousands—that we didn't have—on prom dresses for their daughters. Just paying for Jill's dress was a real stretch. At the dress discussion with Adie, she told us, "Don't worry about me. I've got a plan. Just give me $75, and I'll deal with the situation."

And deal she did. The night of the prom, she was the self-assured center of attention with her long blonde hair cascading over the padded shoulders of a splendid, black, rented tuxedo. Four-inch heels and a big red carnation in her lapel completed the picture. Creativity trumps money anytime.

Right from the start Gale and I just knew that, somehow, we would make it work. She loved my sailboat and I loved her. The clincher was when we scraped together enough money to spend an idyllic week on a chartered Morgan 36 in the British Virgin Islands. Not only was Gale attractive and interesting, she was a real sailor. How did I get so lucky?

Our New Life

These interludes with Gale were emotionally nourishing, wonderfully romantic, and were short reprieves from my daily routine of dealing with angry creditors, unhappy customers, and disgruntled employees.

By now I had become immensely tired of the rat race I had been running all these years. The pressure of scrambling day after day to create a "big business" and be a "big success" had been exhausting and just wasn't working. I had learned from the two years of coaching by Dr. Bill that there were other ways of finding validation, gratification, and contentment.

My sailing experiences showed me the way. The simplicity of the little Rhodes 19 allowed me to start with the basics and build my skills until I was ready to handle something bigger.

Perhaps by just focusing my efforts on simply making my firm "better" rather than bigger, profitable rather than impressive, I could still earn a modest salary and go home each night to a happy family and a life that was solid and well grounded. I decided this would be my path. Now how to get there from where I was?

I found that by shrinking the company down to a more manageable size, I could squeeze out enough money to pay off my creditors and gain better control over the company's operations. And instead of expending so much effort trying to convince everyone to buy everything from us, we focused on selling only the most profitable products to a smaller, more select customer base. This way we had the resources to show our customers we were competently managed and could be trusted to quickly and efficiently take care of their needs. The new goal was quality not quantity. Just as the new plan began to produce results, news from New York threatened to derail the process.

My uncle, who had assisted my dad in running his large company, had suddenly died, and my 73-year-old father wanted me to return to New York, almost 20 years after I had imagined it happening, to help him and to pick up the slack.

Returning to New York was a very tempting possibility. It offered security, a guaranteed comfortable income, and would remove me from my present financial predicament. But I knew that if I accepted his deal, I would be returning as a failure. I would be leaving the Caribbean and the exciting life I had been leading. Not only that, but I would be abandoning the handful of loyal employees who had stuck with me through the bad times, trusting me to save the company and their jobs. "Sorry, Pop," I told him. "I have to stay in Puerto Rico."

So after a year and a half of shuttling between San Juan and New York City, and wearing the engagement ring I bought with my earnings from the TV soap opera *"Angelica Mi Vida,"* Gale and the two little girls arrived at the San Juan airport. This time without a return ticket.

We celebrated Christmas 1984 in a small rented home on San Justo Street in Old San Juan and three months later made our formal commitment to each other by being married in a ceremony on the front steps of the El Convento. In a frenzy of nostalgia, we celebrated our wedding reception on the same Sunset Terrace where we had met.

Old salt that he was, Gale's father offered a nautical toast. "I'm not losing a daughter, I am gaining new crew." I later found out he gave the same toast to Gale's first mate—who was also a sailor— making me her 2nd mate.

The day of our wedding my father offered me two pieces of advice.

First: "There are three rules to follow to assure a happy marriage." Unfortunately, he didn't know what they were.

Second: He had arranged with the hotel to have a dozen oysters waiting in our room for me to eat after the party.

A dozen oysters: it's just a myth. Only four of them worked.

My father was soon to find a positive ending of his own when that same year he sold his company and went on to live happily ever after in a comfortable retirement with his fourth wife.

After a few days spent getting our affairs in order, Gale and I left on a dream honeymoon to Greece.

During our long-distance courtship, we had flown between San Juan and New York so often we had accumulated enough Frequent Flyer miles to fly First Class to Greece. Once there, to cover as much territory as possible in the week we had for our trip, I rented a car. I loved the winding mountain roads, and my driving fit in perfectly with the anarchistic style of the local Greeks.

My knowledge of Puerto Rico's mountain roads—paved and dirt—had a few years before put me in great demand for laying out rally routes for the island's sports car clubs, culminating in my participation in the Carreras 1000 Rally in Jamaica, so I was really in my element in Greece.

At first Gale let me have my head, but on the second day she dropped a subtle hint when she asked, "Do you remember our wonderful wedding ceremony?"

Our quaint house on Calle San Justo in picturesque Old San Juan

"How could I forget?" I replied.
"Remember the part where I agreed 'til death do us part?"
"Sure."
"Well at the time I didn't think it might happen so soon."
I got the message.

Back to the Sea

Honeymoon over and back on the job, any dreams we had of sailing had to take a back seat for a while to our efforts to firm up our finances. Gale rolled up her sleeves and found a minimum wage job in an art gallery then found a better one as the manager of Butterfly People, a restaurant and gallery in Old San Juan, known worldwide for its exceptional creations of three-dimensional art made with real butterflies.

We were lucky to find more work doing small-time acting jobs and minor roles in films and commercials that gave us some additional income. We also found fairly steady work as actors in murder mysteries or playing teacher/chaperones at the "'50s parties" which were so popular then at conventions held at San Juan hotels. All this "extra income" went into a special bank account for the future purchase of a sailboat.

I was very appreciative that as a trained, experienced actress—and graduate of the prestigious American Academy of Dramatic Arts in New York—Gale's skill and advice greatly aided my nascent acting career. But when I got my big break, it was all me.

I am an irrepressible—some might say chronic—joke teller. So when I saw an article in the newspaper that Columbia Pictures, publicizing the release of the Tom Hanks, Sally Fields film "Punchline," was holding a competition to find the "Best Stand-up Comedian in Puerto Rico," I gladly picked up the gauntlet.

I channeled Henny Youngman and Mort Sahl and, after three rounds of eliminations, was chosen as one of four finalists. I thought the odds were against me when they held the championship round at a "yuppie" night club, but when you realize I was the only Jew in the finals, there shouldn't have been any doubt in my mind.

One of the prizes for winning was a guest appearance on "Sunshine's Café," the most watched prime time comedy show on TV at the time. With this on my resume, and the acquisition of an experienced talent agent, I now found myself making some real money doing intermittent stand-up and MC gigs at conventions. The balance in the "Boat Fund" was climbing steadily.

While my TV appearance got me the most recognition, it was a sales convention job for a large technology company at the huge El Conquistador Hotel that I remember most fondly.

At a preconvention meeting, the person in charge of convention entertainment told me they wanted everything done "First Class." (If so, why were they hiring me?) All I had to do was write a five-minute comedy skit around a guy who worked for the company and his wife. Then I would leave the stage, and during the 15-minute fashion show, my stage wife—guess who

I hired—and I would change into formal dress and return for the final comedy closing.

For this they would put us up, all expenses paid, at the hotel and pay us $700. When I admitted to lacking a tux, they bought me one.

Little did I know that the best was yet to come.

The opening skit went off well. It was when we rushed to the small changing room behind the stage to get into our formal clothes that I found out two very significant things. First, the fashion show was a *bathing suit* fashion show. Second, there was only one place for all of us to change. Yeah, me and 15 stunning female models getting in and out of bikinis.

I was so flustered it seemed like it took me forever to buckle my cummerbund and "relax" enough to go back on stage again. I know it sounds like a teenage boy's fantasy, but it really happened. I still have the tux to prove it.

By this time, with our finances now not so desperate, and by sharing the cost with friends from San Juan, we were able to do some sporadic chartering in the Virgins, so our lives, while still waiting for enough money to buy our own boat, were not completely devoid of nautical pleasures.

The British Virgins, whether on land or sea, had lost none of their charm for me, and now there was an added kick. Gale's old Cayman Island friends David and Margaret were now the new colonial governor and his wife, and our arrivals at little Beef Island Airport were treated like state visits. The initial joy of arriving safely was soon eclipsed by the privilege of being met at the plane's door by the governor's driver and royal blue Jaguar Mark 10, flags flying, et al. While the other passengers queued up for Customs and Immigration in the heat, we were giggling like school girls in the Jag's plush back seat, with the air conditioning blasting away while we awaited the driver's return from dealing with the bureaucracy. Then on to our lodgings at historic Government House. Wow.

Perhaps this is a good time to explain why Gale had so many fancy friends and how she had acquired her sailing skills.

Her mother was Boston aristocracy from an old maritime New England family whose rope braid brand is well known to this day. They were such an old New England maritime family that they never had to brag of arriving on the *Mayflower*. They came over on their *own* boat. Her father's French side of the family boasted theater celebrities, heirlooms, silver, and valuable paintings going back as far as the 17th century. Imagine how I felt in their company. The oldest thing my family brought with them from Europe was … Grandma.

So you can understand why I felt a bit intimidated when, about a year after we were married, we received an invitation to attend Gale's cousin's wedding at the family "Camp" on Maine's Belgrade Lake. From Gale's description of the place, I could tell it was a very different setup from the place where I had spent my summers playing softball on a hot, dusty playing field and roasting marshmallows on a dying campfire.

Recognizing the social and ethnic gulf between us, and wanting desperately to project an image that would fit in with this group, I bought a blue blazer, oxford shirt, and khakis. Calling around, I found that the Dollar Rent A Car office at the Boston airport had the perfect vehicle, a nice, conservative Ford station wagon, and I made the arrangements to have it waiting for our afternoon arrival at the Boston airport.

Our flight was much delayed leaving San Juan—what's new?— and I was very relieved to find someone still at the Dollar counter when we finally straggled in at 1 a.m.

Industriously shuffling keys behind the counter, the clerk assured me that if I had a reservation, he would have a car for me. Then with a big "Aha," he looked up and, waving a key with some tags in my face, announced, "Not only does Dollar have a car for you at this late hour, but we're giving you an upgrade."

I thought, "Well, things are looking up."

"Yes, Mr. Patron, you will be driving out of here in a luxurious Cadillac Coupe de Ville."

Oy vey. I had no choice at that point but to accept this icon of Jewish materialism. (Imagine, driving around the Maine woods in a powder blue Cadillac with a bumper sticker that said DOLLAR.) My cover totally blown, we headed north. Once at our destination I was able to find a place in the woods where I could stash the car until the festivities were over.

Gale gets her good looks from her mother. Beverly was blue eyed, blonde, and six feet of elegant classy woman. Her husband, Gale's father, Paul Wilson, son of a wealthy, eminent surgeon, was the somewhat more reserved, more intellectual partner. (Thank God neither he nor any of the others commented on my choice of transportation.)

Paul, who had been expected to follow in his father's medical footsteps, instead left Harvard before graduation to pursue a career as an actor, following in the footsteps of his Parisian maternal grandmother, the renowned French actress, Rejane. Whatever their occupations, it seemed that everyone in the family sailed for recreation.

The recreational sailing my father-in-law did now was a trifle compared to what he had done as a young man. I found out that Gale's dad had served as captain of a U.S. Coast Guard vessel during World War II in the Corsair Fleet, unofficially known as the "Hooligan Navy."

This ragtag fleet was a legendary group of fishermen and sons of wealth with sailing experience who volunteered at the onset of World War II to patrol the North Atlantic in wooden sailboats in search of marauding German submarines. Before the convoy system was instituted, they, searching the seas under sail, stealthily hunted the U-Boats that were preying on Allied shipping off the coasts of North America. For a video and more information on this heroic bunch of guys, just Google "Hooligan Navy" and go to the National Sailing Hall of Fame's site.

As a teenager Gale had spent many a summer weekend as her father's crew in small boat racing on New Jersey's

Shrewsbury River. This was great preparation for boat handling and following orders from a grumpy captain. Oh, and she was a great onboard cook. Boy, had I lucked out.

However experienced she may have been, she still exhibited many nautically objectionable female characteristics, such as enjoying being clean or believing that only nutritious, well-prepared food should be served on board. (No Dinty Moore canned stew.)

Truthfully, I've found that many of the frustrating traits of females on land come with them when boating. The process of getting organized to go ashore could be incredibly frustrating while we waited for the ladies to organize their purses, sunblock, sandals, and selves.

It was no surprise to me, while having a splinter removed in the hospital in Tortola, to see that the other eight patients in the emergency room were all married men, husbands being treated for heatstroke acquired while waiting in the dinghy for women who had said, "I'm almost ready."

Passing Wind

As a result of those early years of hard work and frugality, our finances continued to improve, and the "Boat Account" balance had now reached mid-four figures. We felt at this point we had enough money to begin looking for some economical way to get on the water on our own. Sadly, the result of our initial research was the realization that the four thousand dollars we had accumulated wouldn't buy much boat. But we kept looking anyway.

But then, as so often happens, patience brought luck.

Not wanting to leave any nautical stone unturned, I sought the advice of friend, marine surveyor, and nautical guru Fred Long.

A low-key guy with a comfortable paunch and a biblical beard, Fred seemed always to be dressed in stained cargo shorts and work boots and working on a boat somewhere.

I had met Fred when he arrived in Ponce from San Diego to take over the job of chief engineer at the local tuna packing plant. A few years later, unable to accept his indifference to proper paperwork, management replaced him with what grew to be a staff of five engineers who never performed as well as old Fred did all alone.

Fred would never impress anyone with his slow, measured speech and shuffling gait, but he was a genius at keeping the plant's machines running. He was deep into welding and metallurgy, up to date on electronics, computers, and cost engineering, and could quote the latest studies on industrial ergonomics. But in person he looked more homeless than genius.

After leaving the tuna plant's employ, Fred stayed in town, making a good living with his own non-destructive testing company and taking on marine survey work.

That day I found Fred at the Ponce Yacht Club boatyard, refinishing the bright work on his restored, classic 41-ft. wooden ketch, *Vanir*, a beauty originally built for Nelson Rockefeller 35 years before.

"Hey, Fred," wasn't enough to divert his attention from the fine brush strokes he was artistically laying down.

"Fred, I need your advice. Gale and I are desperately looking for a small cruising boat, but we only have a few grand available. Got any ideas?"

Fred, laconic as always, turned slowly, pointed with the bristles of his dripping brush to a small sloop high and dry behind me, and drawled, "See that one there. She's a Columbia 30. She was abandoned years ago by a guy who came down from Los Angeles and got fired. She'd be a perfect starter for you, but don't get your hopes up."

"Why? What's the problem?"

"Well, there's a big storage bill owed to the club, and it's probably so tied up in legal snarls over the bank loan that you'd never be able to get your hands on it," he explained before returning to his varnishing.

Fascinated by this tidbit of information, I walked over to the abandoned craft. By pushing an old sawhorse against the transom of the abandoned Columbia 30, I could reach the rail, so with a big push I

The Columbia 30 as we found her

hauled myself up and into the cockpit as the sawhorse toppled to the ground.

What I found was a mess.

My first impression was not good. The cockpit drain had filled with debris, and the rainwater and *yeech* were three inches deep, but I decided to investigate further anyway. There was no lock on the weatherboards, so by removing the top one, I was able to peek inside. The interior's condition was very different. The settees were clean, with cushions in good condition, and the salon table and interior wood looked almost new. Climbing in, I marveled at the amount of space inside. Everything needed for cruising appeared to be there: stove, head, cushions, lamps, sails. Everything that is but the engine.

Perched on the transom, I considered how I would come back down to earth. Literally and philosophically. Here was the sailboat we had been looking for. The ideal starting vessel for us at this point. Might it be possible to do what Fred said was impossible?

A visit to the club's administration office only resulted in more headshaking and negativity. The club manager sighed and told me, "It's no use. There's the three years of storage owed to the club, and there's some sort of unpaid debt to a bank in California. We gave the case to a lawyer. You know how tangled these legal things get."

Having come this far, I didn't want to give up. My insistent inquiring garnered the information that Lawyer X, a club member, had been working *pro bono* on the case for two years, and based on the amount of time that had passed without news from him, they assumed this was one of those impossible legal jumbles that would not be worth straightening out.

When I heard this, my heart leapt. I knew Lawyer X. He was a scion of one of the wealthy, important families in the area. I also knew he spent far more of his day at the club bar than he did "lawyering." Having been referred to him when I first arrived in town, I soon turned elsewhere for legal advice when I found, from experience, that he never seemed to actually get around to dealing with the situations I brought him. My guess was that, true to form, he probably hadn't done a damn thing about carrying out the legal process for seizing the boat to guarantee the club's debt, and I was determined to find out if I was right.

Hoping to casually bump into him so I could subtly involve him in a friendly, *gratis* conversation about the boat's status, I planned to hang out where he spent most of his time, the yacht club bar. The very next day I caught him. Gray plaid suit with vest set off by his perfectly clean white shoes, he was hunched over the splendid mahogany bar, somewhere between his fourth and fifth Cuba Libre, his moustache and shoulders drooping.

Casually, I appropriated the stool next to him, threw an informal greeting his way, and tossed off the inquiry, "I hear you're dealing with the abandoned Columbia 30," adding, "Do you think it can be bought?"

Sort of slurring his words, he replied, "As a lawyer, my honest opinion ..."

I cut him off and said, "I don't want your honest opinion. I want your *professional* opinion." Only then was I able to extract from him a date and time for us to meet at his *other* office to discuss this case.

The Deal

Arriving at his workplace at the appointed day and time, I sat nervously in his scruffy office anteroom, awaiting his appearance. During the first hour, I thought I would die from the suspense of not knowing if I were on a wild goose chance or the trail of a Bird of Paradise. As the minutes of the second hour began ticking by, I began to worry that he had forgotten about me and had gone directly to the bar at the yacht club.

Interrupting his secretary's labors, I started by explaining the reason for my visit. Rolling her eyes and shaking her head, she revealed a "here we go again" manner and said, "He hasn't touched that case in two years. Come. I'll show you the file."

Leading me into an office in which every horizontal surface was covered with stacks of documents, she walked directly to the large mahogany desk and opened a side drawer. Rummaging through a healthy collection of unused mustard and ketchup envelopes, she extracted a stained blue folder and with a flourish presented the file to me.

"Here's everything about the boat and the debt." With a conspiratorial tone, she added, "Don't worry. It's Friday, so he won't be in today. You have plenty of time to copy whatever information you want, but you have to leave the file here ... just in case."

Almost shaking with anticipation, I scurried back to my seat, opened the folder, and leafed through the brittle papers. Buried among the bunch of collection letters was a clear plastic pouch, and inside the pouch was exactly what I was looking for, a California Certificate of Ownership dated six years ago, with the name of the Los Angeles bank that held the lien. I jotted down the key important information, and thanking the nice, elderly lady as effusively as was proper with a stranger, I ran out the door and headed for my office.

Trembling with excitement, I dialed the number I found for the bank. At first I thought my balloon had burst when the person answering said, "Sanwa Bank. Good Afternoon." With considerable dread I asked if this was the bank I was looking for and was relieved to learn that Sanwa—a Japanese bank—had very recently bought the old bank and assumed all of its assets, including, I hoped, the one I was after.

After explaining the reason for my call, the employee advised me that she would be passing my call on to the Collateral Recovery Division. Perhaps the phone rang only four times, but it seemed like an eternity until someone picked up. I heard a click then a voice that said just one word. "Akamatsu." *Akamatsu*? Was this a Japanese banking term? Did *akamatsu* mean "Too bad, you poor slob?"

Gathering my courage, I explained to the voice why I was calling. It turned out that Mr. Akamatsu, whose English was only just slightly better than my Japanese, had only started the job that week. He sounded a bit confused when I gave him a description of the vessel and its registration, but he took my number and said he would get back to me soon.

I had not dared to tell Gale about my bet on this long shot. I wanted to surprise her once this newfound treasure was ours. Keeping this situation to myself, I waited nervously for Mr. Akamatsu's call. On the third day, as I was working late, the call came in.

Speaking so slowly and distinctly that I thought I would die of anticipation, it took him about ten minutes of torturous diction to say that, yes, he had found the particular papers—I wondered if the scene in his office was like that of Lawyer X's—and, yes, the bank would entertain an offer for the *"Corumbia."* Would I please tell him how much I was willing to pay and where the boat was located?

Whoa. He doesn't know where I'm calling from or where the boat is now located? If he finds out where the boat is, he can then require an auction and anyone and everyone will be involved. And then who knows what the selling price might be.

Realizing that his ignorance gave me control of the situation—*El sarten por el mango*, as they say in PR—I had the frying pan by the handle—I low-balled him with an offer of $3,000 and totally ignored the question about the boat's whereabouts.

Amazingly, he gave me an immediate "yes" but asked again where the "asset" was located, as the process of transfer in California was very complicated, and he would have to send me papers that required a notarized signature. Not willing to reveal anything, I countered that they could do the closing in California, and I would have someone there to represent me. He should please prepare the documents.

Bypassing Counselor X, I used all my talent of persuasion to get the club to accept $1,000 as settlement for the $7,000 storage debt. With the boat now free and clear from the club's grasp, I closed the deal in California by asking my friend Jim Fowler, a Los Angeles resident, to help me out by delivering my $3,000 check and representing me at the closing.

When Jim called to confirm that all had gone well with the Sanwa Bank, I put Gale on the phone so she could hear for herself that we were the owners of a real cruising sailboat.

With our ownership a reality, over glasses of wine on our apartment's terrace, I proudly told Gale how I had pulled off this miracle. My wife of only four years at the time had already seen quite a few of my wild schemes and projects fall apart, so she was interested but a bit skeptical. That's her nature. They say opposites attract, and although we enjoy many of the same things, we see them from very different perspectives.

For example: We love to travel. Traveling, for me, is a car and a town a day. I have no problem with one-night stands. I'm always ready for the next town. My companion, however, wants to stay, to nest, smell all the flowers, and get to know all the people and all the stores.

She's a "people person." She is still in continuous touch with the kids she knew in primary school. My classmates? I don't know what happened to them and don't miss knowing.

I came from a background of plenty. Her family, with her father struggling to make even a decent living as an actor, attempted to live at the level of his successful father but never had the income. Gale grew up in a penny-pinching, frugal environment where appearances had to be kept up.

However, about a year after we were married, we had a chance to satisfy both our personalities. We stumbled upon what seemed like the deal of the century.

A wealthy local developer had gone bankrupt constructing and trying to sell San Juan's first mixed-use building. The building, called Cobian's Plaza, had 21 floors of offices, businesses, and apartments, and was located in an up-and-coming but still blighted downtown area. This project was to be his master work, and to share it with his family, he built large duplex penthouses on the top floor of this middle class building, just for his children and himself.

Taking a chance that the building's services and integrity would be restored, we signed away our lives by committing to pay the mortgage for a 3,000 sq. ft., two-floor aerie with a huge terrace for the bargain price of only $127,000.

Once it was ours we proudly invited our friends to come see our castle in the sky. And if the elevator worked, and they weren't mugged walking back to their car, they were very impressed.

This deal was a winner but a lot of my wild ideas haven't turned out so well. That's why Gale's first reaction upon hearing about one of my ventures from left field is to take a step back and say, "Wait a minute. Are you sure this is a safe or sane idea?" Unfortunately, I haven't always been able to mollify her concerns.

Maybe it's Mars and Venus, but I'm always ready for something new. I may return bruised and battered from my escapade, but I'm still primed for the next new or exciting idea. Now I—I mean *we*—owned a sailboat. But all of a sudden, instead of fantasies about the future, memories of my past failures came to mind. The stolen sailboat, the failed motorcycle dealership I opened when I should have been directing my attention and capital to my company, the Cal 28 sailboat disaster. Well, what the hell. It's done. I'll figure this one out.

Our new acquisition did need an engine and required remediation dealing with blemishes from three years of neglect, but temporarily forgetting my history of mechanical ineptness, in my euphoria I felt sure we would be able to deal with whatever needed doing. We named her *Passing Wind*.

A Dream's Fruition

We now began a weekly routine that went on for the next six months. Every Saturday at 3 p.m., we would pack Max, our cat, and a picnic lunch into the car and make the one-hour drive across the island from San Juan to arrive at the club in Ponce in time to work on the boat before it got too dark.

The fact that she was only afloat on a sea of asphalt surrounded by a chain link fence, not white beaches, never deterred the enjoyment of our ownership. We would revel in drinks and dinner in the cockpit, just as though we were in St. Bart's or Bora Bora, and then crawl into the V-berth, asleep by 10 p.m.

The next day we would be up at dawn to get in as much work as possible before the blistering tropical sun, baking and radiating heat from the asphalt, made it too hot to work on the boat. And I can tell you, the south coast of Puerto Rico is hot. How hot? Air conditioners made in Puerto Rico have three settings: Low, medium, and Ponce.

Since we had no affordable alternative, any repairing,

reconditioning, and installing had to be done by us. Gale, growing up among boating Christians, just assumed that all men could varnish, knew how to repair water pumps, or swage rigging. But for me the commitment to do whatever work the boat needed to get her going was a giant leap of faith.

I was in love with the dream and like the guy who falls head over heels in love with a girl who's an ardent skier. Although he's never skied before, he hurtles his body down the slope, regardless of what might happen on his way to the bottom.

During those early days, I was better at swearing like a sailor than fixing things like a sailor, but little by little my mechanical and electrical skills improved, and so did the condition of our boat.

It may seem ludicrous to some, but my discovery that an adjustable wrench worked better than pliers was a great step forward, and my first set of sockets truly changed my life. Soon I was haunting the hardware stores for magical items like vise grips and impact screwdrivers, and I gave thanks to St. Dremel a hundred times for my cordless drill.

I will admit, however, to a lingering resentment—jealousy?— towards those slow, deliberate-talking, plaid-flannel-shirted guys with clean workbenches and organized tool cribs who do every-thing methodically and thoroughly so that each project will come out just right. To counter the possibility of becoming one of these plodding, stodgy people, I still just fling stuff into the toolbox and, whenever possible, install one bolt or screw less than is actually called for. I've maintained my independence and non-conformity but, I will admit, at a cost.

As my knowledge of nautical components broadened, I found there was nothing lewd about spreader boots and snatch blocks. A Battcar had nothing to do with the Caped Crusader, and while my boat didn't have any, I just loved the sound of saying "gudgeon and scupper." Although I was getting pretty good at boat repairs, I never even approached the skills of that legendary Jewish boat builder, Noah.

Our Sunday work period usually lasted until 3 p.m. when, drenched with sweat, we would exchange our work clothes for bathing suits and reward ourselves with a swim in the club pool before hitting the road for the hour's drive home and the next week of work.

I can now proudly say that except for the installation of the new Universal 4 diesel engine, we did all the restoration work ourselves. Week after week we cleaned and painted, changed through-hulls (see Glossary in the back of this book for explanation of boat and sailing terms), raised the mast, and gradually restored her to sailable condition.

Finally, the day arrived when everything on the dictatorial "To Launch" list had been crossed off, and the Travel Lift slowly and majestically approached to gather the object of our dreams in its powerful mechanical embrace and convey it to its natural environment, the sea.

The giant machine lifted her off her stands, "Slipping the surly bonds of the earth," and rolled to the launch slip as we followed in procession like a monarch's entourage. It was a Sunday and the club must have been very busy, but all I saw was our project on its way to becoming a real boat.

We may have felt as if we were in a dream world, but the machine's operator had a long list of boats to deal with, and our reverie was rudely interrupted by the need to get her out of the slings and to her home slip. Miraculously, the brand new engine started, and with new fenders and lines, she celebrated her return to the sea by faultlessly motoring to her slip at Dock B. One small trip for a sailboat; one giant step for Gale and Glenn.

Later that day we proudly showed our craft to daughter Ivy, who came to the club to share our excitement. The result of all our hard work was that the Columbia 30 looked like new. The stuff that had been stolen during the time she had been abandoned had been replaced, many things had been upgraded, and everything that needed it had been cleaned or painted.

To celebrate our entrance into the yachting community, we invited our friends from all over the island to a "Boat Inauguration Party." (Sorry, my ethnicity would not allow me to call it a christening.) People brought nautical presents, our musician friends played songs of rejoicing, and Gene Crommet, a consecrated Episcopalian minister, performed an astonishing, bizarre, pagan dedication ceremony.

After a few more days of little nit-picking tasks, we were ready to go sailing. Praying under my breath, I started the engine and we puttered out into the bay. Déjà vu, but okay so far.

Reaching the mouth of the harbor—the site of my disaster in the Cal 28—Gale took the wheel and headed up while I went to raise the sails. They went up without a hitch. More with a cry of pride than a bellow of command, I shouted to Gale, "You can fall off now."

Gingerly, she turned the wheel to the lee. As we fell off, the wind began to fill the sails. Lightly at first, she then hardened to the wind and started to move forward. Gathering energy from what was only a light breeze, she began accelerating then she got up on her toes and really *sailed*.

Ecstatic with our success and not wanting to stop, we sailed back and forth along the coast, testing and learning until dark. It wasn't long before weekend trips to beautiful, nearby Coffin Island *and* safe returns became routine. A far cry from my first try ten years earlier in the Cal 28. "No deaths and no divorces. A successful trip."

We celebrated another milestone when my in-laws visited, and Gale's father and her mother became our sailing guests for the day. The outing, to Gale's great relief, was a success, and the congratulations from her nautical father felt great to me.

Having family aboard soon became routine. When Jill or Adie visited from their mainland colleges, an overnight at Coffin Island was a must. Even Andrew, whose anger at me had softened over the five intervening years, enjoyed a sail and snorkel during his visits.

Ivy, summa cum laude graduate of Brandeis, was now married to the "boy next door," Dr. Ricardo Barnes and was, thank God, willing to accept me as an imperfect father. We were again close, although she and Ricky stuck to their Grady-White 29 fishing machine.

As the months went by, our experience grew, and we learned to deal with an increasing number of sailing and navigation challenges. I became surprisingly adept at fixing stuff on the fly and, if we had engine trouble, could sail our 30 footer into her slip like a veteran. But when a challenge becomes routine, it also becomes tedious. The more we sailed locally, the more I longed to repeat the bliss of our Virgin Island trips, this time in our own boat with my woman as my companion.

We were, at that point in time, in the midst of a four-step evolution of boats through which many others have passed:

First: The Day Sailor, the Rhodes 19: Go out in the morning and come back before dark.

Second: A Weekender, our Columbia 30: Spending a few days and nights, eating and sleeping on the boat.

Third: The Coastal Cruising (next boat): Having the craft, the knowledge, and self-sufficiency to travel longer distances, including being out of sight of land from time to time.

Fourth: Blue Water Sailing (Beyond our dreams at the time): Cross oceans for true long-distance sailing.

It's funny how one's perspective changes. At this time I thought I was a real sailor hitting home runs, but as I look back now, they were really only singles. I still had a long way to go. Owning a boat doesn't make one a sailor any more than landing in a hospital makes one a doctor.

I will admit there was one thing that definitely still needed improving: my tendency to get a little hyper when things got dicey on the boat. Instead of calmly dealing with whatever challenge or problem we encountered, I tended to fly off the handle and scream and berate my crew. I knew I had gone too far when Gale stopped referring to me as Captain and started calling me "Kim il-Glenn."

Loyal friend Peter standing next to women of normal height. Peter and Daly are, great crew but, to be frank, they are, while not quite midgets, very small people. Thanks to our introducing them to sailing they now have lucrative second careers as cockpit models.

Even after I was made aware of this negative behavior, I still had difficulty with my short fuse. Gale found a partial solution by making up a bright yellow T-shirt that said "Designated Yellee." Whenever we went sailing, one person aboard would don the shirt. All abuse for any problems, no matter what their origin or cause, was directed at the person wearing the identifying shirt, who, knowing it wasn't his fault, ignored the mistreatment. As a result, no one felt abused. Remember, it's not whether you win or lose but how you place the blame

(*You can buy a "Designated Yellee" shirt for your crew on my website, www.accidentalcaptain.com*)

Passing Wind Goes Cruising in the Virgins

So it came to pass, about a year after her launching, that *Passing Wind* left her home in Ponce and headed east, traveling along the south coast of Puerto Rico towards the beautiful Virgin Islands.

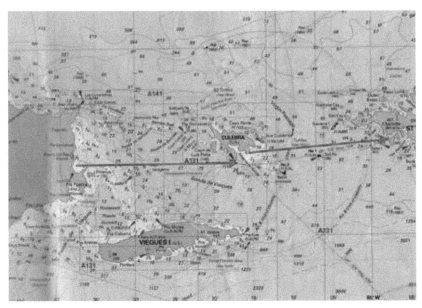

Route to the Virgins

Her normal crew was reinforced by the presence of limey friend Peter Somech. Peter, who looks like the actor Peter Ustinov but shorter and with less hair, was dependable crew. Reserved, stoic, and always under control, he was the antithesis of his diminutive, slender Puerto Rican wife, Migdalia—Daly for short—who exhibited the stereotypical Latin traits of being carefree, impulsive, and musical. What were the children of two such different people like? I can tell you that whatever else they might have been, they were always, precisely, unfalteringly, 30 minutes late. Peter and Daly would serve as loyal crew members for many future voyages.

As this was our first voyage out of our local area, we asked and took the advice of those at the club who had made this trip many times before. They told us the best way to deal with the 50-mile slog straight into the current and wind along the south coast was to motor sail with the mainsail sheeted in as tightly as possible. An overnight stop in Salinas, only 18 miles from Ponce Harbor, broke up the grind a bit.

The next day we left at dawn, buoyed with the knowledge that we had only 32 more miles into the wind before turning the southeast corner of the island sometime that afternoon.

Sure enough, around 3 p.m., with the Punta Tuna lighthouse as a marker, we swung our bow north, and as the 15-kt. breeze moved to the beam, *Passing Wind* took off like a kid let out of class for recess. After taking nine long hours to cover the previous 30 miles, we were thrilled with the fast beam reach that took us quickly to our next stop before dark, Puerto del Rey Marina, 20 miles away.

The enjoyment of this leg was somewhat impaired by some discord with crew member Peter. I learned too late that Peter thinks beer and ale are two of the three major food groups. And when sailing, he usually downs four or five bph (beers per hour). Pre-cruise, when I asked him what he'd like drink on the trip, I took his reply, "Bring a couple of beers," literally, and with only two beers on board, use of British understatement caused him many hours of acute suffering. A disgruntled, parched Peter was glad to leave the boat that night for his home and his refrigerator.

The next morning, Gale and I, full of anticipation, motored out of the marina's channel with sails set, the island of Culebra as our goal. Reaching deeper water, the large swells of Vieques Sound gave rise and fall to our bow—so different from bashing into the short chop off the south coast—and to us more of a feeling of challenging the greatness of the sea. With Peter now gone, Gale and I felt a strong sense of camaraderie. A couple facing the "unknown" together.

The "unknown" may have been a voyage of only 25 miles, but we were being thwarted again by fighting the wind and two knots of current. Finding ourselves only halfway after six hours, we chose prudence over aesthetics and lit up the pint-sized diesel. Dragging our new little, orange inflatable dinghy behind us, we fought our way to windward, hoping to make it to the narrow entrance the chart showed into Ensenada Honda Bay before dark. It was worth the fight, as *Passing Wind* arrived at the channel with enough light to see the buoys that marked the way into Culebra.

Our first evening ever away from our home island of Puerto Rico was spent quietly anchored behind the reef in a bay that had the very un-Hispanic name of Dakity. With a full moon lighting a path on a calm, dark sea, we discussed the day's experiences over dinner. At long last we were cruising, and we were enjoying every minute of it.

While the calm, protected waters of St. Thomas' Charlotte Amalie Harbor awaited us only 18 miles away, getting there the next day would be another battle against the wind and current. Picking our way out of the channel in the dawn's early light with fingers crossed, we hoped our early departure would give us a head start on the usual strong easterly winds. However, once out of the protection of the bay's headland, it was obvious we were in for another uphill battle. The wind was strong and the waves were much higher than those we had experienced the day before. Once again any plans for enjoying the nautical artistry of gliding quietly across the sea were sacrificed to the gods of expediency, and with jib and main set and the engine's additional drive, we fought our way to our next port.

Old hands had warned us that conditions would get even worse as we passed through the area where the current rebounded off the windward side of Culebrita Island. Their advice was spot on. Suddenly, the swells were steeper, and controlling our hobby-horsing little vessel became a real trial. I was finding a steady rhythm in steering when I heard a loud "pop" sound from behind me. What was that?

Quickly turning my head, I was relieved to find the dinghy painter still tied to the stern cleat. Tied but limp as a strand of spaghetti because there was no longer any dinghy on the other end. The jerky motion of the boat rising and falling had pulled the ring and pad from the bow tube. As a result, our brand new inflatable and engine were steadily disappearing in our wake.

My knee-jerk reaction of immediately turning the boat downwind nearly rolled us, but we survived the maneuver and, with the help of wind and engine, turned downwind in pursuit of the drifting tender. We pulled past and then turned upwind close by in its lee. However, getting close was a lot easier than capturing it.

Bucking and yawing in the rough seas, the inflatable mocked us by easily dodging every thrust of the 5-ft. boat hook that was badly in need of some Viagra, as we found it to be too short to reach any hookable protuberances on the wayward craft. Repeated attempts to snag some secure niche or strap or even the engine on the little orange bobber were all futile. It was like trying to capture a balloon with a boathook in a windstorm. Worse, we were so concentrated on the recovery we had failed to notice we had drifted dangerously close to the line of jagged rocks that extend from the point under Culebrita's lighthouse.

It was only when I noticed swells had become breakers that it hit me it was time for us to forget the dinghy and save ourselves. "Hold on," I yelled to Gale and slammed the throttle forward. The flapping of luffing sails added to the sense of danger. Then, as the sails filled, we held our breaths as our tiny craft began to fight her way forward against the current that was intent on carrying her to ruin on the rocks. Inch by inch we put more distance between us and the voracious rocks until we were finally out of the breakers and safely back on our course.

My huge sigh of relief was tempered by the realization that, while we were okay, we had lost our dinghy, our only means of getting ashore without getting wet.

The experience of losing of our little inflatable felt like a death in the family. It wasn't just the cost of the lost dinghy that bothered me. Because I had obtained the exclusive distributorship for Puerto Rico of Dynous, a Japanese inflatable company, and Tohatsu outboards, the monetary loss was minimized. To qualify I had purchased a small inventory of boats and engines, so I had only paid about half the retail cost—my ethnicity coming out again—and I still had some "spares" at home that I hadn't sold.

I was faced with the difficult situation of choosing one of three options available to us:

1. Turn around, go all the way back to Ponce, pick up a tender and engine from remaining inventory, and start again.
2. Continue, dinghy-less, for the next three weeks, even though the only way we could leave the boat would be to swim ashore or pay for a slip in a hot, expensive marina. (Something we detested.)
3. Buy a new dinghy in St. Thomas at—the shame of it all— *retail price.*

Let me explain to those of you who haven't sailed the Caribbean why marinas are anathema to most cruising sailors. As it is I only go to a marina for my annual fuel purchase.

First: Marinas are by requisite located in places protected from the wind. So they're still and hot.

Second: They're chock full of powerboats—the golden calves of watersport—who *must* be there so they can connect to power for their air conditioners, icemakers, stereos with outside speakers, etc. Powerboaters seem to always be accompanied by great amounts of noise, including their crews, who must shout to each other to be heard over the constant din they create.

Third: You've got to put out dock lines, fenders ... and money.

After a few minutes discussing our options, we decided we had no real practical alternative but to go on to St. Thomas and try to find a replacement tender. Gritting our teeth, we slowly made headway towards St. Thomas' Yacht Haven Marina where we would spend the night in anticipation of a dinghy-shopping expedition the next day.

Future trips to the Virgins taught us that, yes, sail south of the island of St. Thomas when going west, but if you are heading east—assuming normal SE winds—choose the north coast of St. Thomas. We found that the east wind swirls around the western tip of the island and blows from the south. This allows one to continue to sail east in calm waters almost all the way to beautiful, nearly deserted Magens Bay.

When we finally lost the wind, we dropped the sails and motored the last two or three miles in the calm waters of the island's lee. Much better than bashing along to windward on the south side.

Once in incredibly beauteous Magens Bay, I suggest you anchor off the south portion of the beach, away from the much noisier public beach on the north end. There's a good chance you'll be the only visiting sailboat in this spectacular bay.

The next morning, leaving *Passing Wind* secured at her rented dock, we left on our tender quest. We were pained to discover that new nine-foot tenders to replace the one I bought for $450 were priced by local dealers at over $1,000 (in those days). Forget about a new outboard. Our suffering was not alleviated until the Avon dealer—boats not cosmetics—condescendingly took us behind the building and showed us a very used, yellow, eight-foot, Italian-made, slat-floored inflatable that had only one small air leak. The price? $200. I jumped at the deal. This little craft became our dinghy, lifeboat, and something akin to Thighmaster, as it needed constant pumping to keep it filled.

Rushing back to Yacht Haven with our acquisition, we paid our bill and were off the dock by noon. Heading out of the harbor, I was reminded of the lesson I had learned on my first charter. I now had lower expectations regarding the speed over ground we could make on the leg to St. John, so this time the slow trip to Christmas Cove was not quite as frustrating as it had been on the little Pearson 26.

However, there was no less of a sense of awe when, the next morning, we passed through Current Cut and the panorama of pristine white beaches, lush green mountains, and turquoise blue seas opened before us. We had arrived. And in more ways than just geographically. After all the failures, roadblocks, and detours I had endured on my quest to sail here, we were finally sailing the Virgins … in our own boat. I was overjoyed. Gale was relieved.

That night, safely anchored in Trunk Bay, St. John, Gale's gourmet dinner under the stars seemed extra delicious, and when a full moon illuminated the water and gave the white beach an incandescent glow, we felt truly blessed to be alive and here.

Anegada: The Drowned Island

When, with a whole week of perfect Virgin Island cruising under our belts, I felt, in a fit of over-confidence, that we were ready for a bigger challenge, I chose to make a voyage to the low, reef-fringed island of Anegada. This low sandspit of an island lay only 14 miles away but out of sight over the horizon. It is an enigmatic, virgin island, rarely visited, as bareboat charter companies, because of its dangerous barrier reef, declare it off-limits to their renters. The old adage, "Success is a dangerous thing as it makes one over confident," must be true because, after only a week here, we decided we were not returning home without a visit to this legendary wrecker's paradise.

Please remember that when I made this decision, Ferdinand Magellan had not yet invented the GPS and that each of our significant but short voyages had until now been accomplished by simply pointing our bow towards the high points visible on the next island.

Anegada, however, was a different story, as it would not really come into view until we were so close we would nearly be upon its long, coastal reef line, a reef littered with the remains of a reported 300 wrecked ships, each one the result of some captain's over-confidence and miscalculation. A safe arrival there would require some serious dead reckoning navigation.

Wanting to stage our departure point as close as possible to our goal, we worked our way east into the British Virgin Islands, along the north coast of Tortola, and into famous North Sound, Virgin Gorda.

Lesson learned #1
In heavy weather tie the dinghy painter short, not long. By tying the dinghy bow high, the dinghy, even with the engine mounted, will pivot gently as its stern rises and falls, and the short tether will keep it from snatching and jerking in the waves. And of course, two lines and two tie-off points are better than one.

Following our trusty *Virgin Islands Cruising Guide's* recommendations exactly, we left before 9:00 a.m. and placed our bow on a heading of five degrees magnetic towards the empty horizon. Now for the first time I understood what it meant to gather enough confidence for a sailor to head off to nowhere.

A southeast wind of about 12 knots moved us briskly along. Glancing over my shoulder, I could still see Gorda Peak behind me, a comforting reminder that land still existed, although I could see none in front of us. We sailed expectantly on, scanning the horizon over the bow, and then a little before noon we were tremendously relieved to make out the tops of the palm trees at the Anegada Reef Hotel, the island's highest point. Now came the scary part: entering through the reef.

To follow our cruising guide's recommendation for a safe passage through the coral heads and ridges that had brought so many tall ships to grief, we had to follow a complicated route. But if we found and followed the buoys that marked the break in the reef, we should arrive without incident at the anchorage.

Being conservative—Gale's idea—we lowered the sails and started the engine. Motoring cautiously forward, wallowing and rolling as the waves rolled under our aft quarter, we searched the irregular blue surface for that first buoy.

To be properly prepared I had memorized the *Cruising Guide's* instructions. But as the distance between our boat and the shore narrowed, and we looked in vain for the markers, I was overcome by a dread realization that at that moment we had no idea where

Don't exit your dinghy the hard way, over the bow. Use a stern line to hold it parallel to the transom for easy egress over the side.

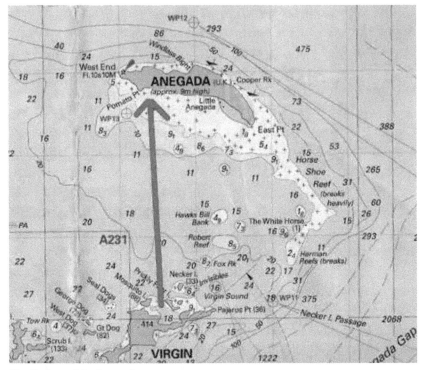

North Sound to Anegada

the hell we were or how we would find our way in. Our anxiety level rose as time went by, and we crept closer and closer to the island without spotting a navigational guide of any kind.

Tense as bowstrings, we scanned the still, white-capped water for some clue that would lead us to the buoys, the channel, and sanctuary. The tension was abruptly shattered when a loud clattering noise erupted from the engine compartment. I dove for the kill switch to shut down our shiny new diesel engine before any other damage might occur. Oh, great. Now we're drifting towards a killer reef with no engine or sails.

Scrambling down the companionway steps, I pulled away the engine's cover and began searching for the cause of the racket. All looked normal until, with the hot engine burning my chest as I leaned over to look at the transmission, I saw that the driveshaft coupling had thrown all but one of its bolts. Still in place on the shaft, the coupling's bolts, nuts, and washers were scattered around the bilge. With a manual dexterity I didn't realize I possessed, I used my hands to re-install as many bolts as I could and was able to get them installed and hand tight in less than a minute.

The experience gained from my years in the industrial power transmission business told me that a shaft misalignment problem had undoubtedly caused the failure, but at low power we could probably motor on for some time before the bolts came loose again. I shouted up to Gale, "Start the engine. Put it in forward, but SLOW!"

By the time I was back in the cockpit, we were again creeping forward fast enough to have steerage. Hunched over the wheel with my teeth gritted, I steered my little wounded vessel slowly forward, expecting at any moment to feel the crunch of coral against keel. Then abruptly, and not where we expected, Gale called from the bow and pointed to a buoy, then another. Trusting that if we got close enough to the buoys we saw, we would soon find more, I turned toward those red and green markers and did the obvious: motored between them. Then, raising our gaze from the depths to the horizon, we could see a cluster of anchored boats just 50 yards away. Eureka. We must be in.

Heading straight for the anchored craft, and finding a space in the small cove, we happily dropped our little Danforth anchor into white sand in seven feet of the clearest water I'd ever seen.

Although the water in the anchorage was still as a lake, my short trip along the deck to the cockpit was made on wobbly legs, adrenalin still very much in evidence. Once in the cockpit, Gale and I at first just looked at each other in silence and then with a shout grabbed each other, hugging and swaying, to celebrate our safe arrival.

Anchored and out of danger now, we ate the sandwiches we had been too nervous to consume while sailing, washing them down with plenty of red wine. Once sated, I lay back and scanned our environment. We were anchored only about 50 feet from a perfect, low beach that extended left and right far into the distance. On shore nearby were a handful of palm trees that shaded a scattering of small, brightly painted wooden cottages and a larger building we assumed was the nerve center of the remote and exotic Anegada Reef Hotel.

Defeating my tendency to be a "Cockpit Potato," Gale dragged me into our—thank God we had one—imperfect but precious Italian dinghy for a trip ashore. We paddled the short distance—we only bought a replacement tender, not engine—to the long dock that extended from shore over the shallow white bottom.

Noticing with some curiosity that we were the only dinghy secured to the slatted wooden pier, and that we could see no one on shore, we nevertheless clambered out onto the dock, anxious to see what this celebrated cruising destination had to offer.

Arriving on shore, we saw no activity at the hotel's main building or the cottages strewn along the beach baking in the sun. There was also a small wooden beach bar surrounded by empty stools. At least we wouldn't have to elbow our way into a crowd to get a drink.

Looking at each other, we simultaneously said, "Where is everybody?" Our question was immediately answered by the appearance of a small black man in a Hawaiian shirt who, blinking at the bright light as he exited from the larger building, ambled slowly across the sand to the shade area under the palm fond-roofed bar. Now that we had a bartender, rum punches seemed appropriate, and we drank them with gusto appropriate to our arrival.

As time went by, an increasing number of disheveled sailing characters drifted down the dock and also took seats at this very informal watering hole. It may not have been the fanciest of places, but the camaraderie amongst those who had the boldness to come here was great, and they served a hell of a good rum punch.

Confidence bolstered by the rum, we left the now busy bar to explore the hotel "complex." Having read that the Anegada Reef's fresh lobster, grilled on the beach, was the big draw, we made our way to the open-air A-frame building that housed the restaurant to reserve two of them for dinner. Behind a small bamboo desk, a nice young lady, place card and pen in hand, asked the name of our boat for the reservation card to be placed on our table. I proudly answered, "Passing Wind." Raising her eyes slowly from the card, she paused and, looking me in the eye, said, "Hmm, I think you'd better give me your name for the card. I won't put those words out for everyone to see. Our restaurant may not have walls, and the customers don't wear shoes, but we do have our standards."

That night's dinner of crispy lobster and laid-back local music made it worth the trip and the fright.

Once back aboard, with no powerboat noise, few lights, and a night sky strewn with stars, we took in the tropical serenity of this special anchorage. And as only one of six boats in the cove, we went to sleep that night feeling like members of a very elite group.

(Though not quite as exciting as the night we were anchored in Honeymoon Bay, St. Thomas and noticed that they were shooting a porno film on the terrace of a villa not 20 yards from us)

The quiet of the next day's morning was only interrupted by the tiny voices of the small children of the owners of the Anegada's other commercial establishment, Neptune's Treasure, who rowed out to sell us delicious, warm fresh bread and cakes. Later, rousing ourselves from this idyllic scene, we returned ashore to the focus of activity and, at the recommendation of hotel staff, took a vintage Volkswagen Kombi taxi to their recommended snorkel spot five miles away, Loblolly Bay, on the north coast.

Our initial disappointment at seeing the scrubby, flat bleakness of the countryside quickly changed to amazement when our driver stopped atop one of the dunes that bordered the beach that was our destination. Remarkable. After so many years in the Caribbean, I had seen a lot of beaches, but none of them had made an impact on me like this perfect combination of sand and sea. The uninterrupted bright white of the endless beach—and only beach, no people—dissolving into the most brilliant shades of blue sea I had ever seen, just took my breath away.

During the next few hours, we delighted in excellent, shallow-water snorkeling on a thriving reef, followed by a long, curative warming up in the sun, and we never saw another soul until our driver and rusty van returned.

Some advice if you go:

Don't be turned off by the moribund coral you first encounter when leaving the beach. Keep swimming out to where the waves break over the shallow part of the reef, and you will be rewarded by the discovery of an underwater world of shallow canyons, arches, and caves teeming with sea life. Like so much in life, perseverance pays off.

Three delightful days spent in Anegada now behind us, we weighed anchor and picked our way out through the no longer terrifying channel and pointed our bow once again towards the mountains of Tortola. We had seen and done so much, but the two weeks we had allotted for the first stage of our cruise were almost over, and it was time for us to stash our boat somewhere that was safe and fly home to Puerto Rico. We also needed to find a capable

Snorkling Lobolly bay

mechanic to realign the engine and driveshaft before we returned in a month for more cruising.

We were fortunate to be able to kill two birds with one stone by taking the Columbia to Nanny Cay Marina for repair and storage to await our return. And return we would. We had tasted the cruising life and we were hooked.

Return to Paradise

Back in San Juan I spent all my non-working time over the next four weeks re-reading my cruising guides. I checked and re-checked the routes and stops we planned to make on our return trip. The month seemed to drag on endlessly.

But eventually, we found ourselves back on an airplane headed to the Virgins, and this time daughter Adrienne was joining us. Adie and Gale, sitting together, chatting a mile a minute, left me to take a seat next to a stranger who soon tried to engage me in conversation. I usually avoid vacuous airplane conversation, but when my seatmate asked me what hotel I was staying at, my face lit up, my chest swelled, and I smiled, realizing I now had a chance to reply with the words that for so many years I had dreamed of someday using. "No hotel," I answered proudly. "We're cruising the islands in our own sailboat."

Once back on Tortola and at Nanny Cay, I went off to check on the work that had been done on the Columbia's driveshaft, while Gale and Adie explored the small marina and its shops. All had gone well, and just as I finished paying for the boat's repairs, I heard Gale call my name. Shouting from the far end of the mechanic's pier, she said, "Hey, captain, come check out this boat."

They were standing next to a substantial-looking, fiberglass, center cockpit sloop with a For Sale sign tied to the safety lines. The mechanic, overhearing our loud conversation, sauntered over and told us, "She's a Caribe 41. We've been doing some work on her to bring her mechanicals up to snuff. She's for sale." Wary but easily seduced by "BBS"—Bigger Boat Syndrome—and Gale's praise of the large, shaded cockpit, I went aboard to take a look.

Although only 11 feet longer than our Columbia 30, she seemed comparatively cavernous. The cockpit space was what you would expect from a catamaran of the same size. Interestingly though, it had a center cockpit design; the normal interior walk-through had been eliminated, leaving a huge amount of open space under the cockpit sole for the engine room. Gale and I gave each other knowing looks that said, "She would be perfect for our next stage of cruising." However, the $50,000 price on the sign put her beyond our reach.

Oh, Lord, thy sea is so great, and my bank account is so small. So content with what we had, we returned to the Columbia, started the engine, loosened the lines, and left for two more weeks of great sailing: Marina Cay, the Baths, and wonderful Manchioneel Bay at Cooper Island. Every day was a new treat.

All too soon, our supply of vacation days was running out, we had no choice but to face the reality of beginning our return.

The plane that took Adie away also brought us Peter and his wife, Daly, who would join us for the downwind sail from St. Thomas back to Ponce. Once Peter had certified that sufficient beer was aboard, we weighed anchor, headed out from Lindbergh Bay, and turned west. The reliable southeasterly trades and a moderate following carried us quickly towards our next anchorage, Punta Arenas on the island of Vieques. The trip was, thank goodness, mostly uneventful ... with one significant exception.

While sailing in poor visibility through a squall, our attention was unexpectedly drawn to a shadowy shape that seemed to be coalescing off our starboard bow. The dark form kept growing in size until it became a huge gray blob rising out of the sea. At first barely visible through the rain, it began to coalesce and, only about 50 yards away, much to our shock turned into a great big, real live submarine that passed us silently.

At first no one spoke, dazed as we were by this awesome experience. A few minutes passed before we attempted to moderate our shock and awe by assuring each other that we probably were never in danger. After all, the United States Navy's subs have all kinds of sensors, devices, and instruments, so they must have known we were nearby, and probably, there was never any threat to us. That confidence was badly shaken when, a few weeks later, we read the news coverage that an American submarine in the Pacific surfaced under a Japanese trawler, sinking it and killing most of its crew.

The next day the same wind and current that two months earlier had hampered our sail eastward now carried us swiftly to Ponce and the end of a voyage that had been a dream come true.

That night as I lay in the dark, I reflected on my new status. Yes, I now owned and had enjoyed the use of my own cruising sailboat. I was no longer "Glenn, the know-it-all fiasco." I had become a reasonably competent sailor. Not because I had the money to buy a boat, but because I had stepped through a portal of change in my life. I had acquired some patience and was now willing to learn and take advice from others. I felt tremendous pride in the knowledge that with my own hands I had been able to fix and install what had been needed to get our boat into the water and complete the wonderful trip we had just made.

Would this change in me allow us to expand our sailing horizons even more?

3

Class Act

As we entered the '90s, things were definitely looking up at work. Altering my firm's product mix to include a greater proportion of more sophisticated "high-tech" products, and changing the name to Powermotion, had opened new doors and resulted in higher profits. We chose to enjoy the fruits of this economic prosperity by spending more time on board our little cruiser, adding to our sailing experience and expertise by navigating the waters near home. But every successful day on the water only reminded me that a greater, more exciting world awaited us if only we had a bigger boat.

In principle Gale agreed that a larger boat would be a good idea, but she was leery of putting tens of thousands of dollars into a larger vessel that would also create more expenses at a time when we were really just beginning to achieve some financial security. Growing up in a family where money was tight gave her a very different attitude than mine towards spending it. To mollify her concerns I promised I would not consider a larger boat if it would stretch our budget. She agreed. Now all I had to do was produce another miracle like the Columbia deal. I started searching right away.

In that pre-Internet year of 1990, finding a new boat, a comfortable cruiser that we could afford, meant searching the classifieds and the brokers' ads in sailing publications. But anything decent I saw over 40 feet was priced well over our $40,000 budget. After several months of futile searching, I was beginning to think I would never find the boat we wanted until, in the classifieds of a local nautical throwaway, I saw a strange ad.

It read: *For sale: Whitney Caribe 35' $20,000 BVI.*

The price was right, but 35' wasn't. Whitney never made a 35-footer. Could this be a sister ship of the 41-footer that had impressed us so much when we saw it at Nanny Cay?

I called the St. Thomas number at the bottom of the ad, and upon hearing the "Hello," immediately let loose a string of questions about the boat in the ad.

"Whoa," the guy who answered said. "I don't know anything about this or any other sailboat." He then explained he was only involved in this sale as a favor to his landlady, the owner of the advertised vessel.

For many years she and her husband had left their home in Connecticut to spend the winter months in the Virgins in their winter home and sailing the boat that was now for sale. Her husband had developed serious health problems, and during his long physical decline that ended with his demise, their boat had languished for five years in the yard at Virgin Gorda Yacht Harbour. Now with her spouse gone, she wanted it sold, and her tenant had agreed to help by representing her locally in selling the boat.

It was my guess that he, as someone knowing nothing about boats, had read the length of the boat from the documentation certificate—which is LWL, Load Waterline Length—and used that figure in the ad instead of the LOA—Length Overall—of 41 feet. I had a hunch that this boat, at that price, was the 41-footer and our Holy Grail, so I made plans to fly to Virgin Gorda to see if I was right.

Realizing that this was too important a decision for us to make alone, I hedged my bet by also buying a ticket for old Fred Long, my nautical expert and good luck charm.

Only a few days later, the flying rattletrap that carried us from San Juan landed, finally, on Virgin Gorda's dirt airstrip. Once relieved of our presence, it gunned its engine, swung the tail wheel, and was soon gone, leaving us with a hot five-minute walk to the marina from the now empty airstrip.

I was concerned that I might have some difficulty getting key information about the boat, but the yard manager at Virgin Gorda Yacht Harbour was a talkative Brit who knew the boat and its owners quite well. "Yes, Captain—massaging my ego—she's a 41-footer. Her name is *Cyncir's Caribe.* Sad story. For the last five years she's just been sitting in the yard here. She's at the far end. I'll get the keys for you."

Keys in hand, Fred and I started across the boatyard. As we walked I was dazzled by the dozens of magazine-cover Caribbean cruising boats—real mooring candy—we passed on our way to the overgrown corner of the boatyard where our quarry awaited us.

There she was. No doubt a Caribe 41 like the boat we had seen at Nanny Cay. Fred, while looking her over from the ground, gave me some key background information on this unusual vessel. Also known as a CSY 41, the now defunct bareboat charter company Caribbean Sailing Yachts had commissioned well-known designer Alan Gurney to come up with a design specifically for the Caribbean bareboat trade. She had to be simple to handle but exciting to sail. Most importantly, she was to be designed for use in the sunny, breezy Caribbean. That meant she had to have a great, big, shaded cockpit, since that's where we spend our days—and often nights too—lots of ventilation, and carry enough water—300 gallons—for a two-week charter that included daily showers.

The 7,500 lbs. of keel ballast that hung from a lightweight Airex foam core hull gave her a very stiff 50% ballast-to-displacement ratio. Stiff enough so their customer's wives wouldn't panic when the wind blew hard.

Now the bad news. She looked terrible. Dirty and dull, her teak was fractured and gray. A broken hatch had allowed

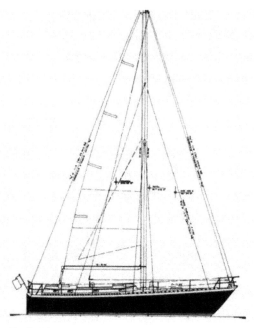

Carib 41

rainwater to enter for months, and some kind of green stuff that definitely wasn't carpeting covered the floor of the owner's cabin. The V-berth showed signs that someone had been living there, and the Perkins 4-107 engine was seized. Fred's verdict? "She's got good bones and this is a lot of boat. Use your cultural wiles to obtain a better price and have the yard paint the bottom. Then with a new engine and some elbow grease, you'll have a big comfortable boat to cruise the Caribbean for far less than her value on the market."

Once back in Puerto Rico, I told Gale about our find and, validated by Fred's positive opinion, convinced her that we should make an offer on the boat. I felt a little guilty offering only $15,000 to the guy representing the unfortunate widow but quickly forgot my guilt when I heard she accepted my price. Now all we had to do was send the check, go to Virgin Gorda, bring her home, and clean her up.

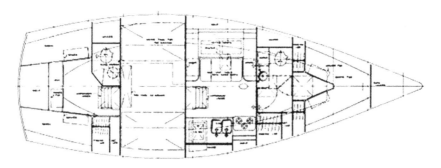

Carib 41

It seemed that the fates were with us, as the Columbia sold within days of my putting her on the market, so I now had the money and time to concentrate on our new boat.

First I dealt with finding a new engine. I called Parts & Power, the Perkins dealer for Tortola, and learned they had a drop-in 4-108 they would install for less than $5,000. Well within our budget. All I had to do was sail our acquisition the 12 miles from Virgin Gorda to Road Harbour where they would install the new engine.

This looked like a reasonably simple project. Thanks to the area's dependable 15-knot trades, the 12-mile motorless voyage from the marina on Virgin Gorda to Parts & Power's Road Town location would be a downwind jaunt that shouldn't take more than three hours. A 9 a.m. departure would put us at their shop by noon, leaving plenty of time to catch the 2:00 p.m. afternoon flight from Beef Island Airport to home.

Seemed Like an Easy Trip

It was early in the morning two weeks later when, joined by son Andrew, Gale and I touched down again at the dirt airstrip near the marina. This time we had brought another of my fleet of orange-colored Dynous inflatables, a 6-hp outboard, and three PFDs, better known as life jackets—which completed the list of necessities I calculated we would need for the short sail to Road Town.

Rushing to finish preparations before our 11:00 a.m. Travel Lift appointment, we removed as much trash and mold as possible from the shabby hull. Then after liberating the sails from their five years' sojourn, we loaded some ice and drinks into the convenient, built-in cockpit cooler and waited.

I was mesmerized by the majestic, slow progression of the Travel Lift as it approached and embraced our new boat in its webbed arms. The long grind to the opposite end of the yard seemed to take forever, but then at last the machine began to lower her to return again to her element, the sea. Once in the water, the poetry ended and the reality of the trip began. She floats. No leaks. The Travel Lift crew stood with arms crossed, impatiently waiting for us to vacate the slings, but I was almost paralyzed. A jaunt that had seemed like nothing in the planning suddenly looked to be full of hazards.

Shaken from my reverie by the impatient reminder, "Hey, Mon, we got three more to launch dis morning," I commenced setting up our propulsion system for leaving the marina, the dinghy and engine lashed firmly to the boat's starboard side.

I gave Andrew the sign to start the outboard, took the lines and fenders aboard, and with a nod from me, he put the little motor in

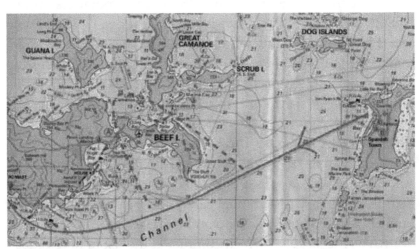

Just 12 miles to Roadtown

gear. Moving forward slowly, we left the pier and began picking our way out to sea along the crooked marina channel towards open water.

My shout of "more power" resulted in more noise and churning from the motor's little prop but not much of an increase in speed; nonetheless, we had plenty of steerage as we took the #1 buoy to port. Turning the wheel over to Gale, I told her to head us up so we could raise the sails, something we had not been able to do in the yard.

Regrettably, on the day we had chosen to travel motorless, the usually dependable easterly trades were trading elsewhere, so in almost perfect calm I went forward to raise the main and jib.

It took some effort to liberate the main from its refuge, but finally, I had it stretched onto the boom and clipped to the rope halyard. It was logical that after five years in a locker, the main might be a bit rebellious about going back to work, so when I felt some resistance, I wound the halyard around the mast winch and applied more tension. Nothing moved, so I added a little weight to my effort, and suddenly, all resistance was gone … and so was the halyard. That is except for the broken section in my hand. The halyard had parted, and what little sail we had raised was now draped over the cockpit.

I had to admit that for a sailing trip, this was a bit of a setback. However, we still had the jib, so all was not lost.

The jib sheets seemed to be okay, but I hadn't noticed in the yard that the jib lead blocks had disappeared during her time on the hard, so the only alternative I had to maintain sail trim was to tie the jib sheets off on the stern cleat.

Saying a small prayer with each turn, this time I carefully and slowly added tension to the jib halyard as the jib rose off the deck until the luff was something that approximated tight. The foresail's shape was pretty saggy, but what breeze there was gradually filled the soiled triangle of canvas, and with the outboard engine now silent, our craft began to move slowly west in a wisp of breeze.

Because the distance we had to cover was less than a dozen miles, I hadn't thought to bring much in the way of supplies other than a few cans of soda for what should be, at most, a four-hour trip. However, when after an hour we found ourselves only a little past Collision Point—maybe a mile from our start—the crew agreed it was time to again use the outboard engine for more speed "until the wind picked up." This strategy was a great success, doubling our speed to about two knots. I say "about" because I had no knot meter to gauge actual speed. In fact we had no working instruments of any kind on board.

I calculated that at the rate we were going, even with the help of the outboard, we might not arrive at Road Town in time to get a taxi back to the Beef Island Airport and fly out the same day. I was reminded several times by my wife that this scenario was

On our way to Roadtown. When we had a puff of wind I sent Andrew off in the dinghy to take this photo. Note the blue tarp bimini and bonus fiberglass dinghy.

unacceptable, as she had to be at work early the next morning. (She certainly had skewed priorities.) My reply that I was doing the best I could—really, all I could do was sweat and curse—didn't seem to mollify her.

Andrew pointed out that at that moment, though far from our final destination, we were much closer to the shore of Beef Island where the airport was located. Why go all the way to Road Town and then taxi back? By dinghy, if she got in right now, he could get Gale to the airport in about ten minutes, which would be in time to catch the 2 p.m. flight to San Juan, after which he could continue west in the dinghy along Beef Island's north shore until we met up at the western end.

Jumping at the opportunity to get off this grubby, drifting wreck, and with no time to spare, Gale did not hesitate. She grabbed her bag and leaped into the dinghy. Letting go the lashings, I watched the dinghy with Andrew in charge as they turned and motored away towards the airport.

Following our plan, I sailed—I mean drifted—west along the south side of Beef Island, anticipating the moment when Andrew would, after his airport stop, pass under the Queen Elizabeth Bridge to meet me on the other side.

At that moment it sounded so simple, but it was only after they were out of sight that I realized that:

1. Andrew didn't know the area.
2. He had no charts.
3. We had no idea how much fuel was left in the outboard's tank.

Deeply concerned that he might not make it to our rendezvous, I did the only thing I could do at that point: worry while drifting slowly westward. How slowly? At one point as I neared our proposed rendezvous spot, two sea turtles swimming in the same direction passed me. The sea was flat, and whatever we lacked in wind was made up for in blazing sun and heat. The cockpit's only shade was a small blue tarp we'd found in one of the yard's trash bins.

When two hours had passed since we separated and there was still no sign of Andrew, I really began worrying. Oblivious to the beautiful surroundings, I just stared at the spot where I prayed Andrew would appear. Dejected by the crisis I had created, I wondered how I would explain his loss to his mother. Then at long last I saw a small orange spot far in the distance. As it came closer I could make out my son and my dinghy. Overjoyed at his arrival, I eventually pulled him aboard and, overcome with relief, hugged him.

After a few minutes of relief, I recovered my normal parent personality, and with a critical and accusatory tone that covered any trace of the affection I felt, I inquired, "Well, what took you so long?"

"Dad, cut it out! You're beginning to sound like your father!"

Chagrined, I put my head down and just listened.

"Pop, we didn't realize it until we got to the counter that in the rush to get into the dinghy, Gale had taken her passport and ticket but somehow had left her wallet behind, so she did not have the cash to pay the $20 departure tax."

"Oh, no! What did you do?"

"There she was, all wet from the dinghy ride, in a bathing suit and T-shirt, trying as hard as she could to convince the airline personnel to let her fly to San Juan with the normal people. No go without the tax receipt. Then I had a brainstorm. I offered to leave my watch and come back tomorrow and pay the tax if they would let her board. That did it. They took pity on us and let her go.

Good job, kid. Don't worry, we'll get the watch back tomorrow.

Emotional reunion now over and our sailing craft again connected to a motorized vessel, newfound hope returned as our speed increased, but not for long. Suddenly, the little engine started to run rough and then went silent as the last of our fuel was used up.

Doing everything I could—cursing the wind—I begged for even

a whisper of breeze. The current, however, was helping in a small way by carrying us slowly towards Road Town.

5:00 p.m. came and went, and just as dusk turned to night, we arrived at the entrance to the harbor. While relieved at now being on the home stretch, we realized we had a new problem. Ghosting along through a busy harbor on a moonless night with no lights was not exactly safe sailing. Every noise or shape moving in the dark was a potential danger to us. We dealt with this problem by yelling, "Hey, watch out!" at the top of our lungs every time something moved in the dark. This must have been effective because by 9 p.m. we were safely moored at the Parts & Power dock.

We collapsed at the nearby Treasure Island Hotel and early the next day caught a taxi to the airport to ransom Andrew's watch and fly home.

Bleeding Fuel

The guys at Parts & Power were great. Much sooner than I expected, I received a call informing me that my new yacht was ready to leave under her own power. But before I could take off for Tortola, I had to dedicate a few more weeks to the job that was paying for all this. So by the time we were able to return to bring our baby home, nearly a month had passed.

With a distance of 120 miles from Tortola to Ponce, I was quite relieved, after our experience on our previous trip, not to have to make the voyage by sail alone. No, this time we had a brand new engine, and before we left I changed the main halyard, so we used that sail too. I also took the precaution of buying a bilge pump, hose, deep cycle battery, and three days of provisions.

Our plan was to make the voyage in two parts. The first leg would be to Culebra, only 40 miles away. At that point old friend and stalwart crew member Peter would come aboard for the longer leg to Ponce.

With everything crossed off my preparations list, ready as ready could be, it was time to top off the fuel tank with diesel. "No fuel, Mon," was the greeting I got when I opened the door of the attendant's little booth. "Fire at de power plant. Power long time come." Unfortunately, without electricity, the pumps wouldn't work, and we couldn't wait for "long time come," as we wanted to make Culebra before dark.

The guys back at the Parts & Power office told me they had put "a couple" of gallons of fuel into the tank to test the new engine and that they had another five gallons they would donate to get us on our way. Seven gallons? Should take me about 30 to 40 miles if needed. But as I now had *two* sails, and the chances of another calm day were a thousand to one, more fuel probably would not be necessary. (Is there something about this that is beginning to sound familiar?)

Standing there with my invoice, new Perkins manual, and a set of spare belts in hand, I watched as they poured the last drop of fuel from their five-gallon jerry can into my tank. The new engine started immediately and, sounding great, powered us confidently out of the harbor, where we raised the soiled sails, killed the engine, and in a brisk east wind, the 41 footer ran down Drake's Passage like a thoroughbred. By the time we reached open water along the south coast of St. Thomas, she was moving at almost hull speed. Wow, she was fast.

And wasn't this fun.

As we approached Culebra, sailing into a setting sun, I gave the wheel to Gale and went below to satisfy my curiosity about what it's like to have a boat so big I could walk around in it while sailing. After one tour around I found that the neatest thing of all was to lie on the bunk in our cabin aft and look through her wonderful transom windows at the boiling wake we left as we flew along. And we were really moving. Transfixed, I kept staring at the wake and St. Thomas receding in the distance.

We were going so fast I barely noticed the first impact, but the second one nearly threw me off the bed. What the f ...? Rushing to the cockpit, I found a terrified Gale, clutching the wheel as our vessel's keel was jolted by something as the boat bumped erratically along like a ball in a pinball machine.

Looking around, I immediately realized what had happened. Instead of paying attention to where we were going, I had been lollygagging below, and we had gone up on the reef that extends southward from the island of Culebrita.

Now we were in deep shit. Shallow water but deep shit.

I quickly started the engine, hoping we could power our way out. I then raised the engine room hatch, fully expecting to see daylight through the hull, but nothing of the kind met my gaze. Jumping down to get a better look, I searched for bad news but couldn't find any obvious damage. The boat unexpectedly lurched again, and I was thrown against the engine, the alternator to be specific. Its toothed fan pulley ripped like a crosscut saw into my side, throwing blood spatter everywhere. You can imagine Gale's reaction.

The small chunk carved out of my right love handle was really only a flesh wound, and aesthetically speaking, my figure would probably benefit from a little more of this accidental plastic surgery—when I walk down the beach in my bathing suit, women *dress* me with their eyes—but this was not the time to bring up the subject.

Now that I knew we were, at least for the time being, not sinking, I shouted to Gale, "I'm okay. I'm going to the bow to look for a way out. You steer."

With a loud "clunk" resounding through the boat about every ten seconds, I knew we had to find a way out very soon if we were going to save the boat. As they say, every time one reef closes, another one opens, and there to port was a long, narrow alleyway of darker water. Each wave that washed over the reef raised our hull just enough to move a few feet towards the channel. To her credit Gale followed my gestures perfectly as, yard by yard, in fits and starts, we worked our way out of danger to open water. Once in deep water we throttled back and, still trembling, made our way to the entrance to Culebra's amazing bay, Ensenada Honda.

Periodic checks of the bilge showed that water was seeping in from somewhere but at a rate slow enough not to put us in immediate danger of sinking. I rigged the bilge pump I had brought, connected it to the starter battery, and we continued towards the town dock where we had agreed to pick up Peter.

As we got closer I was able to make out a diminutive figure standing on the dock: it was Peter. White pork-pie hat, pressed Lacoste golf shirt, immaculate, powder blue Bermudas over white knee socks and, as promised, accompanied by a cooler containing Daly's famous Beef Wellington and—I assume—some extra bottles of beer. And a big smile on his face.

While sloshing a few buckets of water around the cockpit had washed away most of the blood—it had looked more like an old whaling ship than a yacht—I was still bruised and bleeding, and I wanted Peter to know what had happened and how the consequences might affect the rest of our trip.

As the fenders kissed the wharf, I stepped forward to explain our situation, but I was too late, as with a cheery "halooo," our diminutive English friend had already launched himself from dock to deck.

It was only after he noticed the serious looks on our faces that he stopped his chatter. "Peter," I said, looking him in the eye and using my most compelling voice. "We're sinking. And I don't know if we can go on."

"Aw, come on, Patron. You're always joking," he shot back. It took the whole story and removal of my shirt to convince him I was serious.

Peter, a Brit and a CPA, is a much more placid, logical person than I. "Let's think about this," he said. "There's no place in Culebra to take her out of the water and repair the hull, so staying here will do us no good. We might as well try to continue on to Puerto Rico, where there are a number a places we could haul your injured vessel."

Since running the engine from time to time charged the battery, and the pump seemed to keep the bilge pretty dry, what he said made sense, and we decided to stay the night, planning to leave at first light the next morning.

Nightfall found us anchored in the bay, eating cold Beef Wellington and drinking Peter's beer. Going over our options, we decided that if once underway the water in the bilge rose quickly, we would dash to the closest facility on the big island, Puerto Del Rey, on Puerto Rico's east coast. But if we got lucky and could keep her afloat, we should try to make it back to the club in Ponce, where we had connections and our car waiting for us.

That night I slept fitfully, getting up about every half hour to check the water level. Amazingly, the bilge pump had no trouble keeping up with leak.

Up at dawn we weighed anchor—line, not chain, and no windlass—raised the sails, and motored out of the bay, turning west with ten knots of wind to carry towards Puerto Rico.

Could we make it? I was confident that if we arrived in Ponce—though we had no navigation instruments or lights—with its lighted, well-marked channel, we could make port safely even though it was night. However, with no depth sounder or navigation assistance, I didn't want to have to feel our way into some strange cove in the dark. That meant an average speed of about five knots would be needed to cover the 70-mile distance.

Gaining additional confidence in our hull's integrity as each hour passed once we got underway, we decided to go for broke—Ponce or bust.

Running the engine at a little more than idle helped us maintain good speed and we hoped would stretch our meager fuel supply to give the maximum possible hours of running time. Even though we knew we didn't have enough fuel to run the engine all the way to Ponce, we calculated that with a little luck we could make it to the gas dock at the marina at Salinas, which was 20 miles closer along the same south coast route.

Well our calculations were close, but we didn't win the cigar. As we passed Guayama at 6 p.m., ten miles short of the Salinas Bay entrance, we used up the last of our fuel. Once again we were facing a grim situation.

The bay behind the barrier islands along the coast would be a perfect haven for the night. But with just the wind we could not make the additional 15 miles to the normal, safer western entrance of Jobos Bay before dark. We would have to take a shot at the nearby, dangerous eastern entrance, really just a break in the reef, known as "Boca de Infierno." This translates, ominously, into English as "The Mouth of Hell." Add to that it was getting dark, we had no navigation lights or working instruments, and the long hours and tension had taken their toll. We were exhausted.

Racing—perhaps racing is not the right word—the darkness towards the safety of the bay, we glided west as darkness descended. Staring intently at the dark shapes in the gray dusk as we closed on the passage, I realized there really wasn't enough light for me to make out the narrow passage at Boca de Infierno. Try as we might, while we could hear the swells breaking against the reef, we could not see the passage.

I turned to my crew for yet another of those "What do we do now" conferences. Gale, the concern showing in her voice, said, "I don't want to try to sail at night with no lights and no instruments. Is there somewhere we can safely anchor for the night?"

"What do you think this is, Magans Bay?" I shot back. "This coast is steep. Any place more than 50 yards from the shoreline will be too deep, and even if I found a place shallow enough, we'd have no lee for protection from the ocean swells."

"Okay, know-it-all captain. You got us into this, you'd better find a solution. Look at the damn chart."

Cigarette lighter in one hand and chart in the other, I searched in the flickering light for somewhere near the string of islands shallow enough to anchor but still safe from rocks and coral. The chart showed that the only low spot that wasn't a reef was a narrow

This was our planned route West to Ponce

ledge in about 30 feet of water to windward of the western arm of the Boca de Infierno shoal. The only logical way to anchor there would be run towards the reef, and at the last second turn upwind, dump the anchor on its 5/8-inch line, and pray it caught immediately, or we'd be up—again—on a reef. This time in the dark.

With this maneuver I would be playing my last card.

I have to admit that at this point part of me felt that if the boat sank or were wrecked, it would be an act of mercy. We were close enough to swim to shore, our financial loss would be at that point minimal, and the whole nightmare would be over. But giving up wasn't really a viable option, so we ran towards the still visible white foam and, just when we guessed we were in shallow water, swung the rudder, headed up, and with a prayer dumped the anchor.

Sails luffed, and rolling quietly with the swells, I hopefully let out line. Holding the rode in my hand, I could feel the anchor catch then break free. It scraped along the bottom for what seemed like a very long time as we drifted closer and closer to the reef. Then with a strong jerk the Danforth caught, and I shouted, "Hallelujah! We're in."

Our relief was tempered by the realization that although the hook was really in, there was nothing between us and Venezuela but the Caribbean Sea. We were safe for the moment but not very sound. The boat bucked and rolled with the waves that passed under our hull and broke just past our stern. Its constant rolling and leaping was so bad that to sleep we had to tie ourselves into our bunks. Too seasick and scared to eat, that night we filled the empty hours of our watches bailing with a soda can and bucket. At one point a big helicopter clattered over to us. Hovering, its brilliant searchlight created a surreal circle of artificial lights around us, emphasizing our helplessness and broaching the subject of possible rescue. However, the handheld VHF stayed silent, so as we looked too disheveled to be drug runners, they left without calling a cutter to take us to jail …and safety. It was a hell of a night, but as always happens, dawn came and with it hope.

After a breakfast of warm Diet Pepsi—warm beer for Peter—we set about getting the anchor up and the boat back into deeper water. Sails set, with Gale at the wheel and Peter, calm as usual, dealing with jib sheets, we tacked back and forth on the anchor line while I strained at the rode. Each tack gained a few feet of rope until the hook finally broke free. With a collective sigh of relief, we fell off to fill the sails and get up some speed. Now in good light we could see the pass through last night's *bete noir* into Jobos Bay. Once through the pass we were only a few miles from civilization, fuel, and a pay phone, so important in the dark ages before cell phones.

The wind pushed us nicely through the protected waters of the bay, and soon we were in Salinas harbor, picking our way through the anchored boats and their crews, none of whom had any idea what we had just been through. Thankful for our safe arrival, we dropped the hook and I dinghied ashore in search of diesel fuel and some way to get it back to the boat. Luck was with us that day as our favorite sailmaker, Marianne at Tradewinds Sails and Canvas, had—and lent us—a five-gallon jerry can full of fuel. She also graciously offered to drive Gale to our marina in

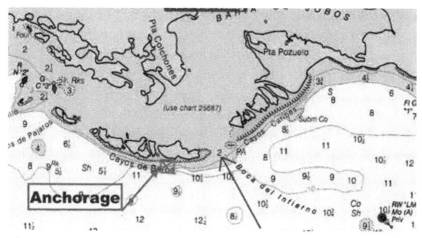

Blue arrow- Boca de Infierno-Red cross our anchorage

Ponce to alert the club's staff to our predicament. There she could make arrangements in person, so upon our arrival we could sail right into the Travel Lift slings and pull our boat out of the water before we really did sink. It would also get Gale off our hapless craft and onto dry land.

Now fueled up and back on board, I spent the first hour learning how to "bleed"—a word that shall live forever in infamy—the air out of the cranky Perkins. Getting the diesel started was to be our last ordeal for a while, as once it started we left the harbor for what turned out to be an uneventful four-hour trip to Ponce, a trip that included a bizarre experience of listening to the Giants vs Bears football game on Armed Forces Radio as we passed the Naval radio station in Fort Allen.

Gale had done her job well, including calling our son-in-law Ricky—that year's club Commodore—who used his influence to be sure everything was ready for our arrival. Once in the harbor we dropped the sails—they were so dirty I was ashamed for anyone at the club to see them—motored past the docks, and aiming the sinking craft for the exact middle, we motored right into the waiting arms of the Travel Lift. In a minute 16,000 lbs. of beat-up boat were out of the water, dripping but safe in the Travel Lift's slings. A small crowd had gathered, I assumed to hail me as the hero who saved his sinking boat. (Not the schmuck who caused the problem.)

With crew and craft on *terra firma*, I felt a giant sense of relief. Nothing could threaten us now. Just then I noticed a couple of uniformed, U.S. Customs agents pointing to the boat and asking questions of the bystanders. Like a ton of bricks, it hit me. Oh, my God. With all the drama I had completely forgotten about the requirement to check in with Customs when returning from the Virgin Islands. I—and my boat—could be in really big trouble.

In a loud whisper I called to Gale, "Tell Ricky we forgot to check in with Customs." Grasping the severity of the situation, Ricky sauntered over to the two federal agents, who were by now pulling papers out of their attache cases, and began chat with them. The churning emptiness in my stomach was only alleviated when I saw, after a few minutes of persuasion, the officers nod their heads, return their papers to their briefcases, and the little conference broke up.

I held my breath until Ricky returned with the news that he had talked them out of seizing the boat by explaining about our emergency and convincing them, as they could see, that the boat wasn't worth much anyway.

Well, our plan had been to get the new boat home and into the yard for refurbishing, and here it was. We just hadn't planned to make the process quite so dramatic.

Now with the Caribe 41 chocked and dry, there was nothing else for us to do but get in the car and make our way through the Sunday afternoon traffic back to the big city of San Juan. As we drove we talked about the adventure, reliving the events of the last two days. Finally arriving at Peter's home, I asked him, "Hey, weren't you at any time scared?"

With a short, clipped tone that emphasized each word, he answered, "No, not until I got in the car with you at the wheel."

Creating a Class Act

As the memory of our thrilling voyage faded into the past, the work of rehabilitation began. Surprisingly, in the calm light of day, careful inspection showed the only damage done by our grounding on the reef in Culebra was a minor crack in the keel that allowed a small but continuous amount of seawater to find its way into the bilge. This damage was easily repaired. We moved on to the most costly part of her renewal, repainting the deck white and the hull flag blue. The professional boat painters we contracted for the job spent almost a week filling and sanding before applying a drop of paint. But when they were finished, the esthetic transformation was incredible. The old Caribe 41 had been transformed from what looked like an old, dirty Clorox bottle into a gleaming, elegant, blue-hulled yacht.

Then we went to work getting the interior up to snuff. After an intense campaign of cleaning and painting, we set about upgrading the interior. New Formica, cushions, lamps, stove, etc. The work was the easy part. You see, while Gale and I usually work well as a team, we are miles apart when it comes to the aesthetics. I'm a practical, "Get it done, clean and simple" guy. Gale, however, insists on adornment frills and "made to order" stuff that costs much more and, in my view, complicates things.

Example. At home I participated in a project that included taking the throw pillows, all 24 of them, off the bed. Then the duvet, bedclothes, and mattresses were removed Why? So we could install a *dust ruffle*. Why do we need a dust ruffle? We need it in case someone should come to our house, go up to the second floor, and down the hall to our bedroom. Then if they go in and get down on their hands and knees and look under the bed, they won't be able to see any dust—God forbid—under our bed.

Do you understand what I'm dealing with?

But I must say, when we finished, she—the boat, I mean—looked like new, No, better than new. There was no way we were going to call this beauty *Passing Wind II*. Alluding to our second

The galley before and after

careers as performers and the boat's unbelievable transformation, we decided to name her *Class Act*.

Once she was floating in her slip, we began the work of upgrading and installing new equipment. Our plans included new sails, ground tackle, fresh new cushions, bright new galley countertop, and a lot of elbow grease. We were lucky to find Alfredo, a relative of one of my employees, who was an elbow grease specialist. Alfredo was a little slow—it took him 90 minutes to watch "The Salsa Hour"—he wasn't very punctual, and had trouble holding a regular job, but he was willing to work for $5.00 an hour. The perfect person for our project.

Each night at home before going to work at the Ponce branch, I would study the manual or instruction sheet of whatever equipment I was taking to him to install. Then before going to the office, I would meet Alfredo at the boat. There, slowly and precisely, I would explain what today's project was and how he should accomplish it. Leaving him with the necessary parts and appropriate tools, I would then head off to my office and leave him to work on his own until 5 p.m. when I would return to the marina to inspect the work and pay him. He was a bargain, and if every once in a while he was a no-show, it was no tragedy for either of us.

Each day was a baby step, but those baby steps added up, little by little, to great strides. I decided to keep the antiquated wire luff jib furled but was ruthless about modernizing everything else. Within two months she was 90% done. She looked like new, and with all the new equipment we had installed, she was ready for the trip we planned to make "down island." I never failed, each time I left *Class Act*, to stop and turn around on the dock to marvel at the miracle we had wrought.

Really Learning to Cruise

Although I had come to Puerto Rico to pursue a business goal and enjoy the broadening experience of living in another culture, my nascent involvement with boating convinced me I should also be taking advantage of our proximity to the delights of the Caribbean. The Virgin Islands, St. Martin, St. Barts, Trinidad. These are dream destinations for people all over the world. Luckily, for us they were just a short flight or, even better, a short sail away.

The many exotic islands of the Caribbean lay before us, a 700-mile chain of romantic destinations that stretched from Puerto Rico to Trinidad. French Islands, Dutch Islands, pirate havens, reefs for diving, Jet Set destinations, surrounded by waters and a climate almost unmatched anywhere else in the world, and all—with one exception—accessible by sailboat without leaving sight of land. Now that we had a proper boat, we would be able to enjoy as much of this as we wanted without paying for a hotel room or an airplane ticket.

Our trips to Coffin Island were now more like comfortable walks to the corner drugstore, and as we worked out her kinks, I felt more and more confident about *Class Act*. With this big boat and the experience we had gained with the Columbia, Gale and I would soon be traveling beyond the Virgin Islands and living aboard for weeks or months. We were ready.

So when I read about the rousing seven days of sailing and partying during the annual Race Week in Antigua, I decided to make this event the goal of our first extended cruise in *Class Act*.

My night table exhibited a constant stack of cruising guides for each night's research to learn about every bay, beach, and snorkel spot between us and Antigua. Cruising guide authors Chris Doyle and Donald Street became my constant companions. I soon knew by memory the course and distances between islands, where I could moor for free, and the best restaurants on every island.

After a week in St. Martin with friends who would fly in, we would stop at St. Barts then on to our destination, Antigua. I could hardly stand the excitement as I wrote down the names and the distances. When the nautical festivities of Race Week ended, we would island hop our way back to St. Martin—via Montserrat, Nevis, Statia, and Saba. Exotic names that I couldn't wait to drop when we successfully returned from this trip.

Finally, food, booze, cruising guides, and charts loaded aboard, we were ready for the trip of a lifetime. How many people dream of perhaps a week in the Caribbean, and here we were about to embark on a two-month trip to a dozen beautiful tropical islands.

A surprise bonus was that Gale's parents wanted to sail with us, so we would pick them up in the British Virgin Islands. This also meant we would be able to count on her father's wisdom and

Hard to believe this is the same boat we found in Virgin Gorda

experience for help on the difficult leg from Virgin Gorda to St. Martin.

In light of our previous experience on this route, and taking into account the suggestions gathered from books and the club barflies, we decided to take their advice and sail along the south coast of Puerto Rico during the night when sea and wind were calmer.

I calculated that by leaving our dock at 5 p.m. and motorsailing through the night, we should arrive in St. Thomas in daylight. I felt more confident about the overnight sail, as I had added to my toolbox of navigational tricks an important piece of technology. With some reluctance I had laid out $1,100 for a new-fangled thing called the Magellan GPS. Now I felt better prepared for any navigational challenges we might encounter.

Departure date came, and as the sun was setting in the west, we left the shelter of Ponce's harbor and turned east. A light wind off our starboard bow gave us some lift without whipping up the waves, and the overnight trip was, with one major exception, smooth and uneventful.

Hearing stories of sailboats that disappeared, probably crushed by some huge ship that ran over them in the night, had made a very strong impression on us. So taking quite seriously the new challenges of night sailing, we endeavored to keep a first rate lookout at all times. Constantly scanning the dark horizon, I spent the first three hours that night searching, like some sort of human radar antenna, for even the smallest light or faint shape in the dark that might pose a danger. Continually scanning left to right, then right to left.

Because I was being so diligent, and had yet to find another craft on our part of the sea, I was a bit bewildered then startled when I noticed the faint thrumming noise of a large ship's diesel engine growing steadily louder as the minutes ticked by.

Sweeping the dark horizon in front of me more carefully, I was still unable to locate the source of the sound. I became concerned and interrupted Gale's galley work with my shouted declaration,

"Hey, Gale. Some asshole in a big ship must be out there with no lights. Please come up here and give me a hand finding it." As she emerged from the companionway, I was surprised to see her face was now bathed in light.

Raising her hand, she pointed past my head towards the stern and gasped, "Oh, God, look!"

There, right on our tail, towering over our little craft, was a sizable coastal freighter. She was damn close and in the process of overtaking us. Before I could take any practical evasive action, the freighter altered course slightly and passed us close, very close, to starboard. How close? So close I could see that two crew members leaning against the rail were smoking ... Marlboro ... Lights. Whew. Lesson learned: Look astern too, or you might be run over by a freighter because "Ship happens."

The long night eventually ended, and sailing into the dawn gave us a wonderful feeling of déjà vu when the high green mountains of St. Thomas, lit by the rising sun, came into view. That afternoon found us safely moored in one of our favorite locations, lovely Maho Bay, St. John. The perfect place to catch up on our sleep and reflect on how well *Class Act* had performed. There was no doubt in my mind she was ready for longer voyages.

With a few days free before Gale's parents were to arrive, we relaxed and explored more of these wonderful islands while preparing for the Anegada Passage, a crossing of fearsome reputation.

The Trade Winds

Before we go on with this saga, I would like to mention, for the benefit of anyone planning to sail there, how important the easterly trades are to the Caribbean sailor. We are lucky that almost every day is sunny and warm. Rain showers are short, and with the exception of the now rare hurricane, nearly every day is a sailing day because the winds are nearly perfect.

I would guess that 90% of the time in these waters the wind will flow from the sector of 100 to 130 degrees at about 15 to 20 knots.

So unlike the fluky winds of other areas, when planning a voyage one has a pretty good idea about what the point of sail will be for the proposed trip.

As you can see by the map, anyone—including us—going east from Puerto Rico along the chain of islands is pretty much going to have the wind in his teeth until Guadalupe. The longest leg into the wind is the voyage from the BVIs to St. Martin.

There are, literally, volumes of books written about how to cross the dreaded Anegada Passage east from the BVIs to St. Martin. One bearded, beer-drinking old salt, who has written many cruising books, devotes page after page to an analysis of currents and crossing strategies. Where there's smoke ...

So we assumed for this first voyage that we should follow his instructions for crossing this notoriously rough, 75-mile strait. We did as he suggested, leaving at dusk so we, with Gale's parents now on board as crew, would have ample time to battle the infamous waves and currents and arrive in St. Martin the next day before dark. This strategy seemed pretty conservative to me. Only 75 miles? Hell, we should be in St. Martin before noon.

A few days of easy sailing and socializing with Paul and Bev had brought us to North Sound, our departure point for the big trip. Everything that needed it was lashed down. Sandwiches were made, foulies donned, and cold drinks placed in the cockpit cooler. We were ready for anything, we thought.

Following the old salt's instructions, we powered through the perilous Prickly Pear Passage. (Try saying that three times fast.) Our course left us motor-sailing very close hauled into 15 knots of wind from 120 degrees. We anticipated

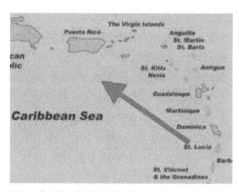

How the Trade Winds affect voyage planning

that the waters would be rough, so we weren't too concerned when the swells became steeper and steeper. Although the sails were filled with wind and the engine was at 1,800 rpm, we were doing only four knots over the bottom, and our track was a disappointing 70 degrees. Oh well, I guess we'll have to make a tack south at some point. We had been sailing for about two hours through intermittent squalls, still 70 miles from St. Martin, when all hell broke loose.

We were plodding along, minding our business, when bang. The upper swivel on the wire luff roller furling jib parted, and all of a sudden it was raining jib. I gave the wheel to my father-in-law, clipped onto a jackline, and crawled forward to gather in the billowing 120. The foredeck was a bucking bronco, and more than once it belted me in my mouth as I struggled to force the useless sail through the forepeak hatch into the V-berth.

Once done, soaked, a bit seasick, and a lot bruised, I worked my way back to the cockpit to dry off and assess our options. With only main and engine, the boat had very little drive, so the steep 6-ft. seas were slowing us down considerably. Returning to the BVIs was not an option, as it was too dark for us to find our way back through the passage in the reef to North Sound.

To make any real progress, we would need to set a foresail. I had prepared for this eventuality by hanking a spare working jib to the forestay and tying it to the starboard safety line and stanchions with sheets already run back so it would be ready to hoist if needed. Crawling again to the bucking foredeck, with the wind in my face and a knife in my teeth, I set about cutting the lashing that held the jib. The job went deceptively well, as the first three pieces of string were easily severed. However, as soon the first few feet of sail were liberated, the wind caught the sail and ripped it from my hands.

The first bow-burying sea ripped the sail from the rest of its lashings, and then the force of the water from the next bow-burying sea smashed into the flogging sail, bending three stanchions and opening a long tear. Scrambling back to safety in the cockpit, I watched as the "storm jib" was converted into streamers, and all I could do was concede to my lack of blue water experience.

With no alternative, now we could only slog on with motor and main. Climbing the waves at an angle then turning to surf down the other side kept us moving, but our ground speed was now down to only two and a half knots, and the hobby-horsing and rolling were so bad my mother-in-law, evicted from the V-berth by the big jib, had to be tied in the bed in our cabin to keep from being thrown to the cabin sole.

My mother-in-law, in spite of the uncomfortable conditions, was acting like most of the women who came aboard our boat as guests: perhaps a little fearful but compliant and willing to follow instructions. My experience with male guests, however, has been quite different.

For some reason when men board a sailboat, they experience an irresistible need to prove they are some sort of Joshua Slocum, or worse, Jack Aubrey. (He's only a *fictional* expert and hero.) These "experts" proceed to comment on everything that happens and don't fail to tell me how I should be doing things on *my* boat.

One guy, an uninvited friend of an invited friend, who had only sailed on other people's boats, spent his time changing the way I had set lines, instruments, and equipment. When questioned about his behavior, in a tone Donald Trump would have found admirable, he informed me he had read and nearly memorized *Chapman*'s. You know what they say: The male ego is the only thing on earth that keeps growing without nourishment.

Another of the attributes of a "real man" is not to sit on the toilet to pee while at sea. Even if the boat is pitching and rolling like a mechanical bull, and there is danger of wetting down the walls of the head space to shoulder height, they have to stand in the head or pee overboard.

So when about 8 p.m. Gale's father announced, "I'm going to the taffrail to take a pee," I wasn't surprised by Gale's cry of, "What?" which was immediately followed by a stern, "No, Dad. You can't. It's too rough."

Obviously unconvinced by the opinion of a woman, the old captain put a foot over the coaming, and in a dismissive tone informed his daughter, "I've been in rougher seas than this and had no problem." Crouching as he scuttled along, he started to make his way towards the stern.

In a tone and using words I have never previously heard leaving her mouth—and I hope I never will again—my sweet, warm, caring spouse stuck her head out from under the shelter of the bimini, growled like something out of the *Exorcist,* and yelled, "DAD, GOD DAMN IT. GET THE FUCK BACK IN THE COCKPIT !"

The old salt, as shocked as I was, meekly wobbled back to the cockpit and sheepishly made his way to the—thank goodness—guest head to relieve himself in a less macho manner as we continued our marathon to windward.

Up and down. Side to side. Through the night. The slap of seawater in the face every third or fourth wave was the only relief from the tedium. Hour after hour we ground on through what seemed like a night without end. When the much anticipated dawn unfolded to light our world, it revealed nothing but an endless expanse of ocean and an empty horizon. The beauty of foam-flecked, deep blue restless sea, bright sunshine, and azure sky went unnoticed as we searched the horizon for a sign of the end to our wet and seemingly endless misery.

Hoping for a morale boost by checking our progress with the GPS, I was dismayed when my calculations showed that, at this rate, we wouldn't arrive in St. Martin until well after dark. Our chart showed that Anguilla's Road Bay was a priceless ten miles closer, and although I hadn't planned a stop there, I altered course in hopes we could arrive there before dark.

Around 6 p.m. the summer sun, now low in the west, still provided enough light to illuminate what looked like a flat tan shape in the distance. Gale saw it first. "What's that? Look."

From the bearing, I knew it had to be ... it was ... land. "That's Dog Island!" I said. "About five miles away, I know it! Anguilla's only ten miles beyond it!" A cheer went up as we slapped each other on our backs. Damn, too late I realized that I had missed the perfect opportunity to shout, "Land Ho!"

Wallowing our way closer and closer to our goal in the last vestiges of light, we were ecstatic to see the lights on Anguilla about five miles away as they flickered on. But seeing *there* and being *there* are two very different things. The wind, waves, and current still conspired to slow our progress, and night found us still a long way from shore. Our spirits were very low.

Thanks to the primitive GPS, we knew where Road Bay was, but although the numbers it gave indicated we were approaching the bay's entrance, in the dark we still couldn't make out any markers for the channel or see any rocks or land. We were left to slowly grope our way in the dark of the moonless night.

The mood was tense as we slowly motored into the unknown bay. Passing shapes in the dark we assumed to be anchored boats, we felt our way toward the only navigational aide we could see: a pair of red and green lights, blinking in the distance. On and on we crept toward the lights, which we assumed marked the entrance into some sort of inner harbor. With the fathometer reading 10', 9', 8', then 7', I was very apprehensive about continuing towards the shore and decided to stop the boat and anchor before anything worse happened. We would discover more by the dawn's early light.

Celebratory drinks—my doctor says that sailing is bad for your liver—and badly needed sleep were the rewards for our safe arrival that night.

The morning's light revealed we were okay, safely moored in the middle of the bay, surrounded by other anchored craft. All okay. However, halting the previous night before attempting to reach the blinking lights turned out to have been an excellent decision, as now in the daylight we could see these lights were not navigational aids at all but wall-mounted attention grabbers flanking the door of the Sandy Ground Beach Bar. I shudder to think what might have happened if we had continued our course towards them.

Relieved to be living examples of "Better late than never," we wasted no time setting out for our original destination. Without bothering Anguilla Customs, we set sail for our destination, Port de Pleasance Marina on the Dutch side of St. Martin, only 15 miles away.

Now certified Anegada Passage veterans—survivors?—we were ready to face the next challenge: the Dutch-side drawbridge.

For most boaters drawbridges are as much a part of your normal environment as docks and light houses. In the Caribbean, however, they are rare, and I was very nervous about dealing with this challenge.

As we approached the bridge, I called Port de Pleasance on the radio to report our imminent arrival. The appearance of a young man in a spiffy nautical uniform in the marina's official pilot boat was a pleasant surprise. Much to my relief, our rescuer was kind enough to explain the procedure for passing though the bridge and told us that, once safely in the lagoon, he would guide us to our place on the quay.

The bridge turned out to be a cinch. Really, all we had to do was follow the other boats in. Less than a mile further on, the pilot boat led us into a beautifully appointed cul-de-sac yacht harbor in a small cove. The quays were lined with large, multi-million dollar yachts all tied up in Mediterranean style. Time to get nervous again. This was to be my first try at berthing with no dock to sidle up to, and a mistake could cause more damage to one of these yachts than my cockleshell was worth.

At that moment the guy in the pilot boat circled back and explained he would act as tug and line handler to slide me into my space. All I had to do was follow his orders. It worked.

Safe at last. And what amazing service. Boy, they take care of everything here. So we weren't too surprised when, instead of our having to schlep across the harbor to the marina office, the dock master, waving both arms, came running to our piece of pier.

Pulling up alongside, after taking a deep breath, he blurted out, "Are you Ivy's father? Are you Ivy's father?"

Momentarily stunned by someone I had never met asking about my family, I was speechless. Then it hit me. I had given my float plan to my very responsible daughter Ivy. It had us arriving, let me see … Oh, God, yesterday. Knowing my super-competent daughter, in the absence of news from us, she had probably called out the Coast Guard, the Navy, and Greenpeace.

Well not quite, but pretty close. Having inquired about arrival several times by phone without any news, she was about to do just that. I apologized to the harbormaster and asked if I could use their phone to call her and turn off the worry machine.

With the last loose end now, literally, tied up, we could calmly relax and check out our new home away from home.

It looked like my pre-departure research was paying off. I chose Port de Pleasance after bumping into a magazine article describing the complete facilities of this recently opened luxury hotel/resort/marina complex. Their introductory price of a buck a foot per day sealed the deal.

And what a deal. The marina was surrounded by attractive neo-Mediterranean hotel facilities and gardens. For our daily dockage cost of $41, the staff fawned on us, gave us free ice and laundry service, use of the pools, spa, and tennis courts. Wait. So you want more for your money? A few days later when we needed transportation to the airport for our flight back to Puerto Rico, they provided a stretch limo to get us there. Having gone through purgatory, we had earned heaven. And we couldn't wait to come back.

Cruising the Islands

By now we were feeling pretty comfortable with commuter cruising. Sail, then work. Sail, then work. For the next three weeks I dealt with my tasks at the office distractedly, but my mind was focused on making plans for our next two legs: St. Martin to St. Barts to Antigua. I had found someone at the marina to repair the jib furler and bent stanchions, so the boat was ready to travel.

Sometimes I had to pinch myself to be sure I wasn't dreaming. We were about to embark on a truly extraordinary trip: starting on the well-known tourist island of St. Martin and ending up at Race Week in Antigua. With a stop in classy St. Barts to dine in fine French restaurants, surrounded by the rich and famous. Does it get any better than this? And now we had a big enough boat to share our good fortune with friends and family.

As a way of saying thanks for his part in the purchase of the Columbia, I invited my unflappable California friend Jim Fowler and his gracious wife, Wilma, to join us. Jim, who looks like Cary Grant—if the actor hadn't dyed his hair—loves people, which is a major reason why he was so successful in his sales career. Wife Wilma keeps him from "giving away the farm." To add some spice to this crew recipe, we invited our San Juan friend Neda Gonsalves. Neda, unpredictable, with her bangs and mischievous smile, is always ready for fun. It was her idea, 12 years later, to sail the islands off the Dalmatian coast from Dubrovnik and visit the island of Corcula where her Croatian family warmly welcomed us with open arms.

But I digress. The excitement built as our date of departure from San Juan approached, and when it arrived I felt so high I could hardly speak. Neda made up for my silence by chattering away all the way to and through Customs at St. Maarten's Queen Juliana airport. Afraid that it might not show up, I had not mentioned the stretch limo. But Port de Pleasance didn't fail us, and our guests were really impressed with the white Cadillac, uniformed driver, and the general elegance of the resort.

Once our luggage was stowed aboard, the girls left to shop for food and supplies in a supermarket on the French side. (They spent nearly as much as the original cost of the boat.) Meanwhile, Jim and I prepared *Class Act* for the next morning's departure.

We had no trouble dealing with the channel and drawbridge the next day, and in bright, sunny Caribbean weather, we motorsailed east along St. Maarten's south coast, fighting our way through five foot seas, almost dead into the southeast wind as we made our way towards new territory: exotic French St. Barts.

We survived the four-hour trip's jarring, plunging motion and arrived safely at Gustavia Harbour, the island's capitol and only town. Glad to get out of the wind and choppy seas, we searched the crowded harbor in vain for space to anchor. Seeing some space on the seawall, I decided to try a Mediterranean moor on my own without a fancy marina pilot boat to help.

Dropping our 45-lb. plow anchor off the bow in the middle of the channel, I reversed gingerly towards the seawall. A miracle. For the first time ever, *Class Act* backed, straight as an arrow, towards the solid mass of concrete behind me. I stopped just in time for Jim to leap to shore and tie the knot that finished the gift of a perfect Med moor.

As this was our first experience checking into a French island, I took Gale, who speaks some French, with me to deal with the legendarily difficult French bureaucracy. Wrong. Here and at the rest of the French Caribbean islands, we were attended to in English and always enjoyed a no-hassle clearance procedure. We were out and back to the boat in five minutes. I'd say the French officials seemed surprised we had even stopped in to see them at all.

Compare this experience to the nightmare bureaucratic process we found in the ex-colonial islands of the British Empire. For example, our first visit to Nevis.

Anchoring off Nevis' scenic Pinney's Beach, we dinghied to the ferry dock and, in the absence of any signage, started asking where to check in. Directed to the Office of Immigration in the police station, a six-block walk from the dock, we sat on old wooden benches until the official finished his paperwork and dealt with us. Thirty minutes later, with stamped papers, we retraced our route to the harbormaster at the dock where, after paying the port fees, we were directed to the Customs office, a short cab ride away. Now with all the necessary forms in hand, we were told to take them back to the police station to have them all stamped as certified. Rand Paul would have killed someone.

Island time. No one else was in a hurry, so why should we be? Back to the trip.

Expecting St. Barts to be some sort of Hollywood in the Caribbean, we were surprised to find the people and businesses were very low key. This famous Jet Set destination turned out to be an expensive but understated island, fringed by lovely beaches and bays, with a plethora of fine restaurants.

It was a good thing we had only scheduled two days here, as we were spending money like saltwater. (A Scotch at a local hotel cost $18.00. Talk about likker shock.) So it was a financial relief when the time came for us to start our second, open water leg, the trip to Antigua, 70 miles away, southeast straight into the trades.

Reminded of our previous hard-on-the-wind experiences, I calculated, with all the tacking we would have to do, we would be making only about three knots over the ground on the rhumb line. I didn't need a computer—even if we'd had one in those days—to calculate that our trip would take … a long time. An afternoon departure was obviously called for if we wanted to make landfall before dusk the next day.

Leaving at 4 p.m., we spent the first hours taking turns being on watch and reading as we pushed through gentle swells in a light breeze. Then came twilight. Perhaps it was the great emptiness of the night that inspired us, but someone started singing, and soon we all joined in, one song after another, as though our voices could fill the great void of sky and wine-dark sea around us. And when the chorus went below for the night, I sat in the bow pulpit, watching the sea speckled with the bioluminescence our bow wave created. It was a very spiritual experience.

But as always happens—so far—day followed night, and soon the green hills of Antigua appeared on the horizon. We made landfall at Five Islands Bay on Antigua's west coast in time to enjoy a swim and sundowners in this perfect anchorage.

However, eyes on the prize, we were anxious to get to our destination, so we left early the next morning for our planned anchorage in Falmouth Harbor, right next to "Race Central" at Nelson's Dockyard.

A few hours later we were enjoying a spirited sail in bright sunlight, heeling nicely as we reached 15 to 20 knots along Antigua's south coast. Our bargain boat was on her sailing lines and making nearly six knots when I realized that conditions were perfect for "Flying the Bosun's Chair." This is an activity I had heard about but never performed.

My dubious crew was not convinced by my self-assured presentation as to how wonderful it would be for them to be swung out over the water, hanging from a rope from the mast of a fast-moving sailboat, but Neda, always ready to try something new, volunteered to be my—pardon the expression—guinea pig.

Now how to rig for the bosun's chair to be at the right height and angle? First I snapped the blue cloth sling to a spare halyard. Since the mast winches were all in use, I ran the tail down through a block that was coupled to a ring at the base of the mast then back to the cockpit and around the only winch I had available. From this winch I could control the height of the bosun's chair.

Neda, expressing her total confidence in my nautical abilities, and not exhibiting one iota of fear, climbed into the bosun's chair and over the safety line. Pushing off the toe rail, she swung way out over the water into a slow, wide arc to leeward.

A cheer went up, and each time she swung out, at the apex she squealed and the girls on board shrieked. I just smiled as I adjusted her height with my winch, keeping her just above the waves. Wonderful. A great idea. Well it was until the shackle holding the down-block on the mast parted, and now there was a hell of a lot of unwelcome slack in the system. Enough to dump poor Neda into the sea that was rushing by so quickly.

Suddenly, there was Neda plowing the surface of the sea, only visible between waves. Gale gasped, "Oh, my God, she's drowning."

I kind of realized that, but instead sharing my opinion on the subject, I was 100% focused on trying to winch in enough line against all the drag to bring her back up out of the water. Cranking madly, with the line at a disadvantageous angle, at long last I was able to raise a coughing and gasping Neda free of the sea—and her bathing suit top—and up and over the safety lines to shelter on deck. Dropping everything, I rushed to see if she was all right. Blinking her eyes and gasping for breath, she listened as I expressed my deep contrition and regret for what had happened. I felt terrible.

But our friend, true to form, just said, "Oh, no. Let's do it again, but I'd rather skip the second part."

By the time everyone was breathing normally, we had arrived at the Pillars of Hercules, and we turned to enter spacious Falmouth Harbor, our temporary new home. With a month to go before the beginning of racing festivities, I easily found a spot near shore, close to where the action would be, and dropped *Class Act*'s hook where we hoped it would remain until our return.

Race Week in Antigua

Four weeks later, with friends Edna, Jim, and Carolyn, we emerged from our Antiguan taxi at the water's edge and were greeted by a very different sight. What had been our solitary anchorage was now the scene of much regatta hustle and bustle and a veritable forest of masts. Falmouth Harbor and the area surrounding Nelson's Dockyard had become the focus of sailors worldwide. The bays were now chock-full of craft that ranged from J22s to large motor yachts, racers, cruisers, and wooden classics. The restored grounds at nearby Nelson's Dockyard at English Harbour were festooned with pennants and the scene of continuous activity. A veritable nautical Times Square.

Parties, parades, and races filled each day. The whole week was a colorful, storybook nautical adventure. And though I missed not being out there racing, there was plenty of other stuff to keep us busy. We enjoyed our roles as just spectators to the hilt. With one exception.

During my comprehensive research for the trip, I had discovered that, before the presentations on Trophy Day, there was a special "Non-mariners Race." The rules for competing were simple. Any non-motorized vessel that cost less than $250 EC—US $100— could be used to compete. I bent the rules a little by purchasing a square-shaped child's inflatable backyard swimming pool for $39.95 and four $10 plastic paddles. We planned to use this contraption to carry four of us to victory and everlasting fame.

Trophy Day dawned quietly, but activity in the area increased in pace until by noon a colorful carnival atmosphere prevailed at the "Non-mariner's Race" start line at historic Nelson's Dockyard. Brawny deck apes and other professional crew in matching T-shirts and uniforms, along with some very strange-looking craft, began arriving at the race staging area. Mostly unnoticed among this crowd of more creative contraptions—including a floating

Rigging for Neda's adventure

toilet—was my paltry racing crew of three mature ladies and me in our so-called boat.

Competitor's craft that varied from just odd looking to downright dangerous crowded the little beach, and strapping young men joshed with each other as the clock wound down toward the start. With only seconds to go, we stood, hands tensely gripping our craft, awaiting the firing of the cannon and the race's Lemans-type start. Once in the water we would be joined by others in a frantic paddle along the shore to the left for 100 yards to the finish line.

Then it came. Boom.

The stampede of flailing muscular arms and legs nearly overwhelmed us as crews shouldered their craft and on a dead run plowed into the waters of English Harbour, nearly trampling my superannuated crew.

Momentarily stunned, it took us a few seconds to get started. Once we reached the water and clambered into our toy pool, we found ourselves well behind the pack that already had their oars or paddles in the water. However, it turned out that being last into the water had given us a surprising advantage.

In front of us, just a few yards from the shore, the other boats were involved in a huge commotion of spray as shouting crews attempted to sink or at least impede the progress of their competition. With all the other serious crews involved in this melee, no one seemed to notice or care about stragglers like us. Seeing a narrow lane of open water between the shore and the brawl, and paddling quietly but steadily, we cautiously made our way around the fray to the forefront, leaving the free-for-all behind us.

Upon turning the corner onto the home stretch, we found only one boat, the crew from a famous 12-meter yacht, ahead of us. By then the fracas behind us had sorted itself out, and a herd of paddling beefcake was bearing down on us. "Go, girls! Paddle like hell or they'll catch us. Stroke, stroke, stroke ..." I was still exhorting my ladies to paddle harder as we crossed the finish line just ahead of the pack to garner a solid second place. Hooray!

Andrew's Fall

The next morning's hangover from the previous night's victory celebration weighed heavily on us as we bid adieu to Race Week and our crew of victorious paddlers who were that afternoon returning to the real world. They were being replaced the next day by my son, Andrew. It was his first time aboard *Class Act* since that initial, dreadful voyage from Virgin Gorda.

Once Andrew was aboard, and in the company of many other boats departing Antigua for Europe, South America, and the U.S., we motorsailed out of the harbor and turned our bow west towards the day's destination, the island of Montserrat, to be followed by planned stops in Nevis, Statia, and Saba before our return to St. Martin.

What a pleasure it was, for the first time in months, to find ourselves off the wind, and with the southeast trades helping, *Class Act* made short work of the 30-mile passage to the anchorage off Montserrat's capital, Plymouth. We endured the very rolly anchorage just long enough to visit the authorities, and then we quickly weighed anchor and left for the calm waters of Old Road Bay. As we sailed we were impressed by the many expensive, beautiful houses perched on the seaside cliffs along the coast of this lushly green island often referred to as "The Emerald Isle of the Caribbean." Who would believe the changes we would find when we stopped there a few post-volcano years hence?

As beautiful as Montserrat might be, we had plans to sail the next day to an even more magical anchorage, Nevis's palm-fringed Pinney's Beach with its stunning view of Nevis Peak.

Nevis has changed little over the last 50 years. After the Byzantine check-in process mentioned previously, we rented a car to spend the day exploring Nevis's hills, valleys, and grand old plantations, many of which have become chic boutique hotels and guesthouses. No other Caribbean island we have visited is so individually picturesque and historical.

With a full day of touring now over, we returned to the boat, stopping only long enough pick up some wine and a Frisbee to take to the beach to enjoy the last few hours of daylight in this enchanting spot. How enchanting? The afternoon of our first day, Gale took her glass of wine onto the deck and just stared, mesmerized, at the perfect green peak that rose, perfectly centered over a black sand beach and a fringe of perfect coconut palms, until the sun sat and darkness overwhelmed the visual splendor.

Andrew and I were trying to work off the effect of Gale's great cooking by tossing a Frisbee when my boy, leaping for my high throw, landed on the hard sand with an audible "crack," followed by his collapse to the ground. He had badly aggravated an old knee injury and now was unable to walk on his own.

The picnic was over, and after a short rest, supported on both sides, we plopped his 6-ft., 240-lb. body into the dinghy. We returned to the boat and, only with a great amount of pulling and grunting, were we able to haul him up the transom ladder and into the cockpit.

Still panting from the effort of getting him aboard, I gulped and said, "I'm worried about your knee. Maybe instead of leaving tomorrow for Statia, we should take you to a doctor here in Nevis."

Looking at me in a conspiratorial manner, my son reminded me with a wink, "Don't you remember you made plans for tomorrow?"

He was right. I had almost forgotten. With some difficulty I had arranged, in Statia, 25 miles northwest, a major celebration of Gale's birthday, which fell the next day. As an expression of appreciation for her complicity in all this cruising craziness, I had planned to spend whatever money necessary for a special dinner the next day at the best restaurant on the island, the elegant Old Gin House restaurant.

The "Gin" in the name had nothing to do with cheap booze but refers to its historical use as a building to process Sea Island cotton that had been grown on the island in the past. The owners had carefully restored the historic factory village and created a small but elegant waterside hotel and restaurant for the elite well-to-do few who visited the island.

Statia—short for St. Eustatius—is Dutch, boasts a fascinating history, a dormant volcano, and a submerged town, but lacks a protected harbor. Boats visiting are forced, as we did, to anchor in an open, rolling roadstead. We didn't want to leave a disabled Andrew aboard in such uncomfortable conditions only 50 yards from the birthday festivities. But his lack of mobility was a real impediment to getting him ashore from our anchorage off the hotel's black sand beach.

With no lee or reef protection, big rollers broke precipitously about ten yards from the beach, so safely landing the dinghy there was out of the question. Looking east along the shore, in the failing light I could see a dinghy dock just before the 15-foot high commercial dock, but it was, at a quarter mile away, too far for Andrew to land and walk back with his injury.

I once read that the most important characteristic for a cruising captain is resourcefulness, so I did some serious thinking and came up with what I thought was an ingenious plan.

Gale, already dressed for the celebration in an ankle-length tropical cocktail dress, would pilot the dinghy to a spot just short of the surf line. There Andrew and I, in bathing suits, would bail out of the inflatable and swim ashore through the combers while Gale, with towels and our party clothes safely enclosed in a big plastic bag, would then motor the quarter mile to the dinghy dock, secure the dinghy, and walk back to the beach with our dry clothes and towels. Once reunited, we would use the hotel beach bar bathroom to dry off and dress. Then properly attired, we would proceed across the road to our elegant dinner and birthday celebration at the fine hostelry and restaurant.

With each of us drilled and prepared to carry out our roles in the operation to military precision, we prepared to board the little inflatable. Slowly and not without difficulty, we helped Andrew into the dinghy from the rolling sailboat. With Andrew and me, each on our own side, and Gale at the tiller, we were ready to establish our beachhead.

Gale started the outboard and, putting it in gear, edged forward as the swells passed smoothly under us. All seemed to be going well as we crept closer and closer to the line of breakers. Because our attention was completely focused forward while we gauged the distance to the "bail out" spot, we didn't notice one great big "mutha" of a groundswell sneaking up behind us. It was the "thluk" sound when the wave hit the outboard that got our attention. Turning around, I could see water pouring in big time over the transom and nearly filling the dinghy. Gale's eyes were as big as bagels, and realizing another wave like this would swamp the dinghy, I shouted to her, "Turn around. Go back," and yelled to Andrew, "Bail out now!"

My boy was over the side in a flash, and I was less than a second behind him. Surfacing, I could see, each time the breakers allowed me to take a breath, that Gale had successfully turned the tender around, was safely outside the surf line.

Tumbling in the surf, I was relieved to finally wash up like beached whale on the grainy black sand beach right next to Andrew. We were effusive in congratulating ourselves on our safe arrival until we noticed that the rogue wave had also flushed the plastic trash bag with our clothes out of the dinghy. The parts of our wardrobe that hadn't already washed up on the beach could be seen sloshing back and forth in waves that lapped the shore.

Gale, distraught, with clammy hair, sopping wet dress, and fearing that we had drowned, took off with the tender at full speed and, missing the dinghy dock altogether, tied up at the high commercial pier. With no ladder to climb up and no wardrobe to bring ashore, her only choice was to stuff her dress in her underpants, her sandals in her teeth, and shimmy up the piling to the dock.

Flagging down a providentially passing Jeep, she begged a lift back to the disaster scene at the hotel beach to find out what had happened to us.

Flying out of the Jeep to where my son and I were standing, she looked us over while I assured her we were safe. I told her I was sorry she was so waterlogged, but at that point all we could do was collect our wet clothes from the beach and get dressed.

Once clothed — the word dressed would not apply to the way we looked — with Gale in tow we made our way across the road and into the hotel. I wish I had a photo of our group as we presented ourselves to the maître d' at the restaurant's entrance. (I don't have such a photo because the camera, put in the trash bag for "safe-keeping," was also lost.) So let me try to describe the scene.

Gale, looking like a drowned cocker spaniel in a soaking long sundress, stood next to me. I did my best to look *insouciant* with my white Lacoste golf shirt liberally peppered with grains of black sand from the beach. (Luckily, no one could see the sand in my underwear, but I could feel it.) Andrew, wet, rumpled and leaning on me for support, was standing on his one good leg, a silly smile on his face.

I've got to hand it to the restaurant's unflappable staff. That night, in addition to their usual group of well turned out, upscale guests, they were also hosting a private dinner for political leaders of the islands of Netherlands Antilles. Nonetheless, the waiter, pretending we looked like normal people, said, "Please follow me," and led us towards a dark corner table.

Already ashamed at our appearance, we attempted to steal as inconspicuously as possible to our table. But each time I took a step, my shoes made loud squishy noises. Still, I was doing better than Andrew, who had to lean on me and hop along on his good leg. Each hop, as we crossed the restaurant to our table, pounded the old, hollow, wooden plank floor with 240 lbs. of Andrew, creating a boom ... boom ... boom ... boom that sounded, to our self-conscious ears, like the chorus of the "1812 Overture."

Well, all's well that ends well. The food was delicious, and while the bill approached the amount of national debt of the island of Statia, it was definitely a night to remember.

Caribbean Heat

The following day Gale and I left the boat early to explore Oranjestad, the island's picturesque capitol. While this small town is chock-full of remnants of its colorful history, we soon ran out of monuments to the past, and we turned our attention to our second mission, a climb to the summit of the volcano, The Quill, whose mass dominates Statia's landscape.

A cab took us the short distance to the trailhead where we would begin the climb to the now quiescent caldera 2,000 feet above the sea. The recognizable path where the cab dropped us was a fairly easy walk at first, and Gale, a plant lover, excitedly called out the names of exotic flora she encountered as we trudged onward and upward. Mimosa, West Indian, Sugar Apple, and Yellow Plum. I grunted to acknowledge each name, trying to sound interested. As the trail became steeper and the sun rose higher, we really began to feel the tropical heat. Both now sweating profusely from the heat and exertion, our clothes had become liabilities, and as we stumbled skyward we began relieving ourselves of our garments piece by piece, hanging the discarded apparel on branches we passed until, reaching the 2,000-ft. summit, we were down to our underwear.

The view was expansive, but with our camera sitting on the bottom of Gallows Bay, we couldn't even take a photo of our achievement, so we were left with nothing to do but turn around and head back down the trail, picking our clothes off the vegetation and reversing the disrobing process until we were completely presentable when the taxi returned to pick us up.

A cool swim off the boat was very welcome at this point, and after a debriefing for Andrew, we settled down for what we hoped would be a well-earned rest. But that night's constant roll made sleep so difficult that instead of staying another night we weighed anchor and set sail for our next stop, the cliff-ringed, extraordinary island called Saba.

Saba rises straight up out of the blue sea like the top of some Swiss Alp. This sparsely populated, green, cone-shaped island, with its peak in the clouds, has a flavor that is more Alpine than Caribbean. Both its history and its present are quite intriguing. Today Saba is much more "Cruiser Friendly," with moorings for visitors placed at Ladder Bay, an indentation that approximates an anchorage. This bay, whose name is derived from the steps hewn into the shore's cliff—the only way to land merchandise until a few years before—is open to the west and has a stony bottom that seems to repel any attempts at anchoring. Holding here was so notoriously bad the cruising guides all recommended that vessels staying here leave someone on board on anchor watch while the crew went ashore. Our choice of who should stay was obvious, as we could not to even think about transferring our onboard cripple into the dinghy to explore ashore.

The three-mile trip in the inflatable to the new, artificial harbor on the south side was a wet one, but luckily, there was a friendly driver with a van and an affordable itinerary stationed at the pier when we stepped ashore.

As the van climbed the steep roads and switchbacks, we marveled at the clusters of neat, colorful homes that made up the small hamlets nestled in high, cool valleys, and thus began our love affair with Saba. Because Saba lacks beaches, tourism is not important, leaving this uniquely Dutch community not much changed from how it was a century ago. Any difficulty in getting to Saba is greatly overshadowed by the wonder that a few days' visit offers.

The tenuous anchorage, and the fact that again my practical wife had a schedule to hew to, forced us to leave after only a one day's visit, so early the next morning we turned our vessel towards our home away from home, St. Martin, and our favorite marina, Port de Pleasance.

Leaving at 7 a.m., we enjoyed 25 miles of picture book- perfect sailing on a beam and arrived at the bridge for its 11 a.m. scheduled opening into Simpson Bay Lagoon and on to the marina. This lagoon is one of the natural features that makes St. Maarten so popular with cruisers. It is a large body of shallow, protected water which makes up the west half of St. Maarten. An excellent anchorage, it also gives cruisers safe access by dinghy to the airport, shopping, and the French side.

The next day the limo was not available to take Gale to the airport, so Andrew and I placed her and her suitcase in the dinghy and dashed to the airport in time to put her, clothed and properly documented this time, on her plane to Puerto Rico.

During the remaining two days before our departure, Andrew and I were left to research the island's bars and restaurants, but all too soon it was also our turn to return to civilization. With the limo again available, we were pleased to make the trip to our flight in the marina's luxury vehicle.

I should explain at this point that any photos of me you may have seen in this book have been carefully chosen not to show my … corpulence. And as the nut doesn't fall far from the tree, my son shares my plumpness and my tendency to break into a sweat with the slightest amount of exertion in warm weather. With a midday flight, neither of us wanted to be wedged into the small seat of a puddle jumper next to stranger—or each other for that matter—dripping in perspiration, so we prepared a plan to arrive dry and unwrinkled at the gate the next day.

The over-arching strategy of the plan was to leave plenty of time to make the trip. Starting early, we would move slowly. No rush, no exertion. Just stay calm and enjoy the air conditioning. For example, to make the 15-minute airport trip for our 3 p.m. flight, we requested a 1 p.m. limo departure from the marina. No hurry; especially, no running. Although Andrew's knee was better, he was still somewhat hobbled.

Just after midday, packed, showered, deodorized, and zestfully clean, we called the marina office for an immediate golf cart pick up at our slip. The breeze that cooled us on our ride to the lobby reinforced our belief that the plan would work, and we would fly frosty as cucumbers back to Puerto Rico.

Handing our luggage to the driver to load into the trunk, we placed our carry-ons with our documents on the back seat, and leaving the driver with instructions to start the engine to get the A/C going, we entered the cool lobby to pay our bill.

Now free of any financial obligations, we returned calmly to the car. The driver was deep in conversation with a very pretty maid, and we practically had to drag him away so we could leave on time.

I pulled on the chrome handle of the back door, anticipating that first blast of cool air from the Cadillac's air-conditioning. The door didn't immediately yield, so I tried harder. Huh? I guess my door was locked. But so was Andrew's. So were all the doors.

Damn. The driver had locked the doors with the keys and our documents inside. Now despite all our planning, we were going to be delayed, and I was getting pretty hot under the collar … and armpits.

I told the driver in no uncertain terms that he'd better get another key or break the window *now*, as with our passports locked inside, we had no way to get off the island unless the car was opened.

He said the car wasn't his, so he would not break a window. Afraid to leave the scene of the disaster lest something worse might happen, Andrew and I just stood there in the heat, trying to think dry thoughts while the hotel staff scurried around, searching for the spare key.

To make a long story short, a key was found at the driver's home, and only a half hour late, we jumped into the baking car's interior—the engine had been off—for the oppressive ride to the airport. In irate silence we endured the snail's pace ride in heavy traffic along the narrow roads to the airport. I could see the sweat stains spreading along Andrew's shirt and assumed I was doing the same. Arriving at the airport drenched in perspiration, we ran —well I did, Andrew limped—to the airline's counter, ran to pay the exit tax, and our dash to the gate got us to the plane's door with only seconds to spare. Drenched and squeezed into the narrow seats, Andrew and I just sat there and dripped on each other. Ah, the Caribbean.

Speed III

Port de Pleasance was to figure in yet another memorable experience on the return leg of our next down-island tour.

I had installed in *Class Act* a refrigeration system that was driven by the engine. Each day we had to run the engine for an hour or so to cool down the fridge. While anchored in Les Isles de Saintes, an off-the-beaten-track collection of charming islets, we were cooling the food when I noticed that even though the transmission lever was in neutral, the drive shaft was turning, and the boat was slowly moving forward. Obviously, there was a problem with the transmission.

Since the next day we would start our trip home, I wasn't too worried about this small glitch. However, with each day the problem got worse and worse until neutral no longer existed. With efficient, qualified mechanical service hard to find on the smaller islands, we decided to make do and deal with the problem when we go to St. Martin where there were many qualified repair shops.

Unfortunately, by the time we arrived at the drawbridge into the lagoon, not only had neutral disappeared but the only way I could change direction was to shut down the engine, move the lever into the forward or reverse position, and then restart the diesel in gear. A little cumbersome perhaps, but it worked.

Arriving at the bridge, I called Port de Pleasance on the VHF to advise them of our problem. The harbormaster replied that they would send a pilot boat help us with maneuvers into our berth in the marina.

My plan was, once through the bridge, to slowly enter the fairway. Upon reaching our assigned space, applying the technique I had been using of shutting down the engine and then restarting in reverse, I would back into our space.

At first all went well. Once the bridge opened I found a place in the file of craft going through and proceeded, accompanied by the Boston Whaler pilot boat, to the marina entrance. There the helper peeled off to wait for us at our assigned space where I would perform my transmission trick and reverse to the quay.

Continuing slowly down the fairway, with Gale at the bow to handle lines, I could see the whaler waiting for us ahead to port with lines in hand. I smiled and waved as I came abeam and pulled the kill lever. With the engine stopped I reached to pull the shift lever back to put the gearbox in reverse. Huh? It won't budge. Seems to be stuck.

Class Act, oblivious of my frantic attempts to put her into reverse, continued her deliberate, stately progress forward. Unless you have had experience handling big boats, you may think that a 40 footer traveling at a speed of only one or two knots in tight quarters is not an emergency situation. Nevertheless, I can tell you that the inertia a big boat develops, unchecked, is an irresistible force to be reckoned with, and we were inexorably moving forward to an immoveable object, a restaurant full of people.

With calamity staring me in the face, using as much strength as I could muster, I hauled the shift lever towards me with both hands. Uuuh. Damn. I felt it move loosely in my hand, meaning that the shift linkage was now broken, I had gone from captain to spectator.

Helpless, I shouted to Gale, "Brace-Brace-Brace." In hopes of somehow mitigating the effects of the obviously imminent disaster, I aimed for the opening I saw between two luxurious pleasure craft as we closed relentlessly on the wide, sweeping Roman steps that led up to the terrace of the elegant L'Espadon restaurant.

Port De Pleasance otherwise known as "Speed III"

Everything seemed to be happening in slow motion. It was just like that final scene from the movie *Speed II*.

Under the restaurant's striped awning, the expressions of the diners who may have been casually observing the handsome blue sailboat entering the harbor were transformed from serene to quizzical, a little startled followed by stark fear, and those close to the railing began to get up from their tables and move away from the balustrade. Closer and closer we glided until with a sharp thud and a shudder, *Class Act's* forefoot struck the lowest step. Bump, bump, bump she went up the steps. Then bump, bump, bump down she came. As Long John Silver was wont to say, "Well, shiver me timbers."

Then total silence.

In a flash the pilot boat was alongside, and shaken now out of my stupor, I began to notice the buzz of chatter from people in the restaurant. Gale, still in "Crash Position," had a cushion clinched to her chest and was repeating over and over again, "Oh, my God, oh, my God…" Me? I was mute … from embarrassment, not fright. If I was going to be involved in a fiasco like this, why couldn't it be at seven in the morning instead of happy hour when everyone who wasn't eating at the restaurant was sitting on their boats with drinks in their hands watching my misfortune.

Luckily, neither the crew nor *Class Act's* Airex hull suffered any permanent damage. You know what they say: "A good docking is one you can walk away from. A great docking is one after which you will be able to use the boat again."

The marina manager arrived and took pity on us by having *Class Act* towed to a spot far from the clacking tongues at the restaurant. Once dock lines were fast, I started to go below to lick my wounds and hide my face, but before I could do so, a stranger ran up to us with a water tumbler full of Scotch in hand and said, "Here, you probably need this." And I did.

The next day, putting the demoralizing memory of our calamity behind us, we concentrated our efforts on finding a solution to the transmission problem. The mechanic's prognosis was that first he would have to remove the transmission from the boat, and then by the time parts arrived and were installed, we would be probably find ourselves spending two unforeseen weeks in St. Martin. That kind of delay was unacceptable.

The only good news was that the route from where we were to our slip in Ponce would not require any docking maneuvers. During our mandatory stop in the Virgins Islands, we could anchor, visit Customs by dinghy, and then go straight home. Back in Ponce we could enjoy the luxury of having the gearbox issue dealt with by a mechanic we trusted without any time constraints.

So taking advantage of the last bridge opening of the day, we headed home. The Anegada Passage, downwind, was an over-night piece of cake, and dawn found us only a few miles from the mooring field at one of our favorite anchorages, Maho Bay, St. John.

Un-beaching the Dinghy
OK. It took four of you to drag the inflatable far enough ashore so the waves won't break over the transom. Returning it to the water is worse because the transom digs in and the waves break into the boat.

DO IT THE EASY WAY!
Using the painter, just lift the bow and PIVOT it into water. It's easier and the boat will stay dry.

MAIKE IT EVEN EASIER
Tie a small anchor to the painter and, once you've unloaded, leave the dinghy anchored OUTSIDE the surf-line.

Over the past few years, we had learned the hard way that picking up a mooring is definitely an acquired skill. On our first trip to the BVIs, we were at a bar on shore at Cane Garden Bay, finally safely fastened to a mooring ball after a dozen failed attempts and a lot of yelling on my part. An old timer sitting next to me at the bar asked which boat was ours. Pointing out our craft brought a shaking of his head and the comment, "I saw you come in. Who's your captain, Stevie Wonder?"

This time things were different. With a little careful maneuvering and advance planning, we successfully picked up a NPS mooring, and once tied off we could relax, knowing we were halfway home.

Max Goes Ashore

Now secured, Gale came to me with a proposal. "We're back in the USA, and Max isn't prohibited from going ashore. Let's take him to the beach."

This was to be a new experience for Max, as his everyday world was a terrazzo tile-floored apartment, except for occasions when he was taken in his plastic travel cage to be released onto another plastic container, our boat. Because most of the places we visited would not allow him ashore without quarantine, all he knew about the Caribbean experience, not that he gave a damn, was what he saw from his perch on the deck.

Our cat passed his days on board, usually curled up in his carrier under the companionway stairs. But at night he would come alive and perform continuous rounds of the boat to be sure all was well. To do his "business" he used the cat box resting on the poop deck. (How appropriate.) The result was that Max had missed out on a lot of great scenery and creamy white sand beaches like the one in front of us. A situation Gale had now decided to remedy.

I agreed that it might be fun and added, "Let's not spook him with the noise of the outboard." So secure in his gray cat carrier, we paddled our Max ashore in the inflatable to experience the luxurious white sands of Maho Bay, St. John.

The dinghy's bow quietly slid onto dry land, and Gale placed an obviously nervous Max, still in his carrier, on the sand and opened the little grille door. Cautiously emerging from his cage, eyes blinking at the brightness of

Max on watch

the scene, he looked down and discovered … sand. Reminded of his cat box, he scratched a bit, took a dump and covered it. Mission accomplished he raised his head and scanned the area again. Noticing more sand, he took half a dozen steps, another dump and cover, and another, then another. Gale and I were paralyzed with laughter. We could practically read his mind. "Look at the size of this litter box! Wow! I'm not quitting until I use it all!"

Here's a more serious Max story.

On our way to Barbuda in *Class Act*, we were tucked in for a night of sleeping in the cockpit while anchored in beautiful Deep Bay, Antigua. About 3 a.m. Max suddenly became a huge nuisance, mewing and walking up and down on a sleeping Gale until she could no longer ignore him. Sitting up to rid herself of this feline nuisance, she was startled awake to the unexpected sight of another boat only a few feet from our rail. We must be dragging anchor and were about to hit someone's boat.

Her scream, "Glenn, wake up. We're going to hit someone!" did its job, and I rushed, stark naked, from the cockpit to the rail.

Shouting, "Gale, get fenders," must have aroused the Dutch couple on board their boat, and, if we hadn't been so concerned about mitigating any possible damage, we probably would have died laughing at the bizarre sight of four, middle-aged, naked people—Gale had a much better body than the other woman—in the moonlight, separating our boats and exchanging comments like, "Sorry. No problem. Good night."

Once clear, we re-anchored and returned to our beds. But I have to admit that if someone else had told me a cat had warned them of impending disaster, I would have laughed at their gullibility, but, well …

What happened to "The Old Days" in the Caribbean?

When I think back at how things were only 20 years ago, I am amazed at the changes that have taken place in the cruising environment of the Caribbean in such a short time. The three major changes I see are:

1. GPS Plotter: While most Caribbean navigation is still line of sight, the plotter helps keep us off that pesky reef that's in the middle of nowhere, or when we arrive very late at our destination and it's dark—or nearly—we can find and navigate the entrance safely.
2. Cellphones: No more changing money and trying to figure out the old Cable & Wireless public phone system while standing in the hot sun. Forget those frustrating VHF calls to your intended marina. We have cellphones. We can reach anybody more easily.
3. Custom Forms: In the old days in Nevis you had to wait while the immigration official transcribed your information from the original form onto another form because they had no carbon paper. Today they have carbon paper.

It isn't only Nevis. In an attempt to get raises, the Customs and Immigration people in Tortola implemented a slowdown. But no one noticed.

Some things never change though. If you are going to spend long periods of time traveling to faraway places, you will have to learn to fix stuff on your boat. Like that old saw, the definition of cruising is "Repairing one's sailboat in exotic places."

It seems that every time we take a long trip, most of the frustrating but not really dangerous problems happen during the first few days of the trip. It is hard to believe, after reading Gale's log—below—that I had spent two weeks carefully preparing the boat for our planned sail to Martinique.

Here are the entries from Gale's log for the first day.

6/1–Ponce Yacht club

We leave at 4:30 AM. Upon unfurling the genoa, the halyard fouled with storm jib. Returned to dock and spent 30 minutes unraveling before setting out again. 1 hour out the fuel line broke. Capt. fixed it and we continued. East wind increasing. Max took a wave in the face and decided that the cockpit was not the right place for him. The BBQ collapsed but was saved from going overboard. I stayed below and made enough sandwiches for two days. Bilge pump clogged but was fixed. There appears to be a leak in the drinking water supply as the carpet in the aft cabin is soaked with fresh (captain tasted it) water. Autopilot is making a noise and the fridge doesn't seem to be working right.

Things continued in this vein for four or five days then stopped. I feel like the job applicant who, when notified that he had been hired, was told, "Initial salary is $10.00 an hour. Then after three months you get $15.00. When would you like to start?" The answer: "In three months."

I wish we could start our trips on the fifth day.

I must say at this juncture that, as frustrating and tedious as the process of keeping your boat afloat and running might be, it does give one a great feeling of confidence. As experience grows so does pride and self-reliance, to the point that returning to civilization can be a very frustrating experience.

The cruising sailor who returns to land finds himself in a very different environment. Now he is at the mercy of the infrastructure. When the electricity fails he can no longer get out his electric meter and fix the problem; he must call for help. Instead of the open sea, he finds himself enmeshed in the web of the landlubber's laws and regulations. The anticipation of new experiences each month becomes the dread of dealing with the tyranny of mortgages, water bills, and association dues. The freedom to accept or even enjoy eccentric behavior must be surrendered, at the risk of being ostracized.

Ah, to return to the sea and again be the captain of your fate.

Is having your own boat worth the hassle?

Yes, you can spend a week on a bareboat charter and enjoy your morning coffee in the same heavenly tropical ambiance as we do. The charter company will supply flippers that might fit, and you'll probably figure out the boat's idiosyncrasies before it's time to board the plane for home. But there's nothing like having your home *with you* when you travel. Travel anywhere *you* want to go and how *you* want to do it.

Even if we just go for a day sail, I know my favorite booze and snacks will be waiting for me. When the sun is low and intrudes, I just put up the special shades I made to keep the sun out of our eyes. And books. We have a library to choose from. Books to fill up those quiet times in the morning before we dive, or explore ashore, or to read at night in the cockpit where I have installed reading lights just to my liking.

Then , in the stillness of the next day's early morning I roil the windless still waters by peeing off the stern, Lord of my territory.

All these disaster stories—mine and others you have probably heard—make for interesting reading, but I hope they will not deter the neophyte cruiser from striking out to experience the marvelous world that can only be accessed by cruising in your own boat.

Here are some places we think are very special destinations:

Brewers Bay on Tortola: There are few places in the BVIs as beautiful as this small bay on the north side of Tortola. The vodka-clear waters are bordered by white sand and are surrounded by colorful tropical vegetation on steep green mountains that still leave a space to enter and look out to sea at the Bali Hai-like shape of Jost Van Dyke in the distance.

It is off limits to bareboat charterers, but having seen it from the land, we vowed when we had our own boat, we would find a way to get in safely. With some planning and careful reconnoitering, we found a natural channel and an anchorage that is safe, even when the wind is from the north. When Cane Garden Bay, just around the corner, is chock-a-block with boats, we're anchored alone in one of the most beautiful bays in the world.

Barbuda: Antigua's snubbed stepsister has a reputation for having dangerous approaches and is rarely visited by cruising sailors. We found, however, that its west coast is largely free of hazards; stopping here on our way from Antigua to St. Martin, we spent two fabulous days as the only boat anchored off its 13-mile, pink sand beach. Porpoises swam through the proverbial gin-clear water to visit us, and for the two days all we wore was what Adam and Eve wore before the snake.

Montserrat: After the violent eruption of the volcano Soufriere, normal travel to this island became almost impossible. However, having our own boat allowed us to return to Montserrat and see with our own eyes the terrible devastation and resultant sterility wrought upon most of the island by the eruption. We will never forget the gray, dusty desolation that replaced the green beauty and fertility of what once had been the "Emerald Isle of the Caribbean" or the indomitable spirit of those who stayed.

4
New Horizons

C*lass Act* had truly become our magic carpet to Caribbean adventure on land and on sea. Above and below the surface. But was there more to see and do beyond our pond?

By 1994 we had made four long trips "down island" with *Class Act* and considered ourselves veteran Caribbean cruisers. Business was good, we had some money in our pockets, and we were also traveling by more normal means, mostly to Europe. Gale and I are both Europhiles. We especially enjoy our trips to England, France, Spain, or Italy, where we can communicate fairly well, feel at home and, unlike exotic lands like India, China, or Antarctica, can rent a car and tour on our own.

The competence I had achieved getting to this point made me feel more secure, both on the boat and off. I felt that it was time once again to expand our horizons and enrich our lives even further. Dare I try? A new boat? A new sea?

I began to fantasize about sailing around Europe.

Suppose, instead of spending a week or two the way we have done, packing and un-packing our bags as we go from place to place, we could use our boat as our RV? Sailing from port to port, we could spend an extended period of time in Europe and really get to enjoy, in depth, the places we love to visit.

It was 1994 and about the same time as I was fantasizing about sailing to Europe, the Puerto Rican and the Federal governments were moving towards a change in their fiscal relationship. A change that I was sure would adversely affect the Industrial Tax Exemption Program that our manufacturing sector enjoyed, resulting in substantial plant closures. Since my company existed to sell products to factories, it seemed logical to me that it was time to get out of that field before it was too late. Crossing my fingers, I put Powermotion up for sale, hoping that my prediction would not come true before I could turn my years of hard work into cash.

I was lucky enough to find someone who had a very different perspective of this tax situation and its effects on my customers. Once we worked out the dollars and cents for the price, he miraculously agreed to buy my company, and he gave me a substantial deposit. I was relieved then ecstatic.

The day of the closing dawned full of promise. That is until I unfolded the morning newspaper that had arrived at my doorstep. There, splashed across the front page, was the alarming headline, "Clinton Signs New Tax Law. 936-Industrial Exemption in Danger."

Along on 13 mile beach Barbuda

My stomach felt as though I had hit an air pocket.

Damn. The cat was out of the bag for everyone to see. Would the buyer now want to renegotiate the price? Cancel the deal?

I was so apprehensive I couldn't even eat lunch—a first I think—before the 1 p.m. closing at my lawyer's office. I halfheartedly went through the ritual of greeting the buyer and his lawyer, waiting for the axe to fall. They seemed untroubled, and in silence we reread the stipulations of the contract we had hammered out and then … then came that unbelievable moment.

I couldn't believe it was actually happening. In effect, someone had come to me and said, "You go home and do whatever you want. I'll come into the office and do your work. I'll take care of any problems that arise. Oh, and by the way I also have this big check for you." Fantastic.

After so many years of day-to-day struggle. So many highs and lows. And the most onerous, every day, living with the constant dread hanging over me that something might happen that would destroy everything I had done. Now I could hardly believe it. The amount written on the check would be enough money to last me the rest of my life, as long as I didn't do something stupid like buy a big boat and go sailing.

Oh, well.

While we loved the Caribe 41, she was designed for a week or two of island hopping in warm weather. Crossing the Atlantic and living aboard for an extended period required a very different type of vessel. So once again I found myself in the market for a new boat. The first person I told about my plan, after Gale, was my old friend, marine surveyor and nautical guru Fred.

I was still in the early stages of discovering what was available when I received a call from Fred. He had been contracted, in his professional capacity as a surveyor, by an insurance company to investigate a claim on a boat he thought might be just what I was looking for. The vessel was a French-built Mikado 56 ketch, and she was temporarily at a dock in the small, out-of-the-way fishing village of Puerto Real on Puerto Rico's west coast. Oh, and she might be for sale. Cheap.

Dropping what I was doing at the time, I jumped into my car for the two-hour drive from my office to Puerto Real to check her out. Leaving the tollway, I then drove along a two-lane highway for several miles until it became a dirt road. I bumped along until I saw, under a row of palm trees, a collection of wooden houses draped in blue fish nets. This was Puerto Real.

Parking my car in the shade, I eagerly walked up a ramp between two houses to the water's edge and was stopped in my tracks, dumbfounded by what I saw. There, cached among small outboard fishing boats, rickety docks, and shacks, was a true queen of a sailboat. Two tall masts and a hull with sweeping lines, she exuded majesty and comfort. I felt like an explorer who had just stumbled upon a magnificent royal city in a remote jungle.

Boarding her from the wooden dock, I did a quick turn around the spacious deck and then went below to check out her interior. I was awed by the 16 ft. x 12 ft. salon and tremendously impressed that to get to the forepeak, I had to walk down a long, hotel-like hallway between the three staterooms and two heads. As if this weren't enough, there was also a small workshop and fourth stateroom under the poop deck for crew.

Climbing back up into the sunshine, I inspected more carefully her split rig, ample deck, and day space. This was a major sailboat. From anchor to pushpit she was nearly 50% longer than our present craft. The engine in the middle of the vessel was almost 30 feet from the transom, so the exhaust discharge was on the port side just like a real ship.

One day this design quirk created an interesting situation while cruising that demonstrated the straits I tend to get into because of my disorganized mind and deficient memory.

We were in the BVIs and had just arrived at Trellis Bay, hoping to find a mooring after a long day's motorsailing with just a tight main in very light winds. The little bay was crowded with boats as we picked our way in and out amongst the 50 or so tethered craft in search of a mooring ball without a boat.

Glancing from side to side as we looked for an available mooring, I noticed more than the usual amount of cockpit denizens checking us out. It was only when I heard the sound of a jibe from the boom while making a 180-degree turn that I stuck my head out from under the hardtop, looked up, and realized I had been doing all this maneuvering in such tight quarters with the main still set. Thank God, there was almost no wind.

I guess, with the boat's engine pumping water from its midship's port exhaust, the people on my left were shaking their heads about the idiot with the big boat motoring around with his main up. On the other hand, the boats anchored on my right, seeing no trace of a running engine, must have thought I was the most skillful captain they had ever seen.

The ketch was big and she was beautiful, a true blue water sailboat. Perfect for what I had in mind, so I called Fred and asked for the lowdown.

The Bays of the Virgin Islands

The bays of the Virgin Islands, beautiful as they are, can get very crowded and, as the damage to coral done by anchoring is an issue, finding a mooring can become a major problem. One can often find oneself in competition, late in the afternoon, with others heading for that last unoccupied mooring.

There's something a bit absurd about the spectacle of the captains of two or three sailboats with top speeds of only six and a half knots, trying to appear nonchalant as they gun their puny engines to beat the other sluggish sailboat to the last unoccupied mooring in the bay. And what happens in case of a dead heat? Dueling boat hooks?

He explained that the owner was a non-sailor who bought her to live aboard with his pregnant wife while he worked at a construction job in St. Croix. Three years and one child later, never having taken the boat out to sea, his contract was up and he decided, with wife and baby, to motor the boat back to his home town more than a thousand miles away on the Gulf Coast of Florida. Based on his lack of experience and the lack of competent crew, this probably was not a good idea.

Their voyage from St. Croix to Puerto Rico had been fraught with problems. When, upon leaving Puerto Rico, he hit the big swells in the Mona Passage only a few miles offshore, three years of fuel tank sediment were churned up, stopping the engine and leaving them adrift in the swells. No fun. I would say the guy was very lucky to find help in the form of a fishing boat that towed the vessel and terrified family to the little fishing port where I found her. The wife and child immediately abandoned ship for their safe, dry home in Tampa. The insurance claim Fred was assessing was for some minor damage to the pulpit that occurred during the tow.

A closer look at the Mikado revealed she was, like the manor house of an impoverished aristocrat, imposing but a bit shabby and worn in some places. Although you couldn't see any traces of it, Fred said she had sunk 10 years ago, which had made mandatory the installation of a new engine, a large 6-cylinder, 165-hp Perkins turbo diesel. The rest of her was very 1972.

It was my guess, based on my knowledge of the circumstances and my experience with women on sailboats, that the owner, and especially his wife, would prefer to sell her where she was for any reasonable price so they could get on with a normal life on dry land rather than again face the dangers and discomforts of continuing their journey home by the water. I was by then an old hand at buying bargain sailboats, so I called the number Fred gave me and made the owner the ridiculous offer of $20,000 for the ketch. He countered with $40,000, and after only a few minutes of conversation, we agreed on a price of $30,000. Such a deal. So thanks to a little dirt in the fuel tank, I wound up with this amazing bargain.

Now that she was ours, it was time to bring her home. Peter and Adam, the usual suspects, agreed, more out of curiosity than anything else, to help Gale and me bring this behemoth back to the club in Ponce.

Gale, apprehensive about yet another one of my harebrained schemes, had to admit, upon arrival at the dock, that she was truly impressed with the boat. Adam and Peter just kept poking around, mumbling about what a lucky shit I was to make a deal like this.

After checking out her rigging and gear, I announced we were ready to go. With feigned nonchalance I started the engine and backed her out into the small bay. Turning the wheel resulted in a slow, wide circle towards what I hoped was the channel that led out of the shallow cove. Once in deeper water we raised sails and turned her south towards the southwest corner of the island we would have to pass to make it home.

Spacious and luxurious salon of Act III

Anticipating the usual windward slog along the south coast, we motorsailed along with just the main set. Although she weighed 53,000 lbs., with her 50-ft. waterline and the big engine, she really moved along at high speed. Well, she did until about an hour after we turned east into the swell at Cabo Rojo. Then just as it did for the past owner, the engine shut down. In all the excitement of closing the deal, I forgot that the same gremlin that made it possible for me to own her could stop me. Short of replacement filters, we set the jib and sailed her home.

Without an engine I was terrified by the prospect of having to sail anything this big into its slip the first time, so we anchored in the bay off the Ponce Yacht Club. Because we were without a dinghy, I had to swim ashore to get *Class Act's* dinghy to pick up my crew. It was quite a feeling to stand on the dock, dripping wet, and look back at our ocean-going, 56-ft. blue water ketch, strikingly beautiful with her 6-ft. bowsprit.

Upgrading *Act III*

Once our new acquisition was in her slip in Ponce, I began the work of creating the lists of what needed to be done. They were long lists because she was so large and because we planned to go so far. As they say, "If at first you don't succeed … crossing the Atlantic is not for you."

Luckily, Alfredo was still considered to be unemployable by the rest of the world, so I put him to work cleaning, painting, repairing, and installing. Since we were starting out with a silk purse this time, we ripped out the sow's ear salon cloth and installed new, white fabric headliners, blue carpeting, a very large stand-up freezer/refrigerator, a 7 ½ KW generator and some miscellaneous boat bling. Dinghy davits, hydraulic autopilot, and new batteries were added, and we did the best we could to clean out the fuel tank.

Again we decided to spend big money to paint our new yacht's hull, this time an elegant British Racing Green. We also spent a significant amount adding lots of dark green canvas for shade.

(At my age I visit my dermatologist more often than I visit my children.) And oh, yes, we installed a Lavac head for me. The Lavac is invincible, the best. Its simple design makes it able to take any crap—literally—you give it, freeing me from being a *Defenaut*[1]. All these repairs and improvements added up to a pretty significant outlay of money and time, but after six months of work, we had ourselves a real head turner of a yacht for only a small fraction of the usual outlay required for a boat as long as a six-story building is high.

Some advice to anyone upgrading a sailboat:

Contrary to popular wisdom, if you are working on your boat, it should not be "the first boat on the dock." Why? Because it is impossible for the human male to walk past a person he sees working on a vessel without offering uncalled for advice. Whatever time might be saved by closeness to the parking lot will be lost fending off stupid, gratuitous advice from passersby. Being further down the dock means fewer meddlers.

While the expense became large, I had been very careful to buy all the refit materials wholesale (*Vat else?*) or using the most practical versions of what was needed. However, I drew the line on bottom paint that, while about half the usual cost, came with the warning "Keep dry for less marine growth."

Because we thought she would be our last vessel, the one we would use to sail off into retirement, I decided to call her *Act III*. I was pleased with my choice; however, my partner in life was incensed that once again I had named our boat without taking her into account.

---

1. *Defenauts* are sailors who, because of frustration with the problematic toilets usually found in the smelly, tight quarters of the usual boat's head, or for the pure love of nature, prefer to skip the "Sit Down and Pump Stage" of the human digestive process altogether. You can usually recognize *Defenauts* by the total absence of toilet paper on board and their propensity for spending long periods of time treading water near their anchored boats early in the morning.

I heard her loud and clear. "You take me for granted. All these boats, and you never offered to name even one of them after me! You don't care about me. You just want me around to keep your dinghy hard!"

I had to admit she was right … on both counts. And if I were going to have peace and nautical cooperation on board, I better, right now, make a commitment to address her complaint regarding her importance in the naming process.

"Sweetheart, I'm so sorry!" I swear I will honor you when we buy and name our next boat. I promise she will be called the "Mrs. Glenn D. Patron."

Shakedown Cruise

With this bump in the road now smoothed out, we turned our efforts to getting some experience with this very big sailboat. It was important we be sure she was ready for "The Big One," the sail to Europe and back. After a few outings in varying conditions, we found that, with her conservative ketch rig and 25-ton displacement, she was stiff, safe, and comfortable, even in winds over 25 knots.

Because the waters around Ponce were child's play for *Act III*, I needed to plan a longer, more challenging trip. Until now we had never sailed to any of the islands south of Guadalupe and the Saintes, so this was the perfect opportunity to raise the bar a bit. How about a 400+ mile trip to the "Spice Island," Grenada? I love the planning process. I can spend five days preparing for a three-day trip. Planning is more fun than sailing because when you're planning, nothing goes wrong.

So instead of working our way to windward down the chain of islands as we had on our previous trips, I planned to get all the misery out of the way at the front end.

Grenada was 450 NM (nautical miles) southeast of *Act III*'s home port. In a straight line that's about a three and a half day voyage. But our course of 140 degrees would be almost straight into the wind, so we would have to do some tacking into the probable

100-120 degree trades. This zig-zagging would, I figured, force us to travel an additional 200 miles.

While I intended, when I crossed the Atlantic, to become a big-time offshore sailor, spending weeks sailing before touching land, I wasn't quite ready to spend so much time out of *sight* of land. The landlubber in me said, "Why not take a few extra days and do a nice trip to the BVIs? It will be an easier route from there." The landlubber was right.

Leaving from Tortola greatly increased the availability of duty free booze and the probability of making the trip on one tack. From there Granada was only 400 miles away, and the course would now be a much improved 160 degrees. Once ready to return home, our island hopping would be a cinch, as the wind would be in our favor all the way, allowing us to pick and choose our stops and route more easily.

For crew we invited our friend, businessman Mariano McConnie, and a Danish couple, Hans and Margaret, whom we had befriended when they sailed through Ponce some years before. They had sold their boat when they returned to Europe but wanted a Caribbean *redux*. With Gale and I, that made a comfortable crew of five to stand watches during the estimated three- to four-day voyage to Grenada.

The sail to Tortola was uneventful. After a stop to catch our breath, we made an early morning departure via Round Rock Passage in light winds that quickly grew to 15 knots from a perfect direction of 110 degrees. In these conditions *Act III* raised her skirts and sprinted south, quickly and comfortably.

Act III, because of her size and design, was a stiff and stable vessel. Most of the time we could walk around the interior under sail without needing to use handholds, even though the GPS showed us consistently moving at speed over ground of five to seven knots. I felt secure and confident about her seaworthiness. I can't say the same for her dependability. A boat this size has so many systems and such a variety of equipment that the fear of some sudden failure

Buying your Caribbean Dream Boat 3.1

The usual process: The average dreamer living in the Northeast buys his 40 footer for, say, $120,000. Then he spends a few months getting her ready and a month or so getting her to Miami. Taking off in November—after hurricane season—he and his skeptical wife beat their brains out against the trades for two more months—and $20,000 in cruising expense—to get to the Virgin Islands.

Better idea: Ole Fred once told me that sailboats in the Caribbean sell on the average for 30% less than they would on the mainland. Curious, I created a spreadsheet with prices I found in ads for Beneteaus of 40, 45, and 50 feet and compared the Caribbean prices with what was being asked stateside. By gar, they almost exactly proved Fred right. So I ask, why not save a year of work and tough travel and buy your dream boat in the Caribbean where you plan to sail her?

Yes, you'll have to rent an apartment, a car, and do some flying to other islands, but while doing so you will learn a lot about your future sailing grounds, probably end up spending far less money, and skip the misery of fighting your way south.

Check out the following theoretical figures:

ITEM	NORTHEAST	CARIBBEAN
Boat	$120,000	$84,000
Trip South	$20,000	-
Special Living Exp. in islands		$12,000 (3 mo.)
Total	$140,000	$98,000

Does this make sense? And when your adventure is over, it's an easy 1,000-mile broad reach back to Florida.

was always on my mind. Sailing the big boat had its advantages in speed and safety, but the anxiety—especially taking into account Alfredo's work ethic—that something important was going to fail was my constant companion. Although I loved her I was constantly tormented by the certitude that sooner or later she would betray me by throwing some sort of breakdown at me I wouldn't be able to fix.

Notwithstanding my fears, we flew on without any of my nightmares becoming reality. Our two-hour watches were relaxed, and companionship was available nearly 24/7, as Hans loved to talk about boats and sailing. Usually, it's nice to have company while on watch, but I found Hans' heavy accent practically impenetrable. His conversation was like listening to a radio call through heavy static. When he spoke I was able to pick out the most common words like "sel" sail, "cus" meant course and "Vayves" were easy, etc., and filling in the blanks, I usually could deduce what he was trying to express.

However, I was continually puzzled when I kept hearing him use the word "Indian." Mystified, I listened more carefully. There it was again. "Indian." What a strange word for a Dane to use on a sailing trip. It wasn't until we had Grenada in sight that I heard five words clearly enough together to understand when he asked, "When you start the Indian."

Comprendo.

I have found that on long trips like this, people revert to type. Gale, when not on watch, spent her time doing her usual galley magic, so we ate well and had plenty of time to read and sleep. However, to combat the boredom and deadening routine of days at sea, Mariano and I, both Type A personalities, would disconnect the autopilot and hand steer when on watch. We kept up a competition to see who could keep the speed up and cover the most miles while on duty. Conversations between us were mostly about how soon we would reach Grenada.

The Danish couple, however, retired school teachers, had a very different attitude. Exhibiting a level of equanimity and patience completely foreign to Mariano and me, they took each hour and each day as it came. Their attitude was that as long as the boat stayed afloat, was moving forward, and there was food to eat, they were contented. Living in the moment and seemingly oblivious of any goal, they were confident that sooner or later we would arrive at our destination. And whenever that was would be okay with them. This experience gave me a new perspective about people and journeys.

Be that as it may, I shouted with glee when, only 70 hours after leaving the Virgins, we found ourselves approaching the entrance to St. George Harbour. Our bargain-basement sailing ship had done all we could ask of her and renewed my confidence in her ability to successfully handle our planned Atlantic crossing.

Grenada and the Trip North

We chose Grenada's Mount Harmon Bay on the south coast as an anchorage because, in addition to having excellent protection and good holding, it offered another important advantage. Because The Moorings had established a charter base, we would have access to the transportation, recreational activities, repairs, and other conveniences they offered their renters. Some of which seemed unappreciated by the short-term cruisers. Example:

One night Moorings management brought in a terrific steel band from Trinidad.

From our anchored boat we were drawn by the compelling beat of Calypso music. There was something magical about those nights when we would leave the intimacy of our floating home and make our way through the darkness toward the sound of steel band music, a beach that was lit like a beacon in the night.

Motoring over, we quietly tied our dinghy and stepped onto the dock. There our world was transformed by the throb of steel drums and the light of candles and tiki torches that reflected from glasses and goblets along with red hibiscus on white tablecloths.

We didn't want to stand out, but there we were, bambooshay, the only couple on the dance floor, surrounded by about a hundred white people who weren't even tapping their feet. What a waste. Then, as though we broke some sort of Caribbean ice, couples began to join us on the floor. Women in white pants, their hair let down, began swinging their asses to the African beat of the pans while their men stiffly stepped to the rhythm. No longer a spectator sport the terrace now seemed like a living throbbing multicolored organism.

We had our fun, and then before the magic ended we returned to our gray inflatable and putt-putted through the vast darkness to where our boat patiently waited to take us back to the world of the sea.

We had spent several days exploring Grenada ashore in depth. The island is beautiful and historic, but still fresh in our minds were the memories of the U.S. invasion of Grenada 15 years before. These memories became reality when we stumbled upon an empty field full of wrecked, shot-up Russian military planes...

Now with our dry land exploration over, it was time to make preparations for the trip north and home. We traded Mariano and the Danish couple for daughter Jill, who was taking a break from the everyday pressures of being a high-powered New York advertising executive.

Having exchanged her business suit for a bathing suit, Jill relaxed on the sun-splashed deck while we ran north along Grenada's west coast in moderate winds. As the hours went by, we could sense Jill's mind and body begin to relax as she watched the brightly colored houses and little children playing on the black beaches as they slowly slid by only a hundred yards off to starboard.

Leaving Granada, we continued north, bypassing Carriacou, with the firm determination that this time we would make it to Palm Island to fulfill an objective of many years: meeting John Caldwell, the author of the book *Desperate Voyage*, and a man who has lived a fascinating life as an unassuming adventurer.

Caldwell's book chronicles one of the great sailing sagas of all time. John's early life had been one struggle after another, but he

Here she is our Mikado 56 with her new hull paint

always met adversity with talent and determination, taking on and conquering a number of prodigious challenges that made for a life replete with extraordinary accomplishments.

After the incredible solo adventure in the Pacific portrayed in the book, he "settled down" as a charter captain in the Caribbean. Settled perhaps but not complacent, because he had a dream. Petitioning and receiving from the government a 99-year lease for small, barren Prune Island, he began collecting fertile coconuts as he sailed the islands with his paying customers. Coconuts that would serve as seeds for his vision of palm groves on his leased desert island.

By the time he was ready to start building his hotel, although he had no experience in construction, his efforts had blossomed into thousands of palms, transforming the barren island into a shaded delight and earning the change of name to Palm Island. As the years went by, shaded by the now mature palms, Palm Island had become a very desirable eco-resort vacation destination.

We arrived at Palm Island in the late afternoon, anchored, and then rushed ashore to see if our hero was in residence. Seeing an elderly gentleman picking up debris as he walked the beach, I landed the dinghy nearby and inquired of the old man if Mr. Caldwell was on the island. He replied with a wry smile. "Yes, he's here. Right here. I am John Caldwell."

Slightly overcome by the surprise of bumping into my hero, I stammered out how much I liked his book and how privileged I felt in meeting him. Easygoing and friendly, he chatted with us until he received a call from the resort and had to leave us. His is a great story, and you can get a good idea why if you Google *Farewell, Johnny Coconut* and read Caldwell's enthralling book, *Desperate Voyage*.

Buoyed by this experience, I felt I could now face the unpleasantness of dealing with Customs on blighted Union Island. Union is the only Caribbean island where I have had such a negative experience that I want to get out as fast as I can.

Do you remember my account of the Grenadines charter many years before when I sent my wife home in a chartered plane from the Union Island airstrip? Truth be known, the sailing wasn't *all* fun and games after she left. The morning after her departure, we awoke at anchor to find that our dinghy, so carefully secured the night before by methodical Dr. Fleming, was gone. Quickly weighing anchor, we motored off to search the sea nearby, and although we saw nothing afloat, every fisherman we questioned suggested we ask for information about our loss in the village of Ashton on the other side of Union Island from the resort.

Motoring around the island, we anchored as close to the town as we could and were soon approached by two locals in a skiff who asked if we were looking for a lost dinghy. My affirmative reply brought an offer from them to take me, alone, for only $5.00, over the shallows into the village to see one that had just been "found." That seemed reasonable, but as I was to learn, this was just the beginning of a process that was to become a major boost to the local economy.

Approaching the shore in their boat, I could see our little Whaler, complete with engine, up on the beach, surrounded by a large group of people who looked as though they had been expecting my arrival.

The group's leader kept negotiations simple. Without looking me in the eye, he declared, "Your dinghy? $1,000 salvage."

"No way! That's not salvage. That's blackmail! No way! I'm not dealing with this piracy!"

Returning to the fisherman who had brought me in, I said, "I'm going back to the boat."

He said, "Five dollars."

Safely back on board, I explained to the others what had happened ashore. All agreed we should notify the charter company. We were able to reach their office on the radio, but the only advice they gave us was, "There's been a lot of that problem lately. Don't let them get away with it."

Yeah, easy for them to say. Faced with no other options, and not wanting to lose our $300 damage deposit *and* dinghy, we pooled our cash and I returned in the fisherman's skiff—for an additional $5—to bargain.

Arriving back at Negotiation Central, I was surrounded by what seemed like a major portion of the local populace who freely shared their opinions of me, my rejection of the $1,000 ransom, and rich white tourists in general.

Bravely—I didn't know I had it in me—I declared to the negotiating commission that this was nothing more than a hijacking and threatened to call the police, at which point a big guy in a dashiki and head bandana strode over to me, smiled, and waved his constable's badge in my face.

Having used up all my bravado, and recognizing my weak bargaining position, I considered myself lucky when they accepted my $300—the maximum damage deposit—offer, and we had a deal. I figure it was more like $295 because I could now get back to the boat in the rescued dinghy without having to pay the fisherman another $5.00.

This time, almost 20 years later, our visit to Union Island was comparatively painless, and taking advantage of near perfect weather, we returned quickly to the boat and headed north again for our next stop, the famed Tobago Cays.

Jill, who as a child spent most of her traveling time being carsick, was turning out to be a pretty good sailor, and her delight in the beauty of this very special part of the world was her reward. The shallow water area around the uninhabited Tobago Cays is unique, like a huge swimming pool dotted with white beach fringed cays and reefs. A true standout in an area of so much beautiful scenery.

Unfortunately, because of time constraints, on this trip we had to by-pass Mustique, renowned island retreat of the rich and famous. But we did return years later to explore this island's

Incredible Tobago Cays

unusual combination of natural Caribbean beauty and the artificial orderliness that great amounts of money can buy.

Everything was going so well I was beginning to get that feeling that some sort of disaster was just around the corner. But there was no disaster in Bequia, and I was gratified to see little had changed at Admiralty Bay since my visit as a charter sailor 15 years before.

We were returning to the boat from a short excursion ashore when we spotted a craft that looked, from a distance, like another Mikado 56. Excited at finding a sister ship, the first we had ever seen, we diverted toward it in hopes of meeting the owners.

We were about 50 yards or so away when Gale, perplexed, said, "Look at the lettering on the side of the pilothouse. It says '45'? Is there such a thing?"

I, for once unsure, replied, "I've never heard they made this model in a forty-five footer, and damn, but she looks just like ours."

Arriving at the enigmatic craft, we roused the occupants by knocking on the hull and explained why we had come to bother them. The owners, a Norwegian family, were not bothered at all and were kind enough to invite us aboard. Plying us with beers and pretzels, they explained that in Europe, where marinas are more often used as overnight stopping places, they saved 20% of the dockage cost by signing in as a 45 instead of 56 footer. And people say we Jews are cheap.

Returning ashore that night as Jill's guides, we strolled past the colorful wooden houses and passed under the Golden Shower trees en route to Frangipani Restaurant where we delighted in a water-side dinner under rustling palms and a full moon. By now Jill's Type A personality had softened to about a "C," and as parents we felt a great sense of satisfaction that she would be returning to work, with its New York rush, deadlines, and pressure, with wonderful memories

The next morning by 10 all that was left of Bequia were the wistful glances over our shoulders as we left this piece of paradise for the next island on our itinerary, St. Vincent.

St. Vincent had acquired, thanks to the cruiser's grapevine, a somewhat nefarious reputation. We had heard from others about the extreme poverty, unruly, aggressive "boat boys," and where recently a cruising sailor had been arrested in connection with a murder. It was with a strong sense of anxiety we sailed on, committed to explore what St. Vincent had to offer.

This little island, despite its social problems, is an aesthetic jewel. Green mountains abound with streams and waterfalls that empty into small perfect bays. Few cars and fewer stores make for a calm, subdued pace of life here.

Broad reaching north up the island's west coast in 20 kts. of wind, we steeled ourselves for the expected onslaught of 20 or 30 teenage boys mounted on almost anything that floats, bumping into our newly painted hull while clamoring to be chosen to take mooring lines ashore or bring fresh bread and ice. The general wisdom is for visiting cruisers to hire the biggest kid in the group, the theory being that he would then keep the others from bothering us. We agreed that would be our strategy.

We were about a mile from our destination, Wallilabou Bay, when Gale poked me on the arm and said, "Look, isn't that a little boat in trouble off our port bow?"

Drawing my attention away from our arrival strategy, I searched the rough sea in front of us. "I don't see anything."

Then Jill pointed. "See the tiny thing there." Then I saw it, a small, one-man dugout pirogue about a half mile to leeward, almost invisible in the agitated sea. Its lone paddler was frantically waving a white cloth at us.

"He's in trouble," declared Gale. "We have to help him."

I had to agree with her observation. The small primitive craft was disappearing in the troughs of the waves, and with the fresh wind it seemed this little cockleshell of a vessel would soon be blown away from any land to be lost until, like many others, his bones washed up 400 miles downwind on the shores of Puerto Rico.

Responding with an urgency equal to what seemed like the obvious terror of the distressed fisherman, I said, "Let's go. Gale, you steer, and when we're close enough, I'll throw him a line."

Starting the engine, we altered course toward the bobbing craft. Knowing from past failures that taking a man aboard in high seas can be very difficult, if not dangerous, we luffed up leeward of the pirogue and shouted to the young man that he should paddle over to the inflatable we trailed and use it to board the big boat. He did so, clambering over our dinghy to the stern ladder, tying off his painter, and hauling himself aboard.

Now, survivor safe with us and feeling a bit heroic, we fell off and headed again for Wallilabou Bay. Busy as we were with sails and looking for the entrance, all we learned about our "survivor," who seemed unusually calm after his harrowing experience, was that his name was Melvin and he lived in Wallilabou.

It wasn't until a few minutes later, while I was concentrating on finding a good spot in the little bay to moor, that Melvin broke his silence. Calling out "Mistah" to get my attention, with a warm smile on his face, he said, "If you need help with moorin' lines, wan' fresh fish, fruit, bread, or ice, I can get dem for you."

Now I get it. I was awed by the brilliance of this simple man's promotional skills. What a great shtick. As soon as he sees a yacht approaching the harbor, he rows his pirogue out into the heaving, wind-blown sea. Then acting out the victim charade we had just witnessed, he gets "rescued" outside the bay, giving him a huge jump on the competition. You had to admire his pluck and creativity.

Melvin turned out to be a gem. Respectful, he had great connections to obtain whatever we needed. More importantly, he kept the other kids completely at bay, which allowed us to enjoy this exceptional cove in peace. And although *Act III* carried ample fresh water for showers, we relished the opportunity for unlimited bathing in the cool fresh water of a nearby natural pool and waterfall we found with Melvin as guide.

Subsequent trips to St. Vincent would always include a stop at Wallilabou. We were never disappointed in its simple magnificence, even after Disney left their "Pirates of the Caribbean" sets on the other side of the bay.

After two delicious days there, the real world again intruded in the form of the need to get Jill to her flight home from the next island, St. Lucia, the "Helen of the Caribbean."

St. Lucia and Our New Crew

An invigorating broad reach of 35 miles—we would not be hard on the wind again for the next 12 months—brought us to a quiet, almost cathedral-like anchorage in the calm azure water of Pitons Bay. Flanked by the natural beauty of two soaring geological spikes, and with Sugar Beach only a few strokes away, we were again reminded why we spent the money, time, and hassle to go cruising on our own boat.

The difference was obvious. Some years later we would join two other couples on a Royal Caribbean cruise that stopped at many of the same islands we had visited in our own vessel. I found little satisfaction in waking up in the morning and looking through our cruise ship stateroom window at the island port we had so easily reached during the night. Sort of like eating pistachio nuts that came already shelled.

My pre-arrival perceptions of St. Lucia had been very much influenced by the literary works of St. Lucian native and Nobel poetry prizewinner Derek Walcott. His writing magically transports the

Waterfall at Wallialabou

reader from wherever he is physically to a realm of warm seas, soft tropical breezes, bright colors, and lilting native music. *Omeros*, as in the Epic of Homer, his masterpiece, inserts the reader into the world of a poor black St. Lucian fisherman who is at the same time both ordinary and heroic.

After picking up a rental car, we had an early dinner and hit the sack, as Jill had to arrive at the Castries Airport at the north end of St. Lucia by 7 a.m to catch her flight home. While I enjoyed the challenge, going as fast as I dared on the predawn, rain-slicked roads, and doing some "on the edge" driving as we passed each of the long line of old trucks drooping with full loads of bananas, Gale was giving me "that look." Arriving just in time, Jill made her plane, but even as we waved goodbye, my mind focused on a new challenge. Our replacement crew would that afternoon be landing at St. Lucia's other airport at the opposite end of the island on the extreme southern tip. There we would pick up our new group of guests: Peter, his wife, Daly, and Peter's elderly aunt.

Peter, as you may remember, was a loyal crew member and had been present for some of our earlier, more disastrous adventures. His wife, Daly—pronounced "Dolly"—is a sweetheart and an incredibly talented natural musician. Want her to play a song? Just hum it and hand Daly any instrument, from a guitar to air compressor. She'll not only be able to play your song by ear but also sing along with you in perfect harmony. We've had many a memorable cockpit sing-a-long thanks to her. The third new addition to our crew was Peter's Auntie Nin, who had flown over from her home in

The soaring "Pitons" of St. Lucia

the UK. Although in her

eighties, Peter's aunt was always cheerful, energetic, a good swimmer, and up for anything.

Their first night on board happened to coincide with Passover. We celebrated a somewhat abbreviated Seder, surrounded by God's gift of so much natural beauty. The next two days were spent exploring the nearby area via rental car, the highlight of which was the breathtaking view from the terrace of the Ladera Hotel.

Having seen the sights on land, we reluctantly weighed anchor and headed north towards Rodney Bay, where we would spend a day dealing with practical stuff like sail repairs and buying additional supplies. Errands taken care of, we turned in early, as we had plans to head north in the early morning's light. *Act III* ripped off the 30-mile voyage to Martinique in five hours, allowing us to arrive in time to enjoy a late lunch while moored at the cove at Trois Islet near Martinique's capitol, Fort-de-France.

My strategy of sailing off the wind for the return trip was working beautifully. No tacks, no bashing to windward. Pushed along by perfect winds off our beam day after day, we were island hopping without pain.

When my sailing guests ask about appropriate wardrobe while aboard, I tell them that most of the time all they will need is a bathing suit and a T-shirt. (In the French islands not even that.) Nevertheless, I advise them they should bring one set of nice clothes for the one festive, fancy night out that we celebrate with each crew during their voyage.

The abundance of cute French restaurants and shops along the Trois Islets esplanade we found during our visit ashore convinced us that Trois Islets was the perfect spot for our BNO—Big Night Out—and we made an 8 p.m. reservation for a waterside table.

Later that afternoon while the three women were actively engaged in preparing and fussing with ... whatever they fuss with—at one point there were so many hairdryers going I had to start the generator—Peter and I spent the hours before our departure for dinner assiduously dealing with the beer surplus problem.

What do you need to know to go cruising? (Or: "Experience is the name we give our mistakes.")

So many guys ask me this question—never women—but from experience I have learned they are not really, truly interested in the few real gems of advice garnered from years of experience that I can offer them.

They see cruising just as I did in the beginning, as a simple thing. Want to sail around the world? Just get a boat and go. Sailing a boat seems to them just like getting into a different type of car and taking off. They ask questions like, "Is starting with a forty footer too small?" "Should I buy a racer so I can get to the Caribbean faster?" I would like to help them so they wouldn't have to suffer like we did as we learned to cruise. (We learned by "Trial and Terror.")

In case anyone reading this book really wants to know...

First: Start small. Practice sailing, anchoring, and living on a smaller boat near home. You get into minor straits when something goes wrong on a small boat; you can kill someone when the same thing happens with a big boat. Not to mention the negative effect on wife and children when a situation arises that results in real terror, screaming, bloody injury, or worse. You'll never get them back aboard. I know.

Oh, and buy a comfortable boat. Lots of living room, storage, and *shade*. Cruisers spend twenty times more hours at anchor than sailing.

Second: Definition of Cruising: Repairing your boat in exotic places. Learn to fix things yourself. There probably won't be anyone nearby to help you when your water pump goes south in Anu-anu. What are you going to do? Fly in a mechanic?

And even if you can't fix stuff, knowing how things on your boat work will keep you from being bamboozled by mechanics who want to take advantage of your ignorance and tell you, "Yep, looks like you're out of mast fluid, that'll be $300."

Yeah, there's other stuff: Navigation, weather, first-aid; but even a novice understands their importance.

People often ask if we keep a gun on board. Never. We believe a gun has no place on a boat. The only legitimate use for assault weapons like the AK-47 is for slaughtering the owners of un-muffled Cigarette-type Go-Fast boats.

Pirates of the Caribbean? The only rapacious, immoral bunch we've ever run into are the car rental people in St. Martin.

About 7:30 the male contingent was brought to their feet by arrival on deck of the three previously straggly-haired cruising waifs now scrubbed, smelling nice, stylishly coiffed, and looking quite elegant in their fresh clothes. We had no choice at that point but to rush below to do our best to transform ourselves—as much as possible—into something that approximated gentlemen.

Returning to the cockpit in fresh duds, we found the ladies assembled at the stern, ready to go ashore. Peter, recognizing the dinghy was not ready to receive such magnificence, jumped into the inflatable to make space for our divas by picking up the beer bottles, snorkels, and other debris that littered the inflatable's hard floor.

Gathered at the stern, we watched as Auntie Nin, outfitted in a long, black crepe dress, white jacket, and with high heels held in her teeth, began her descent of the transom ladder into the dinghy.

Peter, suddenly deciding to act as some kind of nautical foot-man, rushed to the bow of the inflatable to assist her. Sadly, during his cleanup, he had missed one beer bottle in the dark, and that was all it took to send him lurching forward. Like a drowning man grasping at a straw, Peter reached out desperately for something to keep him from going overboard. Unfortunately, the straw his hands found was Auntie Nin.

For a second it looked as though her white jacket might come off in his hands, and Peter's headlong tumble would be a solo event. But the jacket caught, his momentum ripped Auntie Nin backwards from the ladder, and doing a backwards cannonball, she hit the surface with a loud "plunk" to disappear into the dark waters.

Stunned, we all just stood there for a second or so—except for Peter, who was draped over the bow tube—not knowing whether to laugh or dive in after her. We were relieved when she quickly popped to the surface and, though sputtering and gasping, was still able to aim an incredible stream of unladylike cockney invective at her poor nephew. Now *that* was funny.

Once back on board, the other ladies found her enough nice clothes to allow us continue with our BNO, and all went well. But whenever we're all together, someone—other than Peter—usually reminds the group of the incident, and we have a great laugh.

Gale, the Hostess

You, dear reader, might ask, considering the lack of space, resources, and facilities on a sailboat, why we would choose to have guests aboard almost all the time. The answer is simple. In one word: Gale. Gale loves to be a hostess. Believe me when I say the detail and process for the launching of the international space station is only slightly more complete than Gale's list of preparation for visitors on board.

Food, wine, books, extra sunscreen, and research about beaches and restaurants—all to provide the perfect trip for our guests. So when the famous dirt bike shrink Dr. Billy Fleming called on us a few years earlier for help entertaining a VIP visitor, Gale was only too ready to accept the challenge.

Billy was hosting Dr. Simon Sinlich, an authority on human sexuality. Dr. Sinlich, accompanied by his wife, was to speak at an international conference in San Juan. It was the renowned doctor's first trip to the Caribbean, and Billy thought the visiting expert might enjoy a nice sailing trip. "He has Sunday free before his Monday lecture. Can you do it?" Billy queried, adding, "He's never been on a sailboat before."

"Don't worry," I said in my most comforting voice. "The weather forecast is for light winds. I'll keep us sailing, Gale will do the food, and you do the talking."

So at 10 a.m. Sunday morning, Billy, accompanied by a short, stocky, middle-aged man with a goatee—an anomaly in a gray suit—and a fit, younger woman, arrived dockside. Once the couple settled comfortably and safely in the cockpit, we let loose the lines and left the dock under a cloudless blue sky.

The sails went up, white wings against the azure heavens, the boat heeled and began to move gently through the small ocean swells only slightly ruffled by ten knots of breeze. Gale smiled, winked, and whispered, "Perfect," happy to be able to do something for our friend Billy, who had done so much for others.

After leaving the dock, Dr. Bill and our guest had been deeply involved in heavy conversation about Transvestic Fetishism, paraphilia, neuroticism, and other stuff. (I assumed they were talking about me.) I, distracted by raising sails, running lines, and setting a course, at first missed the subtle change in the rhythm of the conversation as Herr Doktor's words became more and more scarce, and eyes closed, he began swaying back and forth.

Recognizing the symptoms of acute *mal de mer*, Dr. Bill got my attention with his shout, "Glenn, where's your bucket." I rushed to retrieve it from the lazarette in the stern but was too late. Worse, with the little guy's mouth at a height of only four feet from the deck, the good doctor's vomit did not go over the rail, and his breakfast of French toast—easily discerned—spattered all over the cockpit.

I was diligently rinsing the area with bucketsful of saltwater, and Gale was trying to make him more comfortable, when he whispered a plea, "Take me back," repeated louder and louder until the plea became an order. "Take me back, damn it. Take me back!" Madam S. quickly concurred and so did we, so wheel hard over, we swung around and returned to the yacht club.

Safely back at the dock after a voyage of about 32 minutes, though a bit shaky, our guest lecturer apologized profusely and, I suppose as a sort of crumb thrown to us, said, *"Dis vas vone of the most incredible egperienzes of mein life. Da imenzity of da sea und man's powerlessness. I tink I shall talk tomorrow about dis egsperienze instead of my planned lectur about gut sex."*

Madam S., a more practical and worldly person, shushed him and said, "Come along, Simon, thank these people and say good-bye." We bade him farewell and, with a sigh of relief, agreed that at least we had tried to show him a good time.

The next day at the hotel, after stubbornly resisting his wife's entreaties not to lecture hundreds of fellow professionals about his recent nautical experience, the doctor marched off alone to the hall, capitulating only at the very last minute to common sense and returning to his planned lecture about "Sensational Sex," as had been listed in the convention program. His presentation received thunderous applause from the attending experts.

Madam Sinlich, not willing to face what she was sure was to be the humiliation of the family breadwinner, had remained sequestered in their hotel room, awaiting what she was sure would be bad news.

Startled by the beeping hotel room phone, with a sense of deep foreboding, she put the receiver to her ear and said, "Hello."

An excited voice, not her husband's, got right to the point. "Is Dr. Sinlich there? I want to congratulate him. I was at his lecture. Everyone thought it was fascinating, and I learned so much."

I wish I had been at the other end of the wire so I could see the expression on the admirer's face when Madam Sinlich replied,

"That really surprises me. He's only done it once. After only a few minutes, he got nauseous, threw up, and said that he would never do it again."

Dominica, Nature's Island

Martinique, a department of France, is known for being one of the more cultured Caribbean islands. Dominica, our next destination, was quite a way down the other end of the scale. A few years previously, Gale and I had spent a week here on land with her parents. The island's narrow roads took us to verdant valleys with hillsides covered with crops. Rivers and waterfalls were everywhere. Sparsely populated and touristically undeveloped, Dominica was unspoiled, a real Eden but almost primeval.

The only place we had missed on our previous visit was the much-touted Indian River, so we continued north along the coast and anchored in the bay at Portsmouth. Its harbor is excellent, and it is also the terminus of the famed stream we wanted to explore.

Portsmouth was another stop made infamous by stories of cruisers who had been besieged by local kids, "boat boys," paddling over on crates, air mattresses, half a windsurfer, anything that floated. Some pleaded. Some begged. Some were angry; all were poor. To bleeding heart liberals like us, this is always a wrenching experience. They're not begging. They want to perform a service, but we rarely need their help, and even if we did, it would be impossible to hire them all.

You can imagine our surprise when, after being allowed to anchor in peace, we were approached by a few locally made boats with outboard motors, piloted by decently dressed young men brandishing some sort of official-looking certificate encased in plastic. Upon close inspection we learned that the government had, thankfully, created a system where the young men were trained and then issued an official certification and permit to legally act as guides. A great step forward.

After chatting with the boys about their services and knowledge of the river, we made our choice, happy to pay his reasonable asking price and reinforce this new, more civilized system. We were especially appreciative when, at the mouth of the river, our guide shut down his outboard and began rowing us silently along the mysterious quiet stream. The flowery primeval jungle slid by as our guide pointed out the highlights. Another extraordinary experience.

The Saintes

With so many "special," "unique," "unforgettable" places, it isn't easy to explain why our next island destination was just as remarkable in a very different way. Easily visible from Dominica but a world of sophistication away are Les Isles de Saintes.

"The Saintes," a small archipelago of mountainous islands, are located just south and are a dependency of the large French island of Guadeloupe. The main town, Grand Bourg, has a flavor that is really more European than Caribbean. We learned it was first settled by fishermen from Normandy, which may explain the multicolored, classic French-style fishing craft that still line the beaches. The history of these islands, like most of the Caribbean, abounds with political intrigues and great sea battles between the European colonial powers that fought to dominate the area. But all this historical focus belies The Saintes' present, unpretentious, off-the-beaten-track charm.

Cars, unless used to transport the hotel guests who lodge at the small hotels and guesthouses sprinkled around the main island of Terre-de-Haut, are prohibited. Everyone walks, bikes, or rides a scooter. Although concentrated along the town's waterfront, the island is covered with excellent, small French restaurants that are all, by choice, open and cooled by the same breezes that bring so many European sailors to this spot.

If we had any doubts about its Gallic character, we lost them when on our first visit we were startled awake in the early light of dawn by the boom of cannons and the swoosh of jets swooping over this previously peaceful, remote bay. Rushing on deck, we were baffled by these military demonstrations until we realized that the date was July 14, Bastille Day, celebrated even in the

French West Indies.

The action, such as it is, is almost all on the island of Terre-de-Haut. *Haut* means high, and anyone who makes the vertiginous climb—by motor scooter is best—up Mt. Chameau is rewarded with an absolutely breathtaking view of The Saintes and nearby islands from its summit.

If the visitor becomes weary of the ever so slightly commercial atmosphere in town, a move one mile down the coast to Pain de Sucre will slake your thirst for a more natural setting. It's so quiet you'll be able to hear the water dripping from your shaft log.

When there we usually also visit the larger but more serene nearby island of Terre en Bas. Rather than moving the boat and re-anchoring, we prefer to dinghy the half mile to quaint, quiet Grande Anse from Pain de Sucre. Once there you will think you have gone back in time to the Caribbean of 100 years ago.

Guadalupe

The Saintes are like a charming buffet of varied experiences, but even a smorgasbord can become boring, so after a few days we usually move on to the big island of Guadeloupe. The eastern wing of this butterfly-shaped island is dry, populated with hotels, and a few nice night anchorages. We find the capitol, Pointe-à-Pitre, not very interesting, so we usually skip the whole shebang and just head north from The Saintes along the west coast of the larger wing called Basse-Terre.

I can't explain why, but every time we sail this coast, wind and sea conditions are perfect. The easterly wind slides nicely over the island, enough to give us good speed, and the land keeps the waves down. It's like sailing fast on rails.

On one trip along this route, Gale decided the calm waters and bright sun provided a perfect opportunity to work on her "all-over tan." She fell asleep and got a really bad sunburn where "the sun don't usually shine," requiring—she said—days of hourly applications of cream by me.

A great stop for snorkeling or scuba on this shore is the Cousteau Underwater Preserve, and farther up the coast the cruiser will find the modest, pretty little town of Deshaies. The bay there offers an anchorage with very good holding. This is good news, as the swirling winds keep moored boats constantly swiveling in a sort of nautical tarantella throughout the night.

From Deshaies, on a continuous, perfect broad reach, we enjoyed short stops along the chain of islands from Nevis all the way back to Puerto Rico and home. But home for *Act III* was no longer on the south coast of Puerto Rico. Our cut-rate cruiser would now be living at a slip in the harbor of Puerto Rico's capital, San Juan, a more logical staging point for the next voyage I had been planning.

Class Act Ends Its Run

While *Act III*, our 56-foot floating mansion, was on her shakedown cruise, *Class Act* was waiting at her slip in Ponce. The good elves, obviously busy elsewhere, had not come and fixed everything while we were away, so I was brought back to reality by the necessity of fixing all the little problems and spiffing her so we could sell what had gone from being our pride and joy to being a superfluous sloop.

Surprisingly, the ad I placed soon resulted in a call from an interested party who spoke Spanish but with an obvious Argentinian accent. He explained he was in Puerto Rico for only two days and would like to see our boat right away. Since I was now paying for two insurance policies and two slips, I was happy to make time to meet the potential buyer at his convenience.

The next day I was at the dock early to be sure everything on the boat was in order. At the agreed upon time, a young man in his thirties, dressed in jeans with a knapsack on his back, sauntered up to my slip and came aboard. "Roberto" shook hands and proceeded to inspect every nook and cranny of our 41-foot ex-pride and joy.

Hoping to find an edge to bring out her best qualities for what-ever he was looking for in a sailboat, I queried him about his plans for his purchase.

"Adventure charter," he replied. Great. With her huge cockpit she was perfect for day sailing a large group that would sleep in tents ashore each night. I guess he thought so too, because he was willing to make a deal at $40,000—greatly exceeding market expectations—right then and there.

I was pleased but cautious because, with his shifty manner and slicked back "Gardel-style" hair, he didn't look completely trustworthy. But when he opened his backpack and showed me that it was full of cash, I suddenly felt a strong surge of confidence.

A buyer who was willing to pay my price and didn't need to get a bank loan? Perfect. I called my lawyer, and he had bill of sale ready by the time we got to his office. To my great relief, Roberto took possession of the boat and I took possession of the backpack full of money. *Carpe cash.*

Concerned by the possibility that the deposit of $40,000 in cash might attract the attention of our government[2], I took the precaution of making four deposits of $9,990 on four different days. However much of a hassle this might have been, it was a hell of a lot better than having two boats.

Our Favorite Island?

People often ask us, "What's your favorite island?" Frankly, we find it difficult to come up with a single, simple answer. So much depends of what the visitor is looking for.

Here are some opinions. I hope they will be helpful.
* A week's easy cruising? The Virgin Islands.
* A place with lots do? St. Martin.
* Natural beauty and history? Nevis.

And on and on …

---

2. You know the saying, "There's nothing sure in this world but Death and Taxes." In Puerto Rico it's just Death. The government of Puerto Rico is about as effective as the referee in a professional wrestling match.

Glenn and Gale's idea of special places in the Caribbean
I hope our experiences will help the first-time visitor enjoy the wonderful islands of the Caribbean. Below are some of *our* favorite stops.

Montserrat
With the better bays now filled in with ash, only Little Bay is available for a (poor) anchoring overnight. However, once ashore you can hire a car and driver and see for yourself the devastation caused by the latest volcanic eruption. A unique experience.

Anse de Colombier, St. Barts
Except on weekends when people from St. Martin come to "get away from the crowds," this bay is peaceful and quiet. From here you can take the vertiginous but spectacular walking trail—starts on the north side of the beach—for a 45-minute hike to gorgeous Flamands Beach. Enjoy the views and have lunch and a drink at one of the little French bistros along the strand before you return.

St. Martin

Isle Pinel
St. Martin is, as Forest Gump's mother said, "Like a box of chocolates." Once you've tired of the stores in Philipsburg, the expensive restaurants on the French side, and the nude bathing at Orient Beach, we suggest heading to the northern part of Orient Bay where there is a small mooring field off delightful, uninhabited Isle Pinel.

Our visits here usually start by spending the morning hours playing tourist on the beach, along with the hundreds of day-trippers who arrive every morning on small launches from the mainland. We rent beach chairs and umbrellas, order rum punches, and the girls shop at the quaint, rustic boutiques under the palms. Then in the afternoon we dinghy around to the north side—you can also walk there—where there is small beach that

Isle Pinel's two beaches

probably will have no one on it but you … and perhaps some nude sunbathers.

At 5 p.m. when the launches arrive to take everyone back to the main island, we return to the tourist beach. With day-trippers and employees now gone, we enjoy the peace and quiet while we have the whole beach and facilities all to ourselves as the sun goes down.

Anse Marcel

This is another just about perfect bay where we rarely see more than three or four other boats. Its anchorage is less than a mile from the Rocher Creole Underwater Preserve, so one can usually dinghy over for a snorkel. Located on its perfect beach is the Radisson Hotel. If you dress decently, with a drink bought at the beach bar in hand, you can probably saunter past security into the pool area and delight as their fresh water pool dissolves weeks of salt from your skin.

Grand Bourg seen, not from an airplane, but from Mt. Chameau

Buck Island, St. Croix, Virgin Islands

We love Buck Island because it's the perfect jumping off point for St. Martin and Anguilla. I don't understand why other captains still choose the demanding route from the BVIs, when the trip from this location is so much easier.

The sail to Buck Island from the northern Virgins is a fast, exciting, 35-mile close reach. While you are awaiting the right weather to cross the Anegada Passage, you can spend a day or two enjoying the delicious beach on the island's western end and the National Park Services' underwater trail on the east end.

When you plan your voyage from here to St. Martin, you will discover that the course from Buck Island to Anguilla is 70 degrees, so when the wind is at its normal 120-130 degrees, one can often make the 83-mile voyage on a single tack. One summer, with the help of the engine, we left at dawn and made landfall in St. Martin before dark. Quite a change from the day-and-a-half slog to weather on our first trip with Gale's parents.

Beautiful Coffin Island

Puerto Rico[3]

Isla Caja de Muertos (Coffin Island)

Don't let the name deter you from visiting this perfect, small islet. Just a few miles off the city of Ponce, it has attractive beaches and good holding. It is as beautiful as almost any Caribbean island. Monday to Thursday you will probably find yourself alone at this wonderful refuge after the hard work of sailing east along the south coast. On Saturday or Sunday, however, you will have to share it with 20 or 30 Puerto Rican families who come over for the weekend in their boats.

Palominos Island (Fajardo)

The majestic El Conquistador Hotel in Fajardo leases the land on the southern part of this almost perfect Caribbean island for their

---

3. Puerto Rico has a very large powerboating community, and they love to spend the weekend on the water, having a good—noisy—time with friends. Monday through Friday you will probably find yourself alone at these locations, but the weekends could be quite different.

guests. North of the ferry dock there is a bay with a nice beach and free moorings provided and maintained by the PR government for the use of the boating public.

However, when we visit we play tourist. Once secured to one of the government moorings, we set off with our plan to enjoy the Hotel's facilities south of the dock.

(Pink Panther theme in the background.)

Nonchalantly, we sit on the public beach, awaiting the arrival of one of the frequent hotel ferries. These boats disgorge their passengers onto the dock, where they enter the "towel line." We slip into the line and each take a *hotel towel*. Then, brandishing our official towels like a pass, we grab one of the hotel's beach chairs under the palms and enjoy the view, the beach, and maybe even a rum punch.

Bahia Icacos, Vieques

Vieques has many exceptional great anchorages, but this special, lovely bay on the northeastern side is quiet and large enough so it won't feel crowded, even on the weekend. A great stop to or from the Virgin Islands, it is protected by a rich, shallow water reef that until recently was an "Off Limits" Navy bombing range. Thus, it has not been tarnished by too many visitors and has spectacular shallow water snorkeling. Don't let what looks like a difficult entrance keep you out. It's deep and easy to navigate by sight.

This bay is our Vieques favorite, but I would be doing a disservice to my readers if I didn't mention the uniqueness of the bioluminescence of the unfortunately named Mosquito Bay on the south coast. A number of tour companies—take the kayak not the pontoon boat—offer marvelous night tours.

Flamenco Beach, Culebra

I don't know why we never see a sailboat here. Yes, it's open to the north, but every time we've stopped, the bay has been like a lake. If you're passing north of Culebra, check out this picture postcard spot.

In general we find that our guests, as long as they are not seasick, are happy with short trips to the beach, a decent snorkel, fresh water shower, and a drink before dinner.

5

The Atlantic

To get us to Europe, I had carefully laid out an itinerary that had us leaving Puerto Rico in January for Florida via the Bahamas. Then up the ICW—Intracoastal Waterway—to New York and on to our departure point, Newport, RI, for a projected June crossing of the Atlantic.

I chose June for the crossing because the pilot charts showed that, historically, that month had the best combination of warm weather and fair winds before hurricane season. Although I had experienced the close passing of a dozen hurricanes during my years in Puerto Rico, our vessels had never suffered any damage. (The damn fish traps had been a bigger hazard.) The middle of the Atlantic was not the place to have a first.

Thanks to global warming, that year the wind and sea conditions would be near perfect. I believe climate change will become a huge determining factor in the future of sailing. If boat manufacturers want to look to the future, they ought to be shifting their media spending from nautical publications to skiing magazines. It's only a matter of time before there will be no snow in the Rockies, and Topeka, Kansas, will be one of the cities competing to host the Americas Cup.

Assuming we made it across the Atlantic, my plan was to have us spend five months in the Western Med before returning, perhaps with a rally or other group, via the easier but longer southern route west back to the Caribbean. As Mark Twain said: "To succeed, you need two things: ignorance and confidence." He must have known me. But I have always felt that staying home is "Survival of the skittish."

People ask me, "Why cross the Atlantic to Europe?" I know they are expecting a reply like that of Sir Edmund Hillary, who said, after conquering Mt. Everest, "Because it's there." So brave and so poetic, and so not me.

Sailing the islands of the Caribbean had greatly enriched and changed our lives. I just wanted more, and I thought cruising the coasts of Europe would give it to me. History, culture, good food, and so much of it accessible from the shoreline. For us, Europe was more than a box of chocolates; it was the whole damn candy store.

Yes, I know. I could rent a boat there or have my boat transported there on a freighter. But I had learned too much and come too far to reduce myself to being a renter or, finding myself in some sailor's bar, having to admit to the other old salts that my boat got to Europe without me.

The excitement of taking on the challenge of the Atlantic crossing was for me somewhat tainted by the specter of having to suffer the terrible, everlasting boredom and loneliness of such a long trip, a trip that was to be three or four times the length of our voyage to Grenada. Burying my dread of the negative aspects of the crossing under the activity of dealing with the long list of tasks and research kept me from wavering in my resolve to go ahead with the voyage.

Strange as it may sound, despite all my whining about being bored, the only instance during which I sailed alone for an extended period had proved to be a delightful experience. We were returning from a down island trip, and because we were a bit behind schedule, I dropped Gale and our guests in St. Thomas to fly home, leaving me to sail *Act III* back to Ponce singlehanded. I was pleasantly surprised to find that instead of the constant monotony I had anticipated, I enjoyed two days of almost spiritual transformation.

Alone at sea the boat, instead of its normal identity as just a platform for our activities, became more like a spiritual companion. Instead of a master/slave relationship—some might wonder who the slave is—where I would use my intellect to direct her to accomplish my goals, there was an easygoing oneness to our passage. I also delighted in the relaxed, peaceful freedom of not having anyone on board to please, placate, or pacify. And I could sail as I wanted without being second guessed. Also the tension of anchoring or docking with help was replaced with the satisfaction have having done these maneuvers—slowly and conservatively—all alone. So different.

When people inquired about the trip to Europe—"Where will you go? What will you do?"—I could regale them with a half hour lecture of places I wanted to visit. But I had no idea what to say if they asked, "What are you going to do when the trip is over?"

Adios, Amigos

Our feelings of anticipation increased as New Year's 1997 came and went. By late January I had completed verifying the condition of all the mechanical and electrical systems and was taking care of the last installations: a new inverter and carpeting for the forward hallway. I think the only thing more expensive than running for Congress must be outfitting a sailboat for a long cruise and ocean crossing.

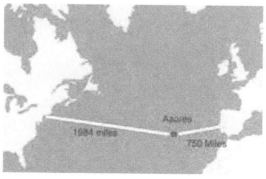

It's a long way across the Atlantic Ocean

With two days remaining until our planned January 30 departure, we found ourselves with nothing left to do except for loading our last personal items, closing up our apartment, and our much anticipated Going Away Party on the eve of our departure.

For Gale the parties took precedence over all the practical boat stuff. Instead of double-checking and organizing boat stuff, she had me running around buying cold cuts, champagne, special napkins, etc. Party day finally dawned, and by 5 p.m. Gale had everything ready. There were platters of delicious food laid out on nearly every horizontal surface and drinks cooling all over the boat.

By dark our 40 invitees, including Peter and Daly, Ivy and husband, Ricky, were aboard, eating, drinking, and being merry. Perhaps it was just because of their affection for us, perhaps it was because there was still food left over, but at 2 a.m. a dozen party-goers were still on board. It wasn't the late hour that concerned me. During the 350-mile leg from San Juan to Grand Turk, there would be plenty of time for me to catch up on my sleep. My dark secret was that I still had to go home and pick up our cat, Max, the last of our clothes, meds, and other personal stuff before our early morning departure the next day.

Finally herding the last stragglers off the boat, we waved goodbye to our closest friends and family, happily accepting their bidding us *Bon Voyage* and *Buen Viaje*. Once alone I jumped into the car and barreled home—no traffic at 3 a.m.—loaded up our stuff and the cat, and 4 a.m. found me back on *Act III*, crawling into my bunk, last task done.

The Long Journey's First Step

Morning came and a groggy but determined crew of six—Gale and I, reinforced by four friends and Max, the red cat—took in the lines and left the dock in a light drizzle that for some reason seemed to me very appropriate.

Crew members Ron and Andy Chevako, with their son Jay and veteran crew Adam McDonough, joined us in the cockpit as we,

Entrance to Icacos bay, Vieques

now freed from ties to the land, made our way towards the mouth of San Juan harbor.

To starboard, somewhat veiled by the mist, was massive El Morro Fort, placed by the Spanish here 400 years ago to protect the entrance to the harbor. Having already seen everything from Spanish conquistadores to great white cruise ships, it took little note of what to us was a historic occasion.

Then just as we reached to point where the rhythmic movement of the ocean's swells gave us that visceral, physical notification that we were now beginning an ocean voyage, the sun suddenly burst from behind the rain's mist, and every one of us gasped at the sight of a perfect rainbow straddling our planned course. What an omen.

As if this weren't enough, just then a group of gray porpoises appeared off the port bow, swimming with us as though they were our escorts to a new world of adventure.

We couldn't believe what we were seeing. The beauty and spirituality of that moment became a talisman that helped me make it through some of the difficult times I went through later in the trip.

It wasn't long before we could no longer see even Puerto Rico's highest mountains, and we were alone at sea. Although we enjoyed fair, fresh winds for most of the time, nevertheless, Type A personality that I am, when the wind dropped I ran the engine. Using this strategy, we dispatched the 350-mile leg to Grand Turk in only 50 hours.

Confucius say: "The longest journey begins with one step." Grand Turk was our first encounter with the low, dry, sandy geography of the island chain along our route all the way to Florida. Not really aesthetically enticing, it was, however, as our first landfall, a very welcome sight.

Anchoring off the beach south of the only town on this barren dry island, we planned a short trip ashore to check in with the authorities before noon and then visit famed Miss Peanut's Café to sample the legendary "rhythm pills"—conch fritter balls—she serves in her restaurant.

The streets of the somnolent settlement were practically deserted under the midday sun, and the few humans we found exhibited a sort of zombie-like character. Inquiries about the location of Customs, the post office, or Miss Peanut's were met with vacant stares and mumblings we could not decipher.

Luckily, with only 3,000 souls—including the "undead"—the town was small enough for us to find Customs on our own. Once the paperwork was taken care of, the government official directed us to continue south along the waterfront to find Miss Peanut's place. Not far away we found a small weathered shack with a sign that announced we had arrived at the revered establishment.

The choice of eating inside or outside was made for us, as only the kitchen actually had a roof over it. The *salle* à *manger* consisted of a porch on the beach that had room for four rough-hewn, umbrella-shaded—thank goodness—wooden picnic tables with benches. The tiny lady who seemed in charge answered our requests for a menu with the reply, "I only have rhythm pills and beer." Well that certainly simplified things. This was the only time I've gone to a restaurant with women where there was no fiddle-faddling about what they were going to order.

We were not her only customers. Somehow a crew of four from a British sailboat had also stumbled upon this paragon of local cuisine. We traded information with them about who we were and what had brought us to this remote place while we waited for Miss Peanut to sort out—judging by the amount of time it took—our complicated order.

Finally, the food for both groups arrived, as did the Budweiser. ("Excellent choice, Monsieur.") Yes, the fritters were very good and so was the cold beer; both worth the wait. Sated, we asked for the check. (American Express? You gotta be kidding.) In an attempt to be, we assumed, ecologically aware, Miss Peanut did not keep the tabs on paper. She kept this financial data in her head, so she was quickly able to come up with the amount of our bill. $150.

Now, five stars or not, $150 for six plates of fritters and six beers in a crumbling, planked dive seemed a little excessive, and we said so. With a sigh that revealed her infinite patience with ignorant strangers like us, Miss Peanut explained that $150 was to cover what all of us white people had eaten, and how we wanted to divvy it up was our problem, not hers.

Now that we understood the system, we successfully negotiated the division of debt with the limeys, paid our bill, wandered back out into the heat, and returned to the boat.

Adam's Journey Over

A short hop west to the even drearier island of South Caicos garnered us some cheap diesel and a visit to the local seafood packing plant where we bought enough lobster and conch at wholesale prices to last a week.

Caicos Bank: Clenched teeth for 40 + miles

Fuel tank and bellies now full, we chatted about what to expect from the next day's run over the Caicos Bank to Providenciales, a voyage that I viewed as somewhat of a challenge.

Learning in and accustomed to sailing in the deep waters of the Caribbean, I found the prospect of the 40-mile Bank crossing, in average depths of seven to eight feet in a boat that drew six and a half feet, unnerving. Sailing into just one rock or patch reef could spell disaster. More so, it turned out. Instead of having the luxury of picking my way along, I had to go as fast as I could because the next day we found ourselves with a medical emergency on our hands.

It happened this way.

We were departing South Caicos Island, sailing south along the shallows towards the entrance to the Caicos bank. Upon reaching the channel, I shouted, "Watch out, we're going to jibe."

Adam, coming up the companionway ladder, evidently didn't hear my warning very well. As he stuck his head up to say, "What?" the main boom swung over and, emitting a sickening *thwack*, clopped him squarely on the back of his head.

Conscious but bleeding profusely, Adam became the immediate focus of a lot of attention. Everyone had a recommendation about what to do. Go back, go on, go below, go get a beer. Gale, in a calm, confident voice announced, "Look, I took stitching lessons from our son-in-law, Dr. Ricky Barnes, and if it has to be done, I am willing to sew up his scalp." Since the rest of us got nauseous at just the thought of the procedure, she got her way.

Putting Adam's head in her lap, she opened the bag of sutures from our first aid kit and stared at the variety of needles for a long, long time. I assumed she was studying them to determine what size to use. But when after several minutes nothing happened, I asked, "Gale, what's up?"

Looking up at me tearfully, she said, "I can't bring myself to do it. But I do believe that if I close the wound by pressing his scalp together, I can stop the bleeding. But we'd better get him to a hospital as soon as possible." That meant engine on and haul ass to Provo. It also meant that Gale would spend the next six and a half hours holding together the split in Adam's scalp.

I tried not to pay attention to the fathometer readings as we raced over the shallow bank, but the desire to know how much trouble we were in was irresistible. Having as little as six inches under our keel intensely tested my faith in the charts, but we flew on anyway.

Blasting into Provo late that afternoon, I headed right for the busiest place I saw in hopes of finding transportation to get Adam to some sort of medical facility. Only after dropping our casualty and Gale, joined like Siamese twins, at the island's commercial dock were we able to take a deep breath and pull away to find a spot to anchor the boat.

Anxiously awaiting news, we watched the wharf until Gale appeared several hours later at the pier, accompanied by an unrecognizable, puffy-faced mummy who swore to us that he really was our Adam. Once in the cockpit, Gale gave us the low-down on the wild taxi ride, the search for someone on duty at the clinic, and then treatment by—an unfortunately named—Dr. Slaughter. Adam's journey was, by doctor's orders, now over. He would have to fly home the next day—not looking at all like his passport photo—and we would carry on northward without him.

Leaving Adam and Provo early the following day, we began the next leg of our trip, the 170-mile voyage to that mecca of North American cruising sailors, Georgetown, Great Exuma. Taking advantage of the excellent weather, we bypassed less interesting places like Acklins and Crooked Islands and found ourselves at the Georgetown channel entrance the next afternoon.

The Exumas

As we found our way along the channel, we could see in the distance a forest of masts. The space between the town and the islands that give this area's waters such excellent protection were teeming with hundreds of sailing craft.

After anchoring, we dinghied ashore to join the rest of the sunburned, deck-shoed hordes that take over this town each spring. Finally finding a table at a crowded restaurant, we delighted in a great, lobster farewell dinner before the rest of our crew left to fly home. Now it would be just Gale and me to take *Act III* all the rest of the way to Florida.

My lack of shallow water sailing experience made the prospect of travel using the calmer "inside" route along the archipelago a bit intimidating, so each of our daily legs north along the Exumas chain was a fast broad reach "outside," without lee and in deep water. We ducked in behind the land only to get protection when we anchored to spend the night.

Innocent—or ignorant—of the Bahamian phenomenon called a "rage," I learned the hard way how dangerous this condition can be ... first hand. I had chosen to transit Rudder Cut just when the ebbing tide and strong opposing wind had created steep, high waves and strong current in the long, narrow passage to our chosen anchorage. Suddenly, we were out of control, sliding down from the crest of a high breaking wave. I jammed the throttle forward, and the big diesel and 24-inch prop bit into the swirling water enough to give us a modicum of control. With the passage narrowing in front of me, and noticing a recently wrecked sailboat on the rocks to my right, every ounce of concentration went into keeping the big ketch away from the rocky cliffs. The 30 seconds or so it took to get to calm water seemed like an eternity. But we made it.

The rest of our trip up the Exumas chain was a real eye opener for *Caribophiles* like us. While these islands lacked the relatively sophisticated resorts, colonial towns, deep waters, and high green mountains we were used to, the waters were gin clear, diving was great, and there were hundreds of deserted islands and beaches where we could be completely alone to do whatever we wanted. And on Valentine's, although Gale took a lot of convincing, we did.

This exposure to the islands of the Exumas gave us a much better understanding of why they are so popular with North American cruisers.

Fickle Fate

The end of February found us past the lightly populated Exumas and docked at The Royal Nassau Sailing Club marina, located next to the Paradise Island bridge in urbane Nassau. Although the marina's name sounds like something out of a James Bond film, the uneven docks, shuttered restaurant, and lack of services were more in keeping with the current economic state of the island nation. Nonetheless, despite the bad press it has received, we enjoyed the historical side of Nassau and the friendly locals and were sad when after three days it was time to leave.

The voyage had been until now mostly devoid of mechanical or electrical problems, so I decided the morning of our departure would be a good time to tempt fate and see if the boat's "day tank" was now really clean and the diesel in it was usable.

The previous day I had witnessed the sad saga of a sailboat that had come loose from its mooring in the narrows. Horrified, I watched as, carried along by two knots of current in the strait, it had bashed its way along the Paradise Island rip-rap seawall and on into oblivion. A sight not easily forgotten.

I wanted to be sure we would not suffer the same fate because of any loss of power, so I took the precaution of running the engine with the fuel supply switched to the untried tank while we went about our business, stowing things for our departure.

After a half hour without a blip, I felt I could assume the fuel was clean and the feed from the day tank evidently was okay. Now sure of engine power, I told Gale to let the lines go, and we headed out of the marina and into the channel.

Regrettably, somehow we had angered the fickle god Petroleumus. No sooner had we cleared the dock than the engine died. Grabbing her arm, I barked, "Gale, take the wheel!" and I made a mad dash forward to try to save our bacon by dropping the anchor.

Now helpless in the grip of the outgoing tide, we were being carried inexorably towards the columns of the Paradise Island bridge. My prayers must have been heard, because as I ran forward to drop anchor, miraculously, the current carried us safely though the span without hitting anything.

Desperately heaving the 65-lb. plow anchor overboard just as the mizzen mast cleared the bridge, I watched as the chain angrily clattered out of the hawse pipe. My second prayer was answered when the anchor caught and the bow swung sharply upstream about 75 yards from the bridge.

I wasn't able to spend much time reveling in our good luck as, while it's true we were anchored securely, we were anchored securely right in the middle of the busy Nassau channel.

I immediately set to work removing the filter that was clogged with sediment and gunk—live by the sword, die by the sword— and set about bleeding the bleeding fuel system. If you have ever owned an older Perkins diesel, you know that bleeding it and getting it started can be operations more difficult than achieving Middle East peace. For most of an hour, I worked and cursed, but nothing I did would get the engine to fire up.

All the while a constant stream of other craft motored by, not so subtly reminding us we were anchored in the middle of the damn channel. Desperate and unable to raise anyone on the VHF, I asked Gale, "While I continue to try to get the damn thing started, just in case, could you please take the dinghy back to the marina, and see if you can find a mechanic who might be able to help me get this M-F P.O.S. going!"

Always willing to help but a bit apprehensive because she has trouble getting the 15-hp outboard going, she replied, "I'll go if you'll start the motor." I did and she did.

Head down, working on the fuel system with the cockpit engine hatch open, I was so intensely focused on the injectors and fuel pumps that I lost track of time. Quite a while later—I don't remember how long—hands greasy, knuckles bleeding, having used every four letter word I knew, the infernal combustion machine for some unknown reason came to life.

With a huge sigh of relief, I raised my gaze to the heavens in thanks just as Gale's face, tears streaming down her cheeks, appeared over the coaming. I may not know how to bleed a diesel engine, but I knew enough about women to understand that these were not tears of joy. Something was seriously wrong.

Between sobs she explained, "Just like the big boat, the dinghy engine suddenly stopped after I got underway." With smaller sobs she continued, "I tried to row back to the boat, but no matter how hard I tried, I was carried away by the strong current and towards the open sea. I desperately waved at every boat I saw, but all they did was wave back! Then just before I was swept into the cruise ship channel, a boat came close enough to see me. I started waving an oar over my head to get their attention, and they heard me pleading for help. Thank God they towed me back here."

To calm her down I prescribed Chardonnay therapy and suggested she go to galley and make sandwiches, one of her favorite pastimes. With the engine now running smoothly on the main tank, and the Chardonnay facilitating her emotional recovery, I felt we could weigh anchor and head out the Nassau channel towards the Bahama bank and Florida. All's well that ends well. Right?

Act III sails the U.S. of A.

The often difficult crossing of the Gulf Stream to Florida was for us a "piece of cake." Our staging stop in Grand Bahama made for an easy 100-mile crossing, and we let the Gulf Stream carry us north right to our planned landfall in Palm Shores, Florida. Why Palm Shores?

Both my elderly divorced parents lived—separately—nearby, and I proudly looked forward to inviting them—separately—aboard to see the vessel what had brought Gale and me—together—a thousand miles to their doorsteps.

This region, commonly known as "God's Waiting Room," is a favorite terminus for elderly retirees, and my divorced parents—my mother, my father with his fourth wife—and his two widowed sisters had all decided to spend their golden years only a few miles apart in the same town.

At this point I would like to share with you a little story that will help you understand my mother's personality and the family dynamic.

Not very close friends even before the divorce, one day the widows found themselves forced to make polite family conversation with Mom during a chance meeting at the hairdresser. I was told that the conversation ended in a dead, cold silence after my mother decided to share her opinion that, "You two are lucky. Your husbands are dead. Mine lives only a few miles away with another woman."

As it was I should have saved myself the trouble of having my parents aboard. I suppose that with no nautical experience they had no frame of reference. Neither Mom nor Dad had any concept of what we had accomplished. Nor did they seem to have any interest in the undertaking that lay ahead of us.

With no glory to bathe in, we decided to say goodbye. We let loose the lines and Waterway guide in hand, pointed our bow north toward our first Intracoastal Waterway marker.

The "Ditch"

For those of you who sail in North America, it may be hard to understand that, despite all the miles we had put under our keel in the Caribbean, we had very little experience with the great variety of channel markers we began to encounter in the Intracoastal Waterway (ICW). At first I had a very tough time figuring things out until I found that by putting away the guide and charts and just following other boats, I could stay away from the shallows—anything less than our 6-ft. 6-in. draft—and learn from these more experienced boaters.

This strategy worked well until we decided to turn off the ICW into the guide's recommended stop, Peck Lake, our first night at anchor on this route. The ICW guide said I should turn left at buoy #12 into a channel with 10 feet of water. I did so and immediately went hard aground. Scratching my head, I read and reread the instructions, realizing too late that the guide is written to be used from north to south, and I had followed instructions from the opposite direction. After a long, embarrassing night sleeping on a 45-degree angle, high tide came and freed us.

A description of our 1,000 mile ICW traverse is very much like that famous definition of sailing: "Long periods of monotony interspersed with moments of sheer panic." Our days averaged eight hours of mind-numbing motoring, only enlivened when we came across one of the many places where, even in the channel center, the bottom came up damn close to or touched our two- meter keel.

Our trip wasn't made any easier by the big powerboats which often blasted down the narrow channel, trailing a huge disruptive wake. There's not much Ying and Yang between sailing and power boating.

The sailor operates in harmony with the environment using the wind as we encounter it to move quietly, calmly along enjoying the smells, colors and movement of the sea.

The power boat is a dangerous high speed machine that bombards its surroundings with noise, stink and disruption except at anchor when loud music and bright lights take over.

I was often reminded of the time we anchored off Little Salt Key. This is what happened.

While Gale was preparing lunch, I decided to swim ashore to check out the beach. When I got to water shallow enough to stand, I noticed an old brown bottle floating near shore, washing up and down the otherwise pristine beach with the lapping waves.

This bottle, the only trace of civilization marring this otherwise perfectly natural scene, was such a—pardon the pun—jarring sight that I decided to pick it up so I could put it in our boat's trash bin. But in my hand the bottle felt very warm and seemed to vibrate. Looking closer, I could see there was something inside that was alive. The stopper came out with a pop and a whoosh like a jet plane, and unexpectedly, there standing beside me was a real genie.

"Thank you for liberating me," said the somewhat rumpled, dark-skinned apparition. "In return I will grant you a wish, one wish, your heart's desire."

What to ask for? I lived with a beautiful woman I loved, had great children, and enough money to enjoy life at my age. Yet there was one thing I wanted that would improve my enjoyment of life.

"Genie, we love to sail to wonderful places, but our sailboat has a maximum hull speed of only eight knots. Could you give me a magic spell to use when I need more speed, say fifteen knots?"

After a glance at our anchored craft, the genie turned towards me and said, "Well, it looks like your boat only has a 45-foot waterline length, so to give you what you want, I would have to change the laws of hydrodynamics in oceans all over the world just to improve your maximum hull speed. I could do that, but the worldwide result would be chaotic and probably dangerous in some cases. Is there perhaps some other desire I could fulfill?"

I thought for a minute, and it came to me. "Yes, genie. Could you make the powerboat people more considerate of others who share the water with them?"

"Humm," said the genie, a pensive look on his face. Rubbing his chin, he turned to me and said, "Would you accept maybe … twelve knots?"

Like so many challenging experiences, with time the difficulty of staying in the channel waned, and I began to feel more comfortable. We were winding our way through the legendary and seemingly endless, sinuous channels in the marshes of Georgia, and I was just congratulating myself on becoming such an expert at navigating a big boat so well in tight conditions, when a goddamn cruise ship came around a bend in the narrow channel in front of me. I swear. Somehow, we managed to pass each other, leaving me with a totally new insight into big boat handling on the ICW.

The Search for Max

Not all our problems had to do with navigation.

Our overnight stop at Florida's Marineland Park Marina included a walk to check out the nature preserve south of the docks. The paths winding through the swamp were studded with signs describing the natural inhabitants. Bobcats, coyote, rattlesnakes, but the only animal we actually saw was an impressive reticulated python.

Up early the next morning for the leg to St. Augustine, I was surprised not to find Max waiting in the galley for his breakfast. When the sound of a cat food can being opened didn't flush him, I became concerned. I awakened Gale, and together we checked every nook and cranny on the boat. No cat.

Max was not a very adventurous feline. His nautical jaunts consisted of moving by car in his travel case to the boat and then back again, his paws never touching the earth, other than the sand in his fantail litter box. And that, with the exception of the litterbox heaven episode in St. John, seemed fine with him.

Now seriously concerned, we spent several hours combing the area near the boat. We asked everyone we met while searching if they had seen a big red cat, but the answer was always no. That night, in hopes of luring him out, we placed cans of cat food in strategic places and took turns until 1:00 a.m. checking the chum with a flashlight. All we accomplished was to feed every raccoon in the area.

Was Max, an apartment cat, out of his element and lost forever? Had someone picked him up? Had he become lunch for the reticulated python? There was no way of knowing for sure, and the reality was that spending more days of our tight schedule in what would probably be a futile search didn't seem to make sense. So after one more search, we had no practical alternative but to leave his cage and our contact information with the park ranger in case he turned up. Mournful and dejected, we returned to the boat and headed back out along the waterway towards our next stop, St. Augustine.

We had only motored north for a few minutes when I noticed a faint smell of burning rubber. Since *Act III* had no tires, the only source of this odor had to be in the engine room. I opened the engine hatch and was nearly knocked over by the stream of acrid smoke that poured out. While reaching for the panel-mounted kill button, I noticed the water temperature had also gone sky high. What was the problem?

Like a ton of bricks, the realization of what had happened hit me. Over beers the night before, another cruiser told a story about how his cooling water strainers were filling up with weeds on the waterway. Aha. I'd better check mine. I did. Closing the thru-hulls, I removed the cover, scraped out the little bit of stuff I found, and replaced the strainer and cover. *But I had forgotten to reopen the thru-hulls.*

I sprinted forward and dumped in the anchor to keep us out of the shallows—I was getting good at this—and once securely anchored, I began to examine our options.

Experience gained from previous situations where I had to perform a repair away from home had taught me much. Instead of trying to fix the engine in the middle of the channel—déjà vu—a more logical strategy would be to return to the marina to make any required repairs. There I could get the help I would—probably—need.

In Puerto Rico they say, *"De los golpes se aprende."* (One learns from the blows one receives.) By now, having had considerable practice dealing with old boats adapted to new engines, we had experienced our share of situations where, with the engine out of commission, entering a marina under sail was not a safe, viable option. It had been a great relief to learn that even with only a 3- or 5-hp outboard, our inflatable dinghy, pushing against the transom, could easily give us enough speed and steerage to accomplish some of the complicated maneuvers needed to find, enter, and tie up to a dock.

So with Gale acting as tugboat captain in the dinghy, and me screaming instructions to her from the con, we puttered the mile or so back to Marineland and eased her into the first open slip we saw.

Happily, I found the only damage done was to the raw water cooling pump impeller. And I was thankful when, after only a moderate amount of finger burning and knuckle busting, I was able to install a new one and get the engine running again. Too late now to head back out on the waterway, we decided to spend the night here and repeat our search efforts for Max before leaving again.

This time we pulled out all the stops for project "Max Hunt." We opened and laid out our entire stock of Max's favorite food, Bumble Bee tuna in water, and crossed our fingers. That night, swaddled in foul weather gear in a driving March rain, we alternated making rounds of the deserted park every hour to check the bait we had laid out.

Sodden and cold, I was returning to our slip just before dawn after completing the last of my three circuits when, back at the boat, a sleeping Gale was jolted awake by a mass of wet fur that landed on her chest. It was Max. Nose to nose with her, he let loose a series of howls of cat anger and frustration that seemed to be directed at her for having abandoned him. Whatever his opinion, we were ecstatic that our crew was again complete. In the years that followed, Max never mentioned his experiences during the two-day disappearance, and we, not wanting to relive the pain, never asked him about it.

A Jersey Girl Comes Home

The peaches must have been dropping off the trees as we made our way through Georgia in weather that stayed below 40 degrees. South Carolina wasn't much better. It got so cold we moved off the boat and into a motel in Georgetown, SC. How cold was it? So cold we had to buy gloves or our hands stuck to the stainless steel ship's wheel. This was probably a contributing factor to the loss of our dinghy when Gale's mittens prevented her from laying a good bight on the stern cleat. We blessed our good fortune and eternal gratitude when our tender was returned to us by a swordfishing captain named "Mad Dog."

After Georgetown, things improved with two days of enjoying the natural magnificence of the Waccamaw River as we crossed into North Carolina.

The rest of the thousand-mile leg to Norfolk was pretty much devoid of great drama. By then I had learned to call the drawbridges on the VHF and say with an authentic southern twang, "This is the sailin' vessel *Act III*, nawthboun' ..." Etc. We had a couple of groundings—and observed quite a few too—enjoyed visits to friends along the way, and had to deal with unbelievable, freak 70-mph winds from a sudden spring squall in the middle of the Chesapeake Bay.

While I must admit that the trip seemed to be excruciatingly slow, we did get to see a lot of our country from a very different perspective. Seeing America from the Waterway was a lot like train travel. We saw the backyards of a lot of houses and buildings.

In addition to traveling north to stage the boat for the crossing, we had another objective during the trip. An important stop on our ICW itinerary was to visit waterfront property in Kinsale, VA, we had purchased as the site of our future retirement home.

The lot, though a bit distant from any major urban area, consisted of two wooded acres located on an inlet of the Potomac River, with water deep enough to moor a sailboat. Anchoring *Act III* off the riprap we had installed on our shore, we dinghied in to plant our feet on our land and to revel at being part of a scene that, in May, was absolutely sublime.

Little did we realize then how much the adventure and experiences of this expedition would change us. At the time, our dream was to spend our later years in this calm, bucolic sanctuary, but by the time this transatlantic odyssey was over, we would become addicted to travel to foreign cities, and the notion of being stranded here in the boonies was no longer tolerable

Our souls nourished, we returned to the Chesapeake Bay and our route towards New York City. Two days later we were plowing up New Jersey's Atlantic coast north—only stopping to check out glitzy/tacky Atlantic City—on the home stretch. It was late May and the finish line was in sight when we doubled the cape at Sandy Hook and arrived at our destination, a marina in Atlantic Highlands, New Jersey, only a few miles from where Gale spent the years of her childhood.

With *Act III* now secure in a slip, and with Max in his carrier, we taxied to Gale's parents' house for what was to be a bittersweet reunion. The satisfaction we felt in having brought our beautiful sailboat all the way here was considerably diminished by the absence of Gale's father, who had died suddenly the year before. There had been many, many times that, as we enjoyed some special nautical experience, we would say, "Too bad Dad isn't here."

I have to admit that after four months on board, being in a house was very comfortable. I slept soundly that night, happily bereft of concern about anchors dragging or dock damage.

Gale's mother, Beverly, had agreed to care for Max while we continued on across the Atlantic and explored Europe, so with cat-sitting now solved, we began sorting through all the mail that had been forwarded from Puerto Rico.

Gale was in the living room going over several months' accumulation of bills and other correspondence while I sat in the dining room with my charts spread all over the big table, planning our route. Her first cry of, "What is this?" must have fallen on husbandly deaf ears, as I just continued with my research. Then, "Glenn! There's a registered letter here from the U.S. Department of Justice, marked 'Official Business' and addressed to you," did get my attention.

Now suddenly very alert, I looked up to see a very serious-looking envelope with a federal logo being waved in me. "Shit, what have I done now?" With shaking hands I picked up the envelope and tore it open.

I mumbled out loud phrases that jumped off the paper at me as I scanned the notice: "… seizure of your assets," "… statute…," illegal substances …"

Gale slumped in her chair, covered her mouth, and said, "Oh, my God!"

Motivated now to apply my full attention to the notification, I carefully perused the voluminous federal verbiage as I worked my way down the page, looking for details. The "asset" they were referring to was *Class Act*, the boat I sold to the Argentinian guy and for which … oh… the penny drops; now I get it. Now I know why he brought all that cash and checked out all those odd spaces. The shifty little shit must have been caught smuggling drugs with my boat.

But why me? It hasn't been my boat for six months. Then the second penny dropped. I had asked my lawyer to make out a bill of sale to sign, but with all the trip preparations going on, I forgot to send the Feds the documentation certificate with the change of ownership. Nervously, I called my lawyer in Puerto Rico who, after hearing my story, told me what steps to take so the DEA would leave me in peace. What a relief.

Now with any fear of federal detention gone, I could turn my efforts back to plans for our arrival the following week in the Big Apple.

Closing Circles

After her divorce in the Cayman Islands, Gale had taken her young daughters to New York City to start a new life. Refusing her parents' offer to come home, she had focused on Manhattan and begun looking for a job and a place to live. In the '80s, apartments in the City were very scarce. Unable to find a safe, affordable place for the three of them, and with school about to start, she moved the little family into the only space she could find, an unheated houseboat docked at the 79th St. Boat Basin on the Hudson River. Their stories about passing the winter on the flimsy, uninsulated craft are epic.

Then with a roof over their heads, she directed her efforts to finding work. Her unbelievable good fortune in finding an administrative/production position at a theater on Broadway was somewhat tempered by the modest paycheck, but it was an exciting, gratifying job with a future in the performing arts, a field she knew and loved.

Surviving their first winter in the City, this struggling, single mother was very relieved when in the spring they found a two-bedroom apartment in a respectable Upper Westside building.

Now settled into job and school, their foothold in the big city strengthened over the following few years. Then came the trip to Puerto Rico and our chance encounter. I would never forget that Gale had left the exciting milieu of theater and New York City to take a chance with me in the Caribbean, so I wanted her Upper Westside friends, colleagues, and family to see she hadn't made a mistake in her choice. To impress them I reserved, at great expense, a transient slip—next to Malcolm Forbes' yacht—at the same 79th St. Boat Basin and made plans for a lavish party on board *Act III*.

It was a sunny Memorial Day when we sailed north from Atlantic Highlands past the Statue of Liberty. I had a strong feeling that all we had done so far was only a prelude to our thrilling entrance into New York Harbor. The view that unfolded in front of us was like a travelogue: Brooklyn to my right, the Statue of

Liberty on my left, and the skyscrapers of lower Manhattan in front of me. What a sight.

This experience was one of several episodes during our travels that left me feeling a bit dizzy and disoriented. My immediate surroundings—the boat—were so familiar, but the territory we sailed through was totally incongruous. Here I was, passing the Twin Towers in the relative luxury of a yacht that had been a ramshackle, disabled vessel I had found in a tiny Puerto Rican fishing village. It was as though I had left home in my car one day for work and unexpectedly found myself driving it through the streets of Paris.

We made our way past the World Trade Center and the Empire State Building, and shortly thereafter reached our berth on the Hudson. With the party boat in place, we could now begin preparations for the festivities.

The following day's late afternoon sun bathed a repeat performance of our San Juan *Bon Voyage* party. But this time we had, along with the champagne and flowers, canapés from Zabars, and a string trio playing Bach from chairs set up in the bow. Gale, in a long blue and white sundress, graciously greeted old neighbors, buddies from work, sister, Wendy, her husband, Steve, and others as they stepped aboard. Living the dream. It doesn't get much better than this.

We Meet Our Crew

The party was also our way to get to know our fellow transatlantic crew members. I was concerned that they, seeing the luxury of this celebration, might get the wrong impression. Crossing the Atlantic would be no party. As a matter of fact, Gale had put her foot down and told me she would be going only as far as Newport. As she explained, "I grew up watching "Victory at Sea," and I don't plan to suffer several weeks of misery on the North Atlantic. Call me when you know your ETA and I'll fly to Lisbon."

Frankly, I didn't blame her. There was no need for both of us to be miserable.

Putting together a crew for this expedition was a surprisingly easy assignment. Once word got out that we were planning to cross the Atlantic, I was inundated with volunteers. All I had to do was eliminate the bad apples from the deluge of requests from young men and women blatantly lying about their sailing knowledge and experience and select four.

For our crossing crew I chose:

Sean: A good-looking, blond, stocky kid, Sean was relaxed and carefree as only a young man without responsibilities can be. Son of old friends of Gale's from the Caymans, and just out of his teens, he had the summer off from his culinary studies at Johnson & Wales. During the long voyage, his gastronomic and joke-telling skills would be greatly appreciated. But his innocence was evident by the awe he showed at the tall tales of sex and adventure the older crew members shared during our transatlantic bull sessions.

Mike: Son of a friend of a friend, Mike actually did have some sailing experience and had free time while home on leave from his banking job in Saudi Arabia. In his early thirties, he often exhibited a small smile that belied a somewhat aloof personality.

Andrea: Short, with straight dark hair, Andrea was the daughter of a well-known classical musician friend of Gale's from her days in New York. Working as crew on a day sail schooner that carried tourists through Manhattan's murky waters would have given her a leg up on a probable spot on the crew list if she had been a guy, but old male chauvinist pig that I am, I at first rejected her application. But since the woman's movement was really gaining steam—and with four women in my family—I got an earful of consciousness raising; I relented and agreed to take her on.

Alex: Tall, spare, and muscular, sporting a crewcut, cowboy saunter and flannel shirts, Alex had an air about him that said, "I'm an outdoorsman, and my milieu is the mountains and forests of the American West." While Alex was an earnest and sincere guy, the views and opinions he expressed about the many subjects we discussed during the long hours of sailing to Europe seemed to me to lack maturity and an understanding of the real world.

Alex was an acquaintance of Andrea, but more importantly, with Adam's head injury experience in mind, he was also an EMT. He and Andrea were in their mid-twenties and had sailed with me once from Ponce to St. Thomas. I was later to find out the other three crew members gave him the nickname "The Washington Weirdo."

Closing My Circle

With the New York celebration now over, with a great sense of anticipation, we left the boat basin the next day to motorsail around Manhattan Island via the Battery, the longer but more scenic route to Long Island Sound en route to Newport.

I have to say that Manhattan was a truly awesome sight as the skyline slid by to port. Also awesome in a way that gave me chills was the sight of the hard, inhuman structures of Rikers Island Prison that we passed as we continued east into Long Island Sound. The scenery began changing from clusters of multistory buildings to individual houses, and the softer, tree-lined coast told us we had arrived in suburban Long Island.

I also had a circle to close, and the afternoon of that first day, we arrived in Manhasset Bay, which bordered Great Neck, the town where I spent all those tempestuous years trying to grow up.

Unlike Gale, there was no one I wanted to invite to share the "triumph" of my return. This was a very personal visit for me, and once anchored I boarded the dinghy alone and motored to the dock of the neighborhood pool and park where I had spent my summer days, swimming and staring at the boats as they sailed by.

Making the tender fast to a cleat on the float, I walked up the ramp and encountered a scene like an image from my memory. A handful of teenagers were stowing sails from their small sailing prams. Some children were in the pool, taking a swimming lesson, and an older couple were stretched out on their beach chairs, enjoying the waning sun. I felt the nostalgia wash over me. Shaking

Retracing the route of my grandparents but in style

myself loose from this reminiscence, I returned to the present and took stock of where I was now.

Yes, traveling a couple of thousand miles in my own yacht had served as kind of a balm to the pain of the failures of my childhood. But what was more important to me at that moment was the realization that, rather than feeling victorious at my arrival here, I relished the knowledge that I was ready for the real test, crossing the Atlantic. And when I got to the other side, I knew I would not be the same person I was now.

Unlike Gale's pleasure from a reconnection with those with whom she shared a history, there was nothing like that here for me. Only a dead past. Pivoting both physically and philosophically, I spun on my heel and returned to my boat and my future.

A Familiarization Cruise

Now back on board after my episode of nostalgia, I gave the orders to get under way, and we struck out for the short hop to Greenwich, CT, from where the next morning we would leave for Newport, RI, our last port before the crossing.

The following day dawned gray and cold. Long Island Sound was choppy and chilly, a far cry from the summer boating playground we expected to find in June. Too bad, because our familiarization cruise would cover 115 miles—a day and a night—ending when we reached the refuge of Newport on Narragansett Bay. The time spent on the passage would provide an excellent opportunity for my newly arrived crew to get some experience with the boat and for me to get to know them better.

It quickly became apparent that our days of sunny, rhythmic broad reaching in the trade winds and placid motoring up the calm waters of the ICW were definitely over. Temperatures were in the frigid forties, and high winds from the east and six-foot waves resisted our efforts to make progress. Although the solid windshield and hardtop of our vessel protected us from most of the cold salt spray, nevertheless, we spent our first day huddled together in the cockpit, miserable, fighting seasickness (they say that the best cure for seasickness is to sit under a tree), and wearing our foul weather gear to ward off the cold, chilling spray as we beat our way east. At that point I thought to myself, "June weather could not be more unpleasant." That is until the rain began and what little sun we had enjoyed disappeared.

The differences between this trip and one of those starry-night, warm-water Caribbean passages soon became painfully more evident in another way as fog enveloped us. Staring through the rain-dappled deckhouse windshield as night began to fall, all I could see was a gray curtain surrounding us on every side. No stars, no shore lights, and no buoys.

Luckily, in an uncharacteristic fit of logical, conservative thinking, while in New Jersey I had had the presence of mind to add radar to the navigation aids we were already carrying. I knew it worked because the technician had turned it on to explain the controls and prove that he should get paid.

So otherwise blind, I decided this was the time to fire up this electronic marvel. Impatiently, I watched the dead gray screen turn to a deep sea green and begin to show dots of light. Great. It worked, but what the hell were all those big and little dots scattered over the screen?

If we were to avoid becoming freighter fodder, I would have to figure out how to use this important technology, *fast*.

Only later, after arriving in Newport, when I had time to spend studying, did I encounter the following statement in the manual:

Using radar for navigation does require practice and experience. Keep in mind that after a few weeks of practice, you will be able to read the scope just as easily as you might a chart.

A few weeks. We're in a busy shipping lane. I don't even have a few minutes.

I felt like I was in one of those dreams when you are falling, falling, and just waiting for the "splat" that will end everything. I could tell by their tight jaw muscles that my crew was also feeling very apprehensive as we stared at the radar screen that showed us to be completely surrounded by blips I swear all looked like they were heading right for us. With all hands in the cockpit—except Gale, miraculously below, cooking—we were five pairs of eyes straining to see if any of those blips might materialize into some large floating object that could crush us like an eggshell.

Every approaching blip prompted a ragged assortment of hailing hollers and frenzied bursts of honking from our little aerosol foghorn, but during all those hours of foggy darkness, we never actually saw another vessel. What a way to spend the night.

Thank God for the dawn's early light. Now we could again begin to discern shapes in the water and their movement. I was exhausted from the tension and lack of sleep, nearly deaf from the constant blowing of the foghorn, and more than a little seasick. (Yes. I do sometimes get seasick.) Not a very positive omen for a North Atlantic crossing.

But as the day progressed, the sky cleared and the sun warmed and dried this now slightly more seasoned crew. This good news was soon tarnished when the engine started running rough as though it had fuel intake problems. Sounding more and more irregular as the hours went by, the big diesel did, nevertheless, continue to punch through the seas, and before noon we had the Point Judith lighthouse in sight. Newport was just beyond.

With Newport now in range, I got on the VHF and requested a slip at the marina I had chosen as our temporary home. Their reply reminded me of Cornelius Vanderbilt's maxim: "If you have to worry about the cost of fuel, you shouldn't own a yacht." It wasn't fuel that was going to put a hole in my budget, it was the $200 a day summer transient rate for dockage. But what the hell, this is Newport.

Newport Departure

Why Newport? Although it put our starting point a hundred miles further from the Azores than leaving from Bermuda, I had chosen Newport as our staging port for several reasons. First, it gave Gale and me a chance to sightsee all the way up the Atlantic coast, visiting people and places as we traveled north. Second, most of our family lived within a half day's drive of Newport, including Gale's sister, who had a summer house just across Narragansett Bay in Saunderstown. (She had generously offered it as a venue for our transatlantic departure party.) Third, and probably most importantly, the availability of marine parts, equipment, and services—like a fuel polishing service—is minimal in Bermuda compared to their obtainability in this New England boating mecca.

A good thing too, as the heavy weather in the Sound—not even the North Atlantic—had exposed two major weaknesses with our preparations.

One: We found during the heavy weather that windows, hatches, and ventilation ports needed some real work to stop all the leaks that had suddenly appeared. The prospect of two or three weeks of wet beds and damp heads was more misery than any of us were willing to endure. Even though it might take more than a few days to get her watertight, we decided to dedicate whatever time necessary to get this problem resolved.

Two: Apparently, Andrea's vision of crossing the North Atlantic had not included the possibility of being cold, wet, scared, or having to wear foul weather gear that made taking a pee a huge inconvenience for anyone with female anatomy. Confirming my original sexist opinion, she quit the team.

This was a bit of a problem because it messed up our watch calculations. I had planned that, rotating days, one crew member would cook and the other four would be on watch, dividing up the 24 hours evenly in comfortable, two-hour watches. Although we didn't know it at the time, fortune was about to smile on us, and this lemon was to turn into sweet lemonade.

The very next day, as we sat in the cockpit discussing Andrea's defection, a short, bald, sort of elfin-looking young man walked up to our boat and asked if we needed crew. He was Dutch. His name was Arie. He was looking for a boat to give him a ride back to Europe after having spent the last 18 months hitchhiking around the world on sailing yachts. Boy, had he found the right boat.

I was at first quite reluctant to take on a total stranger, an outsider with whom we would be confined and intimately involved for several weeks. However, the guys took an instant liking to him and convinced me to take Arie with us. Their instincts were excellent. During the entire trip, he proved to be reliable, uncomplaining, affable, and a great asset.

As the days went by, I worked on our preparations list. Life raft, spare radio antenna, flares, etc., etc. It seemed as if there were no end to the list of safety stuff we would need. The situation reminded me of the Jack Benny bit where he's being mugged and the gun-toting robber says, "Your money or your life."

Benny says, "I'm thinking, I'm thinking."

The last few days were dedicated to straining the fuel again and buying some final provisions and odds and ends. Then out in the bay we practiced our MOB—Man Overboard—drill and tried out the spinnaker, leaving only three items open on my list.

1. Buying a Life Raft
2. The Farewell Party
3. Leaks

1. The life raft. We didn't expect to use it, but just in case …
   Just before leaving Puerto Rico I had read an article in a
   sailing magazine about choosing the right life raft. The
   article's author pointedly emphasized that the cruising
   captain should buy a life raft that was designed for a
   greater number of occupants than the crew who might
   use it. In essence he was saying, "Don't buy a four-man
   raft unless your crew is you and three young, sexy, naked
   women who are willing to take turns being pressed up
   against you."
       To have sufficient space he suggested that the life
   raft be designed for a capacity double the number of the
   crew you want to save. We were five souls, but 10-man
   life rafts were selling for more than $7,000. Standing on
   the showroom floor of "Life Rafts Are Us," I was trying
   to find a way to justify spending $6,000 for a compro-
   mise, eight-man raft, when the company's employee,
   noticing my reluctance, chimed in, "We have quite a
   few used rafts for much less, and they're all certified."
   That was all I needed to hear: "certified" and "less." I
   left a deposit and returned the next day to pick up a
   newly inspected and certified eight-man, used life raft
   for only $3,000.

2. The Farewell Party
   Gale's sister, Wendy, and husband, Steve, really went
   way out of their way to throw a great *Bon Voyage* shin-
   dig at their attractive waterside house in Saunderstown.
   Having my father, sister, and all our children together
   at the same time was truly a rare event. I wondered if

it was because they wanted to fete us as we left on our adventure or because they thought this might be their last opportunity ever to see me alive.

Hell, it was great that our kids showed they cared. With considerable pride and satisfaction, I looked at each of them and reflected on the adults they had become.

Ivy: My oldest. "Goal-Oriented Ivy" and her husband, Ricky. A computer and management virtuoso, and financially secure, Ivy was still living in Ponce and on a positive career and life track from which she would not easily be detoured, no matter what happened to me. I reveled in her respect any time she called me for business advice.

Jill: Still slim, creative, and single, she had chosen to surrender herself to the rigors of having a big time career on Madison Ave. Long hours, lots of pressure, big bucks, and an apartment in Manhattan. I had to laugh though. As a little girl she would use her crayons to draw pictures of houses with gardens and white picket fences where she planned to live when she grew up. Like bamboo, she was both delicate looking but strong enough to bend a long way without breaking.

Adrienne: America's Sweetheart, Adrienne had married a lovely guy the year before and was living in a small house in the suburbs of Charleston, SC. Doing well in an outside sales job, she seemed, after so much woe in school, to be on the road to having a nice, normal family. Normal? Will any of us be "Normal?"

Andrew: Ohio State University had become Andrew's religion. I wondered how this logical, likeable kid, another non-scholar, would do when he graduated with his marketing degree and tried to make a career in the bruising world that awaited him. And would he allow me to give him any guidance?

The party was great. Plenty of conversation, good food and drink, and the festivities ended with a heartfelt emotional toast to our success, some cheers, and some tears.

And finally,

3. Leaks

The fact that we still had a couple of days of caulking and sealing deck leaks made the celebration somewhat anticlimactic, but facing a North Atlantic crossing, we had no choice. I was greatly appreciative that Andrew stayed on. He was a great help, and thanks to his efforts, we would be ready to depart on the following Friday.

Oops. Friday would be June 13th. Could there be a less propitious departure date? Screw omens. We're going.

As I look back at those last days in port, I am surprised that although I was about to embark on a truly perilous undertaking, one in which my survival and that of four other human beings depended on the thoroughness of my preparations and the caliber of the decisions I would make, fear and anxiety were the furthest things from my mind. Completely focused on my lists and the tasks to be accomplished in Newport, I never lifted my gaze from the lists or the boat to take in the huge ocean in front of us and the challenge we would face.

Then Friday arrived. There was no starting gun, marching band, or showy send-off ceremony. No one even mentioned the voyage as we quietly went about our business, stowing lines and fenders as though we were only going to make a short hop across the bay. Then the big boat, motor throbbing, slowly parted from the dock, turned, and directed her bow towards the sea, leaving Andrew standing there alone.

Once underway I turned and glanced one last time to say good-bye to the now familiar Newport waterfront. Once passed the town, I was pleasantly surprised to see that Andrew had jumped into his car and was shadowing us, driving along the shoreline. When at Brenton Point he could go no further, he stopped, got out, and leaned against the little white rental, arms crossed, watching as the distance between us grew.

Only then, for the first time did I experience a strong, hollow feeling of fear. A fear that there was a real possibility I might never see him or the others I loved ever again. A great sob suddenly swelled in my chest. I fought to hold it in. I had to. I could only display to my crew the image of the stoic, stalwart captain that I wasn't.

Andrew and I watched each other until one of the crew asked me a question about a buoy off our bow. I looked, answered, and when I again looked back, Andrew was gone.

Crossing to the Azores

With each wave we crested, we moved farther and farther away from our normal existence and towards weeks of living something totally unknown.

It's interesting that when people find out we spent almost a year sailing to and around Europe, they don't ask things like, "What was it like to sail the Costa del Sol? How did you handle navigating in strange seas? Did you enjoy your exploration of the famed Old World port cities?"

They just want to know what it was like to cross the Atlantic. Okay, here it is:

I can tell you that our first week of sailing was, for me, excruciatingly boring and uncomfortable. It was like the movie "Groundhog Day." Each morning was just a repeat of the day before. The same green seas and gray skies. In my case our continually tilted home and the constant motion of the waves kept me in a state of incipient seasickness. Off watch if I wasn't sleeping, I spent my time reading. About a book a day.

On the fifth morning I looked out my porthole at the immense gray ocean and suffered a massive panic attack. I wanted out. I was so desperate to get off the vessel that I contemplated faking appendicitis in hopes that the Coast Guard would fly out and take me off the damn boat. But the reality was even worse. We were now too far from land for them to reach us. That was really scary.

Oh, God. How I wanted this trip over. Worse, the fresh winds we expected to find in the North Atlantic had gone somewhere else, and for the first seven days, we barely averaged 100 miles a day, adding to my frustration. At this rate we wouldn't see land for several weeks.

Unlike so many long distance sea travelers, I did not use the many hours at sea to peruse philosophical subjects like analyzing my past life or spinning plans for my future. I went through the motions of standing my watch and navigating; I felt I was somewhere else. Living in the books, I read when there was nothing but empty hours. Sleeping. Like the trick of removing my consciousness from my body while suffering in the dentist chair.

None of the other crew complained out loud, so neither did I, the stoic, John Wayne-style captain. I was to find out after the trip that my crew never shared my negative feelings.

For example, here is an excerpt from the log that Arie kept:

The first couple of nights, we watch video's in the evening, the first one some sort of soft porn mix. The first item in that mix is called: "The Dutch Master," so from that moment onward ... After one week the television set got a big shot of salt water and died.

To me it was also heartening to read:

This is really a comfortable vessel, even with towels for everybody, a big fridge and lots of food, fresh as well as canned. In the first two weeks I eat an indecent amount of M&M's, then I go into rehab with dried raisins. Furthermore, there is filet mignon, 5 sorts of cheeses, home fries for breakfast, and so on, and so on. It's hard not to grow really big in this place.

And also:

Best moments: waking up and getting coffee and fresh pancakes or fresh bread; after dinner with coffee and cigar on the poop deck; night watches under a starry sky.

Gale's decision not to be a part of the transatlantic crew had been a good one. She would have been aghast at our lack of hygiene and poor eating habits. A proper diet and proper table settings are not priorities for five guys on a sailboat. She would have been terribly exasperated at our disregard for the amenities she usually provides for our guests.

Despite being big enough to offer ample personal space for each crew member, the boat's hobby-horsing over the large swells made trying to sleep in the bow staterooms like trying to rest on a mechanical bull, so crew members were sleeping all over the boat. (Again, Gale would have been irate.)

Axel and Sean had, unable to sleep in the leaping V-Berth, jammed the huge amount of supplies originally stored in the crew's quarters in the stern—originally called "the garage," later on, re-baptized to "the Den of Punani"—in to this bow space, and moved into the more stable, stern sleeping space.

The other two slept on settees in the salon. Only I, with my mid-ships bed, slumbered in my assigned room, although I sometimes shared my bed with Arie out of pity. This was a mixed blessing, as somehow, even after all the fitting and sealing done in Newport, there was still a constant drip, drip from the hatch right over my bed, so I had to sleep in my foul weather gear.

That was the first week.

The second week stopped being boring. I guess the word "numbing" would be a more descriptive adjective. I no longer thought about ways to improve the lonely, tiresome, uncomfortable conditions; I just concentrated on enduring.

Sailing heeled over for such a long time had become pretty tedious and irritating. It didn't take too long to get awfully tired of living on a 45-degree angle and having everything I put down slide to the floor and break. What's more, even after ten days at sea, I still felt a lingering, constant trace of seasickness. My salvation was that Gale had hidden surprise caches of Snickers bars around the boat, and I enjoyed searching for them, not only for the reward but to break up the monotony. I had no trouble keeping the candy bars down.

Here are some other impressions:

Cooking: It didn't take long for us to realize that Sean's professional cooking talents were being totally squandered by making him stand watch. We all agreed it would be better to adjust our schedules to take over his watch so he could spend all his time juggling pots and pans and continue producing some really excellent meals.

Danger: We saw far more whales then we did ships, and some strange optical illusions put us on edge from time. During the almost 2,000-mile leg to the Azores, I was lucky not to have to deal with anything mechanically serious, as help was a *long* way away.

Recreation: When not sleeping, we read and traded reading matter. We gave up fishing when for the third time sea birds took the lures we used for trolling. Pulling in a half-drowned bird and trying to remove the hook embedded in his bill was a heart-rending process.

Azores Landfall

It is difficult for me to accurately express the emotion I felt at that moment when the latest faint brown smudge on the horizon actually materialized into the land I so strongly wanted to reach. Land that offered safety, comfort, and success.

Our first landfall was the island of Flores, the westernmost of the isles that make up the Azores archipelago. Thanks to high winds our second week out, our speed had increased significantly, and we were able to cover the 1,980 miles to this island in only 14 days. Probably a record for a sailboat that cost us less than a low-end Mercedes-Benz.

The crew celebrates its arrival in Flores, Azores

As we motored into the lee of the steep island and headed up to drop the sails, I was struck by an appreciation of the sudden sensation of tranquility. It wasn't just the lack of ocean rollers. For the first time in two weeks, there was no wind whistling past our ears, the boat was upright and stable, and we had something to look at outside the boat.

The small harbor of the village of Lajes on the island's south coast hosted a dozen or so sailing craft like ours and a handful of work boats. From the concrete pier, a cobblestone lane bordered by diminutive stone houses led up the hill to a small plateau on which was perched a charming little Portuguese village.

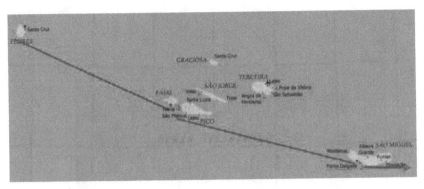

The Azores Islands

A light drizzle did little to dampen our spirits, as each of us experienced, in his own way, the awe of having concluded the greater part of an undertaking that only a small group of—may I say it?—other daredevils have accomplished.

Gliding along in an almost spiritually subdued atmosphere, we searched in silence for a spot to plant our good old American anchor into a European seabed. Standing at the bow, I fed out the chain rode as we backed down. After a couple of shudders, I could feel the anchor set, and I turned towards my crew. Now smiling broadly, I gave the thumbs-up sign.

At my signal an exuberant, simultaneous shout went up, and a savage hugging and back-slapping bout commenced. I rushed below to take out the bottle of champagne I had been saving for this moment. We toasted each other, the boat, the Atlantic Ocean, world peace, and whatever else we could think of until the bottle was empty.

Now secure and having expended all our excess energy, it was time for me to go ashore and deal with whatever authorities awaited me. The crew freed the deflated inflatable dinghy from her confinement below and filled her with foreign air so that she could carry me to a place I never would have guessed I would ever visit.

While they were dealing with the dinghy, I showered and, for the first time in two weeks, put on fresh clothes.

Is it heaven, or Flores?

Landing, I could see the cement wharf was deserted, but just up the hill on the road to the quaint stone village, there was a small restaurant. Wobbling as I walked on dry land for the first time in two weeks, I climbed the steep street to the little café. Upon opening the door to this small eatery, I was hit by a robust blast of light and noise emanating from the warm interior. Inside, a couple dozen sailors were deep in conversation. The proprietor, who must have seen hundreds of glassy-eyed, recent arrivals like me wander in, read my mind. Waving me over, he pointed to a telephone at the end of the bar with a tag that said "Customs-Doune-Aduana," and he said, "Direto." After some clicks I heard a human voice communicating in my second language, Spanish. The official who answered told me

I should handle the formalities by checking in at the main customs office on the nearby island of Faial when I got there.

Red tape temporarily dealt with, I thanked the man behind the bar and returned to the boat to report to the crew and bring them back up to the bistro for drinks and a celebratory meal. Once back at the café, we took turns renting the establishment's telephone to call loved ones and share the joyous news that we were now safe on land, and that the longest, most arduous part of the trip was over.

After two weeks of rocking, rolling, and leaning to one side, the simplicity of moving around on terra firma was a joy. If I took three steps forward, I moved three steps forward. No handholds needed. Anything put down stayed where it was. Including my meals. It was wonderful. Everything was dry and predictable. Delightful.

While we were anxious to move on, we accepted a reasonable offer from a man with a van to take us on a tour of the island the next day. I am so glad we did.

Flores is an aesthetic paradise. The lofty green mountains are a tapestry of foliage in varying shades of green, splashed with swaths of black volcanic rock and an overabundance of blue hydrangea. High wispy waterfalls ended in deep green valleys. Quaint stone villages, abandoned by the natives who had gone elsewhere to find work, were being bought up by rich Europeans who used them as summer vacation homes.

We would have loved to stay longer and see more, but we still had to check in with the main Portuguese customs office 125 miles away in Horta, the capitol of the island of Faial.

Horta, with its large harbor and ample facilities, is the preferred destination for transatlantic sailors who have been so long at sea. Here were stores, restaurants, and an airport from which Mike, whose vacation was running out, could get a flight back to his banking job in Saudi Arabia.

The overnight sail was a cinch, and, although there was a mountain of papers to fill out, we passed customs and immigration inspection without a hitch. A farewell dinner for Mike, and a tour of the town's bars and restaurants, brought us back in contact with the real world.

With a couple of days of the pleasures of the land in Faial under our belts, we left for Ponta Delgada, the capitol of San Miguel Island and home to about half the citizens of the Azores. From here we would begin the final, 750-mile passage to Portugal.

The overnight 150-mile voyage—a puddle jump for veteran ocean sailors like us—was made memorable by a visit from a pod of porpoises during the night. While sailing to the Azores, we had sporadically encountered these friendly marine mammals, but that moonless night was a very different, nearly ethereal experience.

Unseen until spotlighted by a burst of light, like some sort of oceanic meteor, a single porpoise leaped and splashed in the sea off our bow. This was its call to us to watch their show.

In the dark we couldn't tell how many of them were swimming with us, but one after another of these aquatic acrobats thrilled us with their pyrotechnic stunts in the dark sea. Every movement of the playful animals was discernable in the dark water by the spirals of light they and the bioluminescent plankton created as the porpoises swam alongside, spinning just a few feet underwater.

One after another they shot past our bow, leaping into the air and, instead of the usual porpoise clean re-entry, cannonballed back into the water, creating bursts of light when they hit the surface. About ten minutes after the show started, they were gone. What an experience.

The night held no more surprises for us, and the next afternoon found us berthed at the Ponta Delgada seaport's seawall. The setting was very different and the magic gone. The view of our surroundings was dominated by massive concrete docks and walls and the stink of the oily water around us. What's worse, the port was so crowded we and most of the other transient boats were tied three deep to the quay. The crew members of the two boats tied outside us were very respectful, but nonetheless, the constant traffic across our deck at all hours was very unsettling.

As I looked back at the voyage thus far I felt that for a bunch of guys who only a few weeks previously didn't really know each other—especially Arie—we had gotten along well. Spending all that time in the pressure cooker that is a sailboat, sailing far from land with no fights and no resentment, was an accomplishment. I was very proud of my crew.

However, during the last few days in the Azores, my interaction with Alex seemed to include a growing element of conflict. On the boat, decision-making was, by plan, a process in which I always tried to include all the crew. I would listen to comments and suggestions, but as the oldest and most experienced sailor on board—not to mention being the owner—in the end my decision was final.

Now as we prepared for a voyage of "only" 750 miles to Lisbon, we clashed when Alex heatedly disagreed with some of my choices about the preparations for the voyage to Portugal. With a week of sailing still ahead of us, I was concerned about what seemed to be a deterioration in our relationship.

The Chickens Come Home to Roost

With our last leg about to start, I left the boat to call Gale and give her an estimated ETA based on probable arrival six to seven days hence. The finish line wasn't in sight, but it sure was closer.

As I walked back to the boat after the call, and our moment of departure for Europe loomed, another panic attack swept over me. I was overwhelmed by a flood of emotions. Unidentifiable dangers clouded my mind, and the prospect of another week of wretched boredom made me want to vomit. The world was spinning, and I had to lean against a wall to steady myself.

"Why take on the risk and misery again?" I thought. "Maybe I could find someone to buy the boat here so I would not have to go to sea again. Then I could fly home and leave all this behind me."

Yes, that frightened little crybaby kid was still inside me, but now, as a man and with my responsibility as captain, I had no choice but to find some way to bury this feeling of terror and fear of defeat. I felt that if I didn't, the structure of the adult I had fashioned over the last 15 years would fracture, and I would splinter into something that might never be put back together again. I took a deep breath, composed myself, and walked towards the boat.

Once there I busied myself with the details—half hoping the list was longer—of readying for our imminent departure. A few hours later we had been liberated from our concrete corral, and in bright sunshine and moderate winds, we left the harbor.

The wind was averaging 15 kts. from the north, just the conditions that *Act III* loved. Soon the majestic 8,000-foot summit of the volcano on the island of Pico, the easternmost Azorean island, was behind us, and there was only ocean in front. At this rate we should be in Lisbon in just five or six days.

It was July 4th, and that night we celebrated Independence Day at sea with fireworks we had stowed aboard for the occasion. There was great gaiety as we toasted the USA, Holland … and the Cayman Islands, for good measure.

A pod of large whales found us the next day, passing so close we could smell their fishy breath. Wow. What a trip. What a great experience. And in less than a week, we would be in Portugal. We were feeling so high, with everything going so well, that the nagging spectre of departing on Friday the 13th had been forgotten.

July 5th was to be our day of reckoning. Never in my life had I felt so alone as I did at that moment in the dark of night, hundreds of miles from dry land, when I realized I was now on a sailboat that was sinking. The crisis snuck up on us in a very insidious way.

It was early in the afternoon, and Sean was on watch as we beam reached at high speed in six- to eight-foot seas. I was in my bunk, reading what must have been my 20th book of the trip, when I felt a stout thump that came from the area of the bow and resonated through the hull.

Leaping from my bed, I rushed up the companionway to the cockpit and asked Sean what had happened. Appearing very nonchalant, Sean shrugged and replied that he also had felt the shock but had noticed nothing out of the ordinary in the sea.

If a boat begins to leak, the water will accumulate in the bilges. If our hull had been breached, by opening the interior engine room doors, I would be able to see water in the bilges. Checking to be sure we had not suffered any damage, I shined my light into every corner of the boat's hull and, finding nothing unusual, went back to my bed, my book, and the sleep that lessened the terrible monotony of the trip.

This was to be the perfect example that proved the authenticity of that old saw: "Definition of Sailing: Days of boredom punctuated by moments of stark terror."

It wasn't until Arie left the cockpit at midnight to wake me for my watch that we had our first inkling something was very wrong. Descending the four-step companionway ladder in the dark, he was stunned when his last step created a loud splash. Believe me, he had no problem getting my attention with his urgent cry. "Glenn, wake up, I think we're sinking!"

Jolted immediately awake, I leaped off my bed and with my bare feet confirmed Arie's observation. I grabbed my flashlight and strode through the ankle-deep water to the engine room access doors. Snatching them open, I could see, even in the dim light, an ocean of water sloshing back and forth in the bilges, nearly lapping at the tops of the batteries. Once the water reached their terminals, the batteries would short, and we would lose lights, radio, and most importantly, the pumps. Without pumps our chances of saving the boat were slim.

I felt that—pardon the expression—sinking feeling again, the same emptiness filled with dread I had felt when I had dropped the ball, brought home a dreadful report card, lost my little sailboat, or hit the reef off Culebra. But this was not the time for self- recrimination. I had to *do* something.

The first thought that popped into my head was: Oh, shit, I'm in the middle of the Atlantic Ocean with three people on board who trusted me to take them safely to land, and now we're sinking. Perhaps saving $3,000 by buying a used life raft wasn't such a good idea. That's only $750 a life. How am I going to get out of this mess? But then a calmness came over me as I started to formulate a plan.

Step #1 was a no-brainer. Get the damn water level down so we wouldn't lose our electrical system. (Apologies to Robert Redford, but the film "All is Lost" was a load of improbable crap.)

Step #2: Empty the boat to uncover the source of the leak. I roused the rest of the crew.

The crew, galvanized by what was obviously a very serious situation, quickly presented themselves for my orders. Any lethargy accumulated during the weeks of tedium was swiftly shaken off as the three now alert guys in their underwear sat about carrying out the tasks I gave them. Sean was sent to get to work on the manual emergency pump. Alex and Arie became a two-man bucket brigade, using buckets and pots to empty seawater through the cockpit. I set about rigging a spare electric bilge pump, only taking two minutes away from my task to call Lisbon radio with a Pan-Pan and give them our position.

"Lisbon, we have a problem."

Step # 3: Find the source of the entry of so much water.

On my knees in the dimly lit engine room bilge, with my mouth barely above water, I crawled around, probing like a blind man with my hands for any flow of water that would give me a clue to the location of the leak.

Hunting in vain for what seemed like an eternity, I paused for a moment, and looking towards the stars I could see through the now open hatch, I pleaded, "Lord, if you'll get the water level low

enough so the batteries won't short out, I'll give up drinking!"
Then, lowering my head to a more prayerful, pious pose, I noticed
the water had now gone down enough for me to see that the batteries were safe, so I quickly added, "Thanks anyway, Lord, but I
think we've got this under control."

As time passed we were greatly relieved to note that our efforts
seemed to be having a positive effect. The height of the water inside
the hull was receding, slowly but surely. By 3 a.m. we had the
bilges dry enough to be able to detect a small but steady stream
of water was flowing into the bilge well from somewhere forward.
Elated, we knew that if we followed the water upstream—towards
the bow—we would find the source of the leak.

Quickly ripping up the carpet covering the center hall cabin sole
to look below the floor only served to remind me that a previous
owner had glued in a solid wood parquet floor as a cabin sole,
and there were no longer any hatches to open to inspect the hull
below. If we wanted to find out what was happening under the
fancy floor, we would have to chop it up.

Despite the urgency of our circumstances, I couldn't get out
of my mind the concern that even if we were successful and
made it home safely, I would have to explain to Gale why we had
destroyed the interior of her boat. But for now, however, this task
was a matter of life and death, so we got out a circular saw and
crowbar and start cutting away at the thick wooden floor tiles.

We began by ripping out a section of the engine room bulkhead.
This gave us a place to start. Connected to our precious 110-v
supply of electricity, the spinning teeth of the power saw tore their
way into the beautiful walnut veneer with a wailing sound that,
while disconcerting, also gave us the feeling that we were taking
serious steps to solve our problem.

The team of three took turns: one cutting the floor, one prying
up the cut sections, and the third with a flashlight, inspecting the
hull as we went along. Three big guys wedged into the passageway
moved slowly forward, concentrating on cutting a slot along the

wooden sole. Foot by foot we slowly worked our way forward, creating a gouge about two inches wide as we went.

Methodically, we continued cutting our way towards the bow. Past the master stateroom, then past the guest stateroom. I cursed that same long hallway that had so impressed me when I first saw the boat. By 4 a.m. we had cut 20 feet of floor, and still all we had found was the same small, steady stream coming from further forward.

Past the guest head we continued, cutting and hacking our way beyond the bulkhead and door frame to the V-berth, but we could go no further, as the bow stateroom was jam-packed with stuff that had been relocated from the "garage" in the stern to accommodate Alex and Sean. Before we could make any further headway, we had to form another bucket brigade to move fenders, tools, fishing tackle, and other assorted junk to somewhere else to clear the floor. With the sole now finally exposed, we continued cutting past the V-berth bulkhead, and then we saw it. Hallelujah.

Just above the keelson on the starboard side, a few feet back from the stem, was a bulge about four inches in diameter and one inch high, indicating that something had hit us with considerable force. Splinters of fiberglass surrounded a small hole in the middle of the bulge that allowed a small but steady trickle of water to enter the boat. With the automatic bilge pump switch not working, during the eight hours before discovery, a hell of a lot of water had accumulated, creating a serious problem.

The elation of having found the cause was tempered by the challenge of finding a way to stem the flow.

Alex, probing the lump commented, "The blow seems to have softened the fiberglass in the bulge. Maybe if we apply some pressure to it, the lump will flatten out and close the hole."

Sean chimed in, "Okay, but we still have to seal it somehow."

A light bulb went off in my head. Making lemonade out of our lemons, I suggested, "Suppose we cover a piece of wood from the chopped up floor with a slice of the torn carpet. If we slather silicone sealant on the patch of carpet and press it into place with the car jack we have—how about that for being prepared—I think it will stop the seepage."

That's what we did, and it was 100% effective at stopping any water from entering the boat.

While it was the crew's consensus that our patch would hold, we did not feel confident enough to tarry, so with the engine at fast cruise, we moved at nearly hull speed toward land and safety.

The dawn again gave us confidence, and after a little catch-up sleep, we quickly returned to our routines with no mention of the life-and-death drama we had experienced the previous night. The fright of that night was replaced by focus on our imminent arrival in Europe and the security of dry land. Back to watch rotation, preparation of lunch, and a sense of normalcy. The one exception sort of dropped out of the sky when we least expected it.

Feeling that the crew deserved a reward for their all-night battle to save the boat, I told the guys we were going to break the "one drink a day" rule I had imposed upon commencing the voyage and celebrate our success with a party at sunset.

Even at 6 p.m. the summer sun was warm, and the boat was moving along beautifully. Pulling from the fridge a special brie Gale had given us, I put it on a plate, along with the least soggy crackers I could find, and broke out four bottles of Tinta Barroca Portuguese red wine I had bought in the Azores.

Laying out our gaily-colored deck cushions, I called the crew to the deck lounge for a real celebration. "Come on, guys. Let's drink like civilized people do on land!"

I didn't have to say it twice.

We poured and toasted, and by the time we had emptied two bottles, we were feeling very relaxed and loosey-goosey. We were discussing what we must have hit (the majority thought a floating shipping container) when suddenly, the VHF radio came alive, and I heard a call. "*Act III, Act III*, this is Portuguese Air-Sea Rescue 912. Do you read me? Do you read me?"

Stunned, I put down my glass and rushed to the radio. "This is *Act III*. Over," I said, mirroring the puzzled look I was getting from the crew. A vaguely Latin-accented voice replied, "*Act III*, this is the Portuguese Air Force. We will arrive at your location in approximately two minutes. Stand by."

Oh, shit. What have I done? My radio call last night was a "Pan-Pan"—urgent problem—not a "Mayday," which, because lives are at stake, would have called for an immediate response from rescue personnel. Damn, now they've sent someone out here, and I'll probably get a huge bill.

Well if they flew all the way out here because they thought we were in trouble, we better look like we're in trouble. My order, "Hide the wine!" sat the crew to stuffing the wine and snackies out of sight. The last bottle had just disappeared under the cushions when a huge, four-engine, propeller-driven transport plane broke out of the clouds behind us.

If I hadn't already realized how quiet sailing is—even with the engine going—it was underscored by the incredible roar emitted by the aircraft as it zoomed past us at just about masthead height, shaking the deck and everything on it. Once I could hear again, I reached for the mike, but before I could open my mouth, the same voice was on the speaker. "*Act III*, is all well?"

"Yessir," I replied. "No more emergency. Over."

"*Tudo bom*. We had to do a training flight and decided to use your vessel as a target. Bye-bye." And then as though it had never been there, the plane was gone, and there was no noise but our engine and the waves as they slid by.

Now safe from critical, disapproving eyes, we retrieved the wine and cheese from their hiding places and returned to our celebration. As the bottles emptied, the conversation turned again to the extraordinary happenings of the last 24 hours.

Having survived a life-threatening event may have been what prompted Alex to share with us a story that gave me a better understanding of his hostility to my management style.

Three years before he and a friend had made a trip to do a technical climb of a 14,000-ft. peak in the Rockies. Arriving a little later in the day than would be optimum, they were debating the pros and cons of starting immediately or waiting for an earlier start the next day when a guy about my age stepped up and told them he knew the mountain well. "I have lots of experience. Don't worry, come with me, it will be okay to start now."

He was convincing enough that they decided to follow him up the mountain. The sad consequences of putting their complete trust in him was that, instead of safely returning to the base camp, nightfall found them roped together, trapped on the mountain in the midst of a raging storm. Thunder and lightning was all around them as they hugged the rock face, scared and miserable in the bitter cold. Then when they thought things couldn't get worse, the "older, experienced" leader was struck by a bolt of lightning. The victim went limp and dropped off the escarpment, lifeless. Roped together, only the extraordinary strength of the two young men kept them from a fatal fall.

When day dawned, unable to descend with this dead weight, they decided that to save their own lives, they had to cut the corpse loose. The boys shuddered as the body tumbled down the rocky mountainside, causing considerable mental trauma to both young climbers.

Now I could make sense out of the situation when we were leaving the Azores when as captain I had made a number of decisions that affected all of us. Lacking unanimous agreement among the crew, after explaining my logic I had terminated the discussion with the phrase, "I am older and have the most experience. We will do it my way." It was clear his experience had a lot to do with the undercurrent of conflict I had sensed from Alex.

Of course I still had plenty of reason for self-recrimination regarding the near sinking. I should not have accepted the circumstance of the automatic switch on the bilge pump not working. I hadn't wanted to face the problem, as I wasn't sure I could repair it, and working on it would require me to be head down in the smelly, sloshing bilge. A sure way to induce serious seasickness.

So not being a stodgy guy in a plaid flannel shirt, I had ignored the problem. Worse, since I had done nothing to repair it, I should have been more attentive to the condition of the bilge.

With the engine now running at fast cruise speed and the wind on our beam, we cut through the moderate seas like a destroyer at flank speed. The remaining days flew by in fast forward.

Axel's story and the memory of my failure stayed with me for several days but all this was forgotten on the sixth morning when the mountains of the Extremadura rose from the straight horizon. A wave of elation washed over me. There was Europe, right in front of us, and nothing was going to stop us now.

Lisbon-The Finish Line

During all our years sailing the Caribbean, to me our landfalls never became routine. The anticipation of reaching our next destination, and the fulfillment I always felt upon arriving, were a thrill, even after a passage of only 25 or 30 miles. However, none of these previous experiences had prepared me for the sudden flood of emotion that engulfed me when the coast of Portugal began materializing on the horizon through the gray dawn.

Deep in my emotional vault, hidden so they would not bring bad luck, were the emotions I planned to let free once we had safely crossed the Atlantic. Now like bubbles in a champagne glass, all the excitement and satisfaction I had suppressed while planning and making this voyage percolated up into my consciousness. Not an explosion exactly, more like a steady seeping of exhilaration into the empty spaces in my soul. I felt, for the first time in my life, complete.

The day was summer bright, and Lisbon's Tagus River was an almost Caribbean blue. The autopilot, dependable as always, was in charge of the boat, so we were free to let go of our responsibilities to our craft and lose ourselves, each one in his own way, in his own thoughts. Shaken from our reveries by the gradually heavier river traffic and the sight of the buildings, cars, and people walking along the shore, we again picked up the thread of our voyage to deal with the last steps. We were approaching a bustling city, and there, somewhere on this foreign continent, our loved ones awaited our safe arrival. Included were Gale, Sean's parents, and Alex's girlfriend, who had flown over to be with him.

Despite all my meticulous preparations, somehow I hadn't researched places to dock, so I had only a vague idea about where we could land. The cruising guide suggested the Alcântara docks. Hand steering now to dodge the tugs and freighters of this major port, we searched the endless commercial waterfront for a haven, but each time we stuck our bow into what seemed like a potential place to tie up, we were waved away. Finally, on July 10, 1997, near noon, locating an open space among a bunch of local fishing boats on the cement wharf, we hung our fenders and sidled up to the quay.

Unlike the merriment of our arrival in the Azores, my mood was somewhat subdued. I sensed more feelings of fulfillment, satisfaction, and relief than jubilation. I will never forget the sight as our first dock line lassoed to the huge cast iron mooring cleat; we were actually connected to the land on the other side of the Atlantic Ocean.

Now with a whole continent holding us in place, and before dealing with the chores of organizing and cleaning the boat, we set about finding a way to inform our families that we were alive and had arrived in Lisbon.

I could see a discolored old aluminum and glass telephone booth tucked in against one of the dirty, corrugated steel buildings on the wharf, and as captain I got to use it first. Dumping my Escudos into the strangely shaped machine, I heard a dial tone and, after a few false starts, was thrilled to reach the front desk at the hotel where Gale had been waiting since the day before.

I desperately didn't want to leave a "We're here" message and was exuberant when, after the forth European-style chirp, I heard Gale's voice saying, "Hello."

All I could think of to say was, "We're here!"

A statement only slightly dramatically exceeded by her reply, "Thank God!"

"Get Sean's parents and Alex's girlfriend and get into a taxi. Tell them to go to the Alcântara docks ... where the fishing boats are. You'll be able to see our mast from the road."

I could hear a combination of relief and joy in her voice when she said, "We'll be right there!"

Not long after I hung up, I saw a taxi picking its way through the detritus on the wharf towards us. Then it stopped maybe 50 yards away. I watched as a door opened, and there she was, her bright yellow dress a joyful welcome banner against the background of dull gray buildings. Sean's parents then exited the cab and began scanning the wharf for us. Our eyes met, and just like one of those hackneyed, sentimental TV commercials, we turned and ran towards each other, and as we embraced I swung her around 360 degrees. Her hair smelled of perfume, her skin was soft. After weeks of wrangling a large, fiberglass sailboat across the ocean in the company of men, I was mightily reminded how wonderful it was to be in contact with smooth, pliant, fragrant femininity.

After tears and hugs all around, our little group hurried to *Act III* where Sean, Alex, and Arie waited. An orgy of hugging and handshaking soon ensued. (I felt sorry for Arie, having no loved one to greet him). There was no simple answer to give Sean's father when he asked, "How was it?" There was too much to tell so, we begged off and asked for time to organize and clean ourselves and the boat, promising to "Tell All" over dinner that night.

Arie, having no one to share the night with, kindly offered to stand anchor watch on the boat so the rest of us would be free to leave. Grabbing a bag with essentials, I found another cab, and the group headed to our hotel.

Excited to be ashore and in Lisbon for the first time, I eagerly watched the scene outside the taxi's open window change as the gray backdrop of the wharf was transformed into a busy urban port scene of dark stone buildings. Continuing on, the cab climbed steep streets, and as though we had broken through a layer of clouds, we reached the higher center of modern Lisbon. Passing elegant white marble buildings, statuary, and rich green foliage, the cab stopped in the stylish Campos section where Gale had reserved our room at a hotel.

I could feel what had been a month's long need to be in a constant state of alertness drain away as I entered the stylish, carpeted lobby of the Rex, an attractive boutique hotel across from the Eduardo VII Park. An even more welcome sight was our cool, clean, spacious room, and the two bottles of red wine that awaited us. I closed the door, threw my bag on the desk and, reaching for Gale, declared, "Gale, baby, I have been waiting a month to get you alone!"

Not surprisingly, this pitiful attempt at foreplay did not achieve the desired result. Wrinkling her nose and fending me off, my usually affectionate spouse stopped me cold, saying, "Whoa, Captain, you smell like someone who hasn't had a bath in a long time." All too true. And I was wearing the pants I had worn for the previous two weeks.

"Get into the shower," she ordered. "You can wait a little longer. I know I can."

A short while later, showered, and with our physical relationship re-kindled, we lay between the soft sheets in our comfortable bed, sipped wine, and chatted.

"What have I missed while on the bounding main?" I asked.

"Not much. Your Mother is complaining that she doesn't feel well. Max and the kids are fine, and war hasn't broken out anywhere new. You're the one with the stories to tell. How was it?"

Wrapped as I was in a warm cocoon of comfort and love, I was far more focused on where I was in my life at that moment than the places I had recently been. I hesitated. Then as she snuggled up against me, she said, "Tell me what it was like."

I struggled to refocus my conscious mind from where I was at the moment to the memories, the highlights, trials and adventures we had experienced since leaving Newport. I began by sharing the details of our departure and the weeks of subsequent boredom. I tried to describe the excitement of landfall in the Azores and the loveliness of Flores. Little by little I worked my way along, setting the stage for the dramatic high point of my narrative: the near sinking. As I approached that part, I glanced down at her to emphasize the drama and was relieved to see she had fallen asleep.

The room was quiet and only the golden light and shadows created by the setting sun invaded our sanctuary. Alone with my thoughts and feelings, I rewound the day to that emotional moment in the morning when I saw the mountains of Portugal rise from the sea, the pleasing feeling of completeness I still felt, and I thought to myself, "What's next?"

I was a transatlantic veteran, truly ready to take on our next challenge, the 750-mile cruise along Europe's Mediterranean coast, before the crossing west and arrival at home.

But then what? What will I do when the trip is over? The penthouse at Cobian's Plaza in Puerto Rico was waiting for us. Would it continue to be our home? And having spent far too much of our money on this trip, how would I make a living?

At that moment I didn't know the answers and I didn't care. I just felt sure that whatever might happen, now I knew I could handle it.

Epilogue

We had arrived safely in Portugal, but the saga wasn't over. We would incur a bill of over $300 to dry clean all the clothes that had been saturated by the oily seawater sloshing into the closets and drawers on the night of the "sinking." The vessel had to be hauled for repairs up the Tagus River to a Portuguese shipyard. The refrigeration couldn't be run, months of frozen food supplies had to be offloaded and given away. Many thousands would be spent repairing the shipping container's damage to Act III's hull. The little hole in Act III's bow would suck up a lot more money than we could have possibly imagined and would set us back several weeks in our schedule.

We would, not without incident, successfully make our 750-mile tour of the ports and coasts of Western Mediterranean to Sardinia accumulating a rich store of experiences and memories until early November, when the placid waters of the summer Mediterranean suddenly turn into violent and volatile winter seas.

Unable to catch the seasonal window to return across the Atlantic and home because of the repair delay of three weeks, we pushed west through rapidly deteriorating weather from the Ballearic Islands back to Spain where we again hauled Act III.

Safely stored on land in Almeria for the winter while we returned to the USA, we planned to return the following spring.

But we would never see Act III again. Once home, we became so caught up in life on land that when the time arrived that we should have been making plans for our return, the emotional gap between us and the transatlantic homecoming of Act III had grown too wide to bridge to be sensible and so she was sold.

Gale went back to her "on hold" advertising and public relations business. The proceeds from the boat's sale came in very handy as I needed every cent I could scrape together to start a new business. Following many months of research and my customary cavalier attitude of "Oh, yeah, I can do this," I decided to open Puerto Rico's first Private Duty Nursing Agency. Needless to say, those who knew me well (especially Gale), were skeptical of this radical change in careers. But, the "new Glenn" made the switch from keeping machines running to building a business of 200+ employees who took care of older people in their homes. The timing was just right.

In less than ten years, we cashed out comfortably and retired. What did we do with the money? Bought a new sailboat, of course. And so the story continues.

But for now, thanks for listening. Have another drink.

ACKNOWLEDGEMENTS

I found that writing a book was relatively easy. However, writing a GOOD book has been devilishly difficult. Whatever this work may be, it would have been much worse without the wisdom and knowledge of literary professionals like Editor Nancy Barnes and my coach Professor Rachel Panton and friend Stacy Dymalsky.

Successful authors and journalists Jeff & Jinx Morgan took the time away from enjoying their perfect life in the British Virgin Islands to point out my mistakes and suggest improvements. Cousin Chris Bradley ruthlessly noted my many errors & blunders so I would not suffer the shame of publishing a less than perfect book. My brother Eugene, Kees Sanders, David Serrell, and the Sailing Chavurah did their part and Peter Somech delighted in pointing out the the few manuscript's shortcomings he could find.

Creative genius Rick Barrow tweaked the cover that my son Andrew shot.

But most of all I must acknowledge that I am a very lucky guy to have a forgiving, loving family who support me despite all my foolishness. Thank you all.

GLOSSARY

A

Anchor — Sleep-sensitive mooring apparatus that releases its hold when crew is no longer awake

Aye-Aye — Yes-Yes What the Bachelor says when a cute girl agrees to sail with him

B

Battcar — Bruce Wayne's pimpmobile

BBQ — Place to store uncooked meat

Bilge — Area on boat that exerts strong attractive force on nuts, bolts and important tools

Bilge Alarm — A water sensing device that emits a alarm when no one is within hearing distance

Bilge Pump — Vacuum-like apparatus for collecting paper and other loose objects in the bilge

Bunk — Statements from a Yacht Broker

Buoy — green & red (as in Anguilla) — Floating objects randomly placed by the Coast Guard

C

Catamaran — Oddly configured boats owned by fanatics

Caulk — Sound one hears when someone on board is seasick

Channel — Suggested perfume gift to be given to wife for yelling at her for dropping car keys overboard

Compass — Decorative item on power boats

Crew	Term used to describe on board helpers instead of what you really think of them
Customs and immigration	Government agency responsible for convincing foreign visitors not to return to their country

D

Dinghy	A small boat that has the ability to untie itself from docks or boats
Dinghy Dock	A dock never less than 6 ft high
Ditch" Bag	Container for carrying items to be used on the ICW

F

Fender-Bumper	Inflatable cylinders left hanging overboard while sailing to signify a novice boater
Fishing gaff	Being discovered fishing illegally
Fix	A rum punch to be imbibed when one's position can not be determined
Flashlight	A tool for ruining dry cell batteries
Fresh Water	Corrosive liquid to be mixed with alcohol before imbibing

G

Galley	Preferred area aboard for storing women
Grounding	An embarrassing situation that only happens to others

H

Harbor	Geographic term: Any coastal indentation that has a restaurant

Hatch	A horizontal aperture in the deck to attract rain when left open
Head (toilet)	A tiny space on a sailboat used to store human waste
Heel	What a husband must do for his wife if he wants permission to buy a boat
Hull speed	A theoretical maximum speed only attained when describing a boat that is for sale

I

Ice Chest	A cold space for storing food you need under 50 lbs of comestibles that will never be used.

J

Joker Valve	Component of marine toilet installed to assure the retention of human waste (see head)
Jury Rig	As in Hung Jury

K

Keel	Hull appendage used to determine the depth of a body of water
Knots	What you will find in a line you need to use RIGHT NOW

L

Lazarette	See "Ice chest"- A non-refrigerated version
Log Book	A nautical diary usually has writing only on the first few pages

M

Mooring whip	Item used to punish crew members who fail to picking up a mooring

Motorsailer	A sailing craft whose engine will not start when the wind dies

O

Oilskin	The first thing women do to their bodies during a Caribbean Sail

P

Poop Deck	Where a cruising crew keeps their cat's litter box
Porthole	An opaque aperture with inoperable enclosure
Prop Nut	Power boater looking for the perfect compromise speed vs economy
Propeller	Revolving device to move stern of a sailboat quickly to the side

R

Racing	Activity disparaged by cruising sailors unless encountering another boat on the same course
Regatta	A sporting event for people expelled by the Taliban for being too strict about rules
Rhumb Line	People awaiting their drinks in an organized fashion
Right of way	A well planned system to avoid collisions -Totally unknown to people in power boats
Rum Punch	Nectar of the gods

S

Seacock	Capt Jack Sparrow
sextant,	An important navigational device best left on the mantelpiece at home

Snatch Block	A chastity belt
Solo Sailing	Having to no one else to blame for anything that goes wrong
Spinnakker	A large sail used to reduce boat speed by being dropped into the water
Spreader boots	The nautical version of the Broadway musical
Stateroom	What a yacht broker calls a pilot berth

T

Tang	Orange juice for cruisers with no refrigeration
Travel Lift	A huge machine always occupied elsewhere when you need it

W

Wind Generator	Noise emitting device used to scare birds from a boat's stern to poop on the bow
Windlass	Apparatus used to entwine anchor rope around a drum so it can not come loose